PENGUIN BOOKS

THE WEIMAR REPUBLIC

Dr Peukert (1950–1990) was a lecturer in history at the University of Essen from 1978 until 1988, when he became Director of the Centre for the Study of Nazism in Hamburg. He was responsible for setting up in Essen a museum on the history of resistance and persecution in the city from 1933 to 1945. His special areas of interest lay in German history, the history of youth, the theory and teaching of history, and Latin America. His earlier books on the resistance of the German Communist Party and of German youth to Nazism have become standard reading on these subjects in Germany. His book *Inside Nazi Germany* is also published by Penguin.

DETLEV J. K. PEUKERT

THE WEIMAR REPUBLIC

The Crisis of Classical Modernity

TRANSLATED BY RICHARD DEVESON

PENGUIN BOOKS

PENGUIN BOOKS

Published by the Penguin Group
Penguin Books Ltd, 27 Wrights Lane, London W8 5TZ, England
Penguin Putnam Inc., 375 Hudson Street, New York, New York 10014, USA
Penguin Books Australia Ltd, Ringwood, Victoria, Australia
Penguin Books Canada Ltd, 10 Alcorn Avenue, Toronto, Ontario, Canada M4V 3B2
Penguin Books (NZ) Ltd, Private Bag 102902, NSMC, Auckland, New Zealand

Penguin Books Ltd, Registered Offices: Harmondsworth, Middlesex, England

First published as *Die Weimarer Republik* in Germany by Suhrkamp Verlag 1987
This translation first published in Great Britain by Allen Lane The Penguin Press 1991
Published in Penguin Books 1993
3 5 7 9 10 8 6 4

CONTENTS

VI. REVIEW: THE CRISIS OF CLASSICAL MODERNITY *274*

LIST OF FIGURES

LIST OF FIGURES

PREFACE

═══

> Even stories with a sorry ending have their moments of
> glory, great and small, and it is proper to view these
> moments, not in the light of their ending, but in their own
> light: their reality is no less powerful than the reality of their
> ending.
>
> Thomas Mann, *Joseph und seine Brüder*

Scarcely any period of German history has been as closely studied as
the years of the Weimar Republic. With Eberhard Kolb's general
survey we now also possess a reliable guide to the state of research on
the subject.[1] The present volume does not, and is not intended to,
compete with Kolb's book. It may be useful, none the less, building
on the substantial body of work that now exists, to put forward an
interpretation of the Weimar Republic which tackles the questions
raised in the debate over the so-called 'deutscher Sonderweg', or 'special
German path of development',[2] and which also offers a response to
the recent controversy about nationalistic tendencies in the writing
and teaching of contemporary German history.[3] In addition, recent
research in the history of everyday life, personal experience and *mentalités* has shed much fresh light on the tensions of the Weimar
period[4] – an era born of war and destroyed by economic and political
crisis – and the present volume will address itself to the themes that
are raised in this new literature.

It is standard practice in a preface to bemoan the fact that considerations of space preclude a fuller treatment. Clearly, however, the
only way to write a history of the eventful years between 1918 and
1933 in fewer than three hundred pages is to use essay-like concision:
to highlight some questions and to be brave enough to leave out
others. The reader, indeed, will find that some important aspects of
the period are dealt with only cursorily here, or are not touched on at

all. At the very least, then, I am under an obligation to explain the criteria I have used for purposes of selection.

This essay is guided by three central considerations. In the first place, almost all previous histories of the Weimar Republic have been written in the light either of the Republic's beginnings or of its end. The November revolution and the Versailles peace settlement have been seen as birth traumas of the Republic whose effects were translated into structural weaknesses and, ultimately, into the causes of the Republic's collapse. Alternatively, the factors that led to the seizure of power by the National Socialists have been projected backwards, with the causes of the 'German catastrophe' being sited, again, in the early years of the Republic or even in the years before the Republic was founded. These approaches have been legitimate and fruitful, but a change of perspective may open up new kinds of insight. 'Weimar' is more than a beginning and an end. The fourteen years of its existence constitute an era in its own right. It is the distinctive character of the Weimar era, and the era's relationship to the longer-term continuities of German history, that will be at the centre of this study.

A second guiding consideration in this book has to do with the shift towards social history that took place within German historiography during the 1960s and 1970s. This change has generated a wealth of information which it is impossible to ignore; but at the same time the concept of the 'deutscher Sonderweg' that is commonly bound up with this approach is a contentious one. The collapse of the Weimar Republic has been explained in terms of the exceptional dominance in Germany of traditional and authoritarian social relationships and old power élites which, it is argued, dated at least from the collapse of the bourgeois revolution of 1848 and set Germany on a different path from the more democratic route followed by western Europe. More recent research, however – including detailed studies and discussions by supporters of the 'Sonderweg' thesis themselves – has yielded a picture with considerably subtler nuances than this. For one thing, the distinctive national characteristics of German history do not all point in a direct line to the Nazi seizure of power in 1933. For another, it is not at all clear what relative weightings should be assigned to distinctive German features, on the one hand, and to common European phenomena, on the other, as causes of the fatal intensification of the crisis of modernization that occurred in the early 1930s. And in any case, historians are now increasingly abandoning the whole notion of a 'normal' model of modernization against which individual non-normal 'deviations' can be measured. There is now less inclination to see the process of modernization within industrialized society as one that is liable to be harmonious. This study, too, presents a picture of a crisis-racked, modernizing society in which teetering over the abyss was the norm and the resolution of conflict was the exception. In this sense, accordingly, there is no need to explain the fall of the Weimar Republic and the rise of National Socialism chiefly in terms of a 'special' long-term process of development. At the same time, to say that German society underwent a relatively normal version of the modernization process is in no sense to declare National Socialism, or the events that gave rise to it, innocuous. On the contrary, it provides a warning against the mistaken notion that there is anything innocuous about 'normal' industrial society as such.

A third guiding theme of this book is the paradox, rarely explained, that informs the historical image of Weimar: the hopeful picture of avant-garde cultural achievement and the bleak picture of political breakdown and social misery. This paradox is an integral feature of the era and cannot be explained away. But it may be possible to trace connections between its elements, despite the fact that they are commonly viewed in isolation and, indeed, kept as the preserves of different academic disciplines. The new growth of interest in the history of everyday life and research into *mentalités* is of service here. I shall try, for example, to analyse a cultural phenomenon such as rationalization and to trace its contradictions and counter-currents in different areas of historical reality: in the world of work, in changing sexual roles, in political and philosophical thought and in the projects of architects and writers.

In emphasizing continuity here, we are also highlighting the crisis that the modernization of industrial society represented. With their charged atmosphere of social and cultural innovation, the years of the Weimar Republic can now be seen as a critical phase in the era of 'classical modernity'. The concept of modernity is taken from the history of art, but is also a useful way of labelling the social and cultural character of our entire epoch. Until the 1890s the advance of industrial society in Germany had taken place in the socio-economic sphere; what followed was the triumph of modernity in society and culture generally. Developments that occurred after the turn of the century in science and the arts, in town planning, in technology, in medicine, in ideas and in daily life were a trial run for the form of life that remains our own today: indeed, they were a first, classical statement of it. In the years between the First World War and the world economic crisis of the early thirties, classical modernity advanced on all fronts: its contradictions were intensified, and its profoundest crisis was played out. Weimar was a brief, headlong tour of the fascinating, and fateful, choices made possible by the modern world.

These, then, are the guiding ideas I shall follow in this essay as I try to open up pathways of historical explanation through the bewildering mass of material that the Weimar era has bequeathed us. My exposition will be a blend of the chronological and the thematic. In keeping with the style of this series, notes have been kept to a minimum.★ I have dealt only briefly with certain topics which are central to the historiography of Weimar but which can be easily read up elsewhere. The same applies to topics which form the subject-matter of other complete volumes in this series. For this reason, too, the years 1918–19 and 1930–33 have been given a more cursory treatment.[5]

The author is indebted to numerous friends and colleagues for the stimulus, criticism and support they have provided while this book was being written. I should particularly like to thank Hans-Ulrich Wehler for encouraging me to undertake the task, and for his persistent interest, open-mindedness and readiness to discuss questions that have arisen. I am very grateful to those colleagues – especially August Nitzschke, Gerhard A. Ritter and Rüdiger vom Bruch – with whom I collaborated, while working on the second half of the book, in a series of interdisciplinary broadcast talks about the years 1890–1930, a project in many ways parallel to this one. I also wish to thank the Kommission für Forschung of the Universität-Gesamthochschule in Essen for its support. Last but by no means least, I should like to mention my students at Essen, who have been thoughtful and articulate

★ Translator's note: the original volume is part of the Neue Historische Bibliothek published in Germany by Suhrkamp.

participants in the courses I have taught on the Weimar Republic. To them, and to Amir Lewin, with whom I have enjoyed a continuous conversation on the subject, I am indebted for having been given the chance of 'finding out what I think by hearing what I say'.

TRANSLATOR'S NOTE

═══

I am extremely grateful, as I have been on previous occasions, to Dick Bessel for his generous help; and I am deeply indebted to Clare Deveson for putting up with my constant stream of questions. I should also like to express my thanks to Helen Jeffrey, who has saved me from numerous slips and awkwardnesses and has been a model of editorial alertness and tact.

A translator's work is always dedicated to his author, but I should like to dedicate this translation, in so many words, to the memory of Detlev Peukert, who died before the work was finished, with so much more of his own work still to give.

Richard Deveson

LIST OF ABBREVIATIONS

====

BVP Bayerische Volkspartei; Bavarian People's Party

DDP Deutsche Demokratische Partei; German Democratic Party

DNVP Deutschnationale Volkspartei; German National People's Party

DVP Deutsche Volkspartei; German People's Party

KPD Kommunistische Partei Deutschlands; Communist Party of Germany

MSPD Mehrheitssozialdemokratische Partei Deutschlands; Majority Social Democratic Party of Germany

NSDAP Nationalsozialistische Deutsche Arbeiterpartei; National Socialist German Workers' Party (Nazi Party)

RM Reichsmark

SA Sturmabteilungen; lit., Storm Sections, i.e. Storm Troopers

SPD Sozialdemokratische Partei Deutschlands; Social Democratic Party of Germany

USPD Unabhängige Sozialdemokratische Partei Deutschlands; Independent Social Democratic Party of Germany

I. INTRODUCTION

===

An age is always a farrago of different ages. Whole parts of it are unleavened and undercooked; it contains the husks of old forces, and the seeds of new ones.

Alfred Döblin, 1924

1. THE WEIMAR REPUBLIC AND THE CONTINUITY OF GERMAN HISTORY

To define a phenomenon is to specify its boundaries. But it is an indication of the problems that the Weimar Republic poses for historians that even its temporal boundaries are open to dispute. The demarcation of a period of history necessarily rests on a particular conception of the period, explicitly underpinned to a greater or lesser extent by theoretical analysis. What different dates, then, can be proposed for the beginning and end of the Weimar Republic, and what analytical conceptions of the period are implicit in these different datings?

POLITICAL TURNING-POINTS

Some accounts of Weimar actually begin with the Imperial monarchy:[1] to be precise, with the October reforms of 1918, which, as military defeat loomed, introduced parliamentary democracy into the constitution of the Reich and brought to power the governing coalition of Social Democrats, Catholic Centre and liberals that was later to usher in the Weimar constitution of 1919. In such an account, the continuity represented by the socialist–liberal–Catholic settlement takes centre stage, and the November revolution appears as a false trail.

On the other hand, to take the revolutionary proclamation of the Republic in Berlin on 9 November 1918 as a starting-point[2] is to emphasize the break with the imperial monarchy and to highlight the role of the mass revolutionary movement. This approach was adopted early on by the political right, with the *Dolchstoßlegende* (the legend of the 'stab in the back') and the Nazis' vilification of the 'November criminals'. The left, on the other hand, has been faced with the dilemma whether or not to define the period by reference to a revolution which the Weimar Republic itself was responsible for terminating.[3]

Similarly, for those who view the creation of the Weimar Republic as the result of a verdict in favour of bourgeois parliamentary democracy and against Bolshevik dictatorship,[4] the crucial event of the new era is the election of the National Constituent Assembly on 19 January 1919 (or perhaps even the promulgation of the Weimar constitution of the Reich on 14 August 1919).

Historians who deny that this was the only choice and whose interest is in the untapped potential for democratization that was present during the early period of upheaval, notably in the *Räte* movement (the soldiers' and the workers' councils, or soviets),[5] inevitably focus their attention on the mass movements of the winter and spring of 1919, or even, indeed, on the so-called March revolution of 1920 that followed the Kapp putsch.

To do this, however, is to prolong the moment of the Republic's birth until it becomes identical with an entire phase of the republican era, namely the revolutionary post-war crisis. This crisis can be said to have ended with the Reichstag elections of 6 June 1920, in which the Weimar Coalition responsible for enacting the constitution lost its electoral majority, or perhaps to have lasted until the stabilization of domestic and foreign policy that was achieved at the close of the crisis-ridden year 1923.

Although stability arrived in 1924, contemporaries were not prepared to regard it as more than 'relative'.[6] Certainly, it is only in comparison with the several near-fatal crises of the early post-war period, and then with the world economic crisis at the end of the decade, that the years 1924–9 can be termed 'stable'. The cracks in the fabric of the Republic remained fully visible, an outward sign of hidden weaknesses that might prove fatal when the structure was next subjected to severe strain.

Clearly, then, the way in which we judge the years of the mid-1920s are of crucial importance when we come to assess the extent to which the Weimar Republic was, on the one hand, prone to crises and, on the other, able to withstand them.[7]

In similar fashion, verdicts differ as to how long the colla[p]
Republic was really averted after the renewed bout of crisis th[...]
in 1929. The fall of the Great Coalition on 27 March 1930 can be
viewed as the end of 'Weimar', if the relevant criterion is taken to be
the capacity of the political system to produce a stable parliamentary
majority and of the representatives of employers and workers to sustain
the compromise on economic and social policy that was reached in
1918.[8] The decision by Heinrich Brüning, appointed Chancellor two
days later, to govern on the basis of emergency decrees and the backing
of the Reich President, and not to depend on majority support in
Parliament, was – and was intended to be – the first step in a change
to a quite different form of constitution.[9]

Only after (though not before) the sensational success of the National
Socialists in the Reichstag elections on 14 September 1930 (followed
by their later successes in 1932 and the *Machtergreifung*, or seizure of
power, of 1933) is there a case for the argument that the different
form of republic which Brüning and Hindenburg wanted offered an
alternative to Hitler as well as to Weimar.[10] On this view it was not
until the fall of Brüning of 30 May 1932 that the precipitous slide towards the Third Reich can be said to have begun. By the same token,
there were the Hitler–Papen cabinet on 30 January 1933, the emergency decrees following the Reichstag fire on 28 February 1933,
the *Ermächtigungsgesetz* (Enabling Law) of 23 March 1933 and the
amalgamation of the posts of Reich Chancellor and Reich President
in the person of the 'Führer' on 2 August 1934 – before the functions
and significance of the constitutional order of Weimar were finally
nullified.[11]

In terms of political history, then, the Weimar Republic has neither
a clearly defined beginning nor a clearly defined end. From the his-
toriographical point of view, as we have said, periodization is always
dependent on interpretation, and historical controversy on the interpretation of the Weimar era is still very passionate.

But these very ambiguities also tell us something about the character of the Weimar Republic. The beginning of the Republic was not
marked by an event that served as an old-fashioned but politically
unifying symbol of a pivotal moment in national history, along the
lines of the American Declaration of Independence, the *quatorze juillet*

in France or indeed Sedan Day after the creation of the German Empire in 1870–71. On 9 November 1918, the day when the German Republic was established, there were competing symbolic proclamations by the Spartacist Karl Liebknecht in front of the Hohenzollern palace and by the Social Democratic parliamentarian and minister [12] Philipp Scheidemann in front of the German Reichstag: the revolutionary masses see-sawed between the two. The fact that the Republic had no legitimizing founding ritual implies a lack of legitimacy in general: it suggests that there was a lack of active commitment to the new order.

MODERNIZATION AND ITS TRIBULATIONS

The Weimar Republic did not come into being as the result of an heroic act, or of an act which national mythology could represent as heroic; it was not conceived as a brave new world. Rather, it was the product of complex and painful compromise, of defeats and mutual concessions. And yet the unspectacular new arrangements might have survived if, or as long as, acceptable living conditions had prevailed. When, however, economic activity and social conditions reached the point of crisis, there were few reserves of public legitimacy on which the Republic could draw, and the search for stabilizing political solutions proved fruitless.

In addition, the Republic had to bear the heavy historic burden of a lost war, and this particular legacy of historical continuity, bequeathed to it in its role as the successor state to the collapsed Wilhelmine empire, was made more weighty by new social tribulations and economic upheavals that began to make themselves felt in the years – and decades – after the First World War. With hindsight, it can be said that the Germans embarked on their republican experiment at the most unpropitious possible moment: a moment when the political and social system was already about to be tested to the limits.

To understand the Weimar era properly, we must therefore go beyond the sorts of political and constitutional interpretation that underlie the standard models of periodization we have just discussed: we also need to adopt a social and historical approach that takes account both of long-term continuities and of patterns specific to the Weimar period itself. I shall attempt to do this in a number of complementary ways. By way of introduction, we can select three areas of socio-historical continuity and change which would seem to be particularly significant indicators of the distinctive social make-up of the Weimar Republic. These are the shifting demographic pattern, the level of modernization, as reflected in the structure of employment, and economic growth (see figures 1–3).

THE DEMOGRAPHIC REVOLUTION

From the turn of the century people in Germany were becoming more and more acutely aware that they were living in an age of new kinds of demographic change. Unexpectedly, it seemed possible that the population would no longer naturally reproduce itself. For decades the German population had grown regularly at a high annual rate. The process of industrialization had been accompanied by a high surplus of births over deaths (see figure 1), made doubly dramatic by the migration from the countryside into urban areas. The population of the cities, in particular, had become highly youth-dominated.[13]

Despite the cessions of territory that took place after the First World War – which entailed a loss of population of about 10 per cent – the overall population of the German Reich continued to expand under the Weimar Republic.[14] The number of people living within the 1920 borders rose from 62.4 million in 1925 to 65.2 million in 1933, the latter figure exceeding the total for the maximal German borders of 1910 (64.9 million). More important, during the 1920s the pre-war 'bulge' age-groups came flooding on to the labour market. The proportion of young people in Germany had never been so high, nor had the potentially active section of the population – 14- to 65-year-olds able to work – been so large. The labour market in the 1920s was therefore exceptionally crowded (see also chapters 4 and 5). This surplus of labour, and the particularly bleak outlook facing the virtually redundant generation of those born around the turn of the century, lent the nationalistic slogan 'Volk ohne Raum' (a people without space, or territory) a certain specious plausibility.

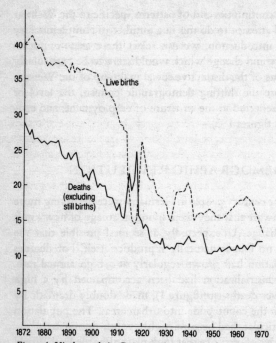

Figure 1. Vital trends in Germany (per 1,000 of population), 1872–1970

Source: K. Bade, 'Arbeitsmarkt, Bevölkerung und Wanderungen in der Weimarer Republik', in M. Stürmer (ed.), *Die Weimarer Republik. Belagerte Civitas*, Königstein, 1980, p. 162

And yet from another angle the picture seemed to be very different. Another catchword was also coming into currency: the German people was ageing; it was undergoing terminal decline: 'Volkstod', or the very death of the nation, was said to be looming. This sort of cry from demographic commentators was provoked by a dramatic fall in the birth rate, which had in fact begun in about 1900 although its full extent had become apparent only gradually.

As long as the death rate fell in parallel with the birth rate, the surplus of births over deaths remained constant. But when the surplus itself began to decrease and a new demographic balance began to emerge, bitter complaints about women's refusal to perform their child-bearing duty began to be uttered. Women – and their partners –

had, indeed, come to adopt in a relatively short space of time the new ideal of the two-child family, and small families were rapidly becoming the statistical norm. Stated in summary terms, the new demographic structure in the Weimar Republic was one of rising life expectancy (or falling mortality), a falling birth rate, a new ideal of the two-child family, a partial removal of the reproductive burden from women and a more pronounced segmentation in the age make-up of the overall population. As if these changes were not enough, there were also the drastic demographic effects of the First World War: the loss of young and middle-aged men created a surplus of women, and also caused a fall in the birth rate during the war years.

These complex processes were the result of far-reaching changes in social values and forms of social behaviour that had already been under way for some time: changes in attitudes towards sexuality and contraception, for example. Society, however, had not yet evolved new values and forms of behaviour in response to these new demographic patterns. Accordingly, there were increasing conflicts between the generations, and growing tensions between the sexes. (We shall return to these questions in chapter 4.)

SOCIETY AT THE CROSSROADS

As far as the social structure is concerned, there was not the same dramatic transformation during the years of the Weimar Republic as there was in the case of population. The long-term processes of industrialization and modernization continued in force. Nevertheless, the period had its own specific tensions and distortions. If we look at the distribution of employment among the main sectors of the economy (see figure 2), we can see that the primary sector, agriculture and forestry, at first continued to decline in importance, in accordance with long-term trends. During the hard times of the 1920s and the post-1929 slump, however, the percentage of workers employed in agriculture temporarily rose, mainly because employment in the secondary sector of industry and small business declined. But in the 1930s industry and small business regained their dominant position, although they were now followed in second place by the steadily

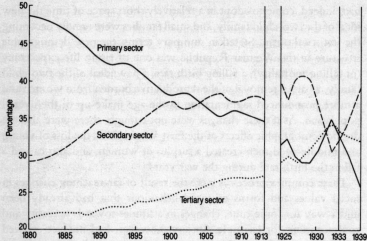

Figure 2. Proportions of those employed in the principal economic sectors in Germany, 1880–1933

Source: K. Bade, 'Arbeitsmarkt, Bevölkerung und Wanderungen in der Weimarer Republik', in M. Stürmer (ed.), *Die Weimarer Republik. Belagerte Civitas*, Königstein, 1980, p. 161

expanding tertiary sector of services, commerce and administration.

The class structure similarly evolved in accordance with the long-term process of modernization. The proportion of the self-employed in the workforce fell from 19.6 per cent in 1907 to 15.6 per cent in 1925, although the proportion of family members working in family enterprises temporarily rose from 15.4 to 17 per cent during the same period. The percentage of white-collar workers and public officials rose perceptibly within the period, from 10.3 to 17.3 per cent, betokening the arrival of the 'new *Mittelstand*' (middle class), while manual workers only just maintained their standing as an absolute majority of those in employment, with figures of 54.9 and (in 1925) 50.1 per cent.

Migration figures likewise continued to conform to the modernization pattern, though migration from the countryside into the towns, which had been a central feature of the decades around the turn of the century, began to abate. By 1925 one German in three was a city-dweller. A further one-third lived in smaller towns, and the remaining one-third in the country.

If we take the distribution of employment among the main sectors of the economy and the geographical distribution of the population between town and country as indicators of the extent of the growth of modern industrial society in Germany, then the national debate that took place around the turn of the century as to whether Germany's future would lie in agrarianism or industrialism cannot be dismissed as an irrelevance. From a present-day perspective, certainly, the situation in the 1920s can only be viewed as one of transition towards a fully fledged industrial society. But at the time the future was still imponderable, its course by no means settled. Agrarian romanticism and hostility to the big city were responses to genuine problems created by industrialization and modernization. Roseate nostalgia and reformist calls for alternative life-styles were both, in their own way, addressed to a pre-modern form of society in which a substantial proportion of German people still lived.

We should be wary of using generalized statistical data as a basis for drawing conclusions about the state of society. Developments which can now be seen to have been part of a long-term process of modernization were perceived by people at the time as events whose outcome was far from clear. Aggregate statistical data also obscure the existence of great disparities, and often conflicts, between regions and specific social groups. Thus contemporaries were unable to see the wood for the trees, and the debates on modernization that took place during the Weimar era itself produced highly disparate responses. (We shall discuss these debates more closely in chapters 4–9.)

Some social critics had already voiced their unease at industrialism and modernization during the late-Wilhelmine period; others had welcomed 'progress' with bombastic imperial enthusiasm. Both attitudes became more pronounced in the years after the First World War. The apologists for modernization now trumpeted the 'Americanism' of the 'golden twenties', while the pessimists embraced the more extreme doctrine of *Blut und Boden* (blood and soil) and denounced the 'asphalt jungle' of the cities. And yet it is not possible to make a simple division of attitudes towards modernization into two polar categories, 'progressive' and 'reactionary': the processes of modernization were too heterogeneous and inconsistent themselves. The point that needs to be stressed is that the inter-war debate on

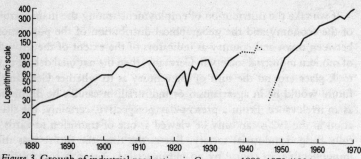

Figure 3. Growth of industrial production in Germany, 1880–1970 (1936 = 100)
Source: D. Petzina *et al.*, *Sozialgeschichtliches Arbeitsbuch*, vol. 2, Munich, 1978, p. 43

modernity became both fiercer and more inconclusive precisely because modernization itself had reached a state of crisis.

THE HALT TO ECONOMIC GROWTH

The crisis is most clearly apparent if we look at economic growth. The expansion of industrial production, which can be regarded as the principal motor of modern economies,[15] breaks down into three distinct phases in Germany during the past hundred years (see figure 3). Thirty years of practically uninterrupted industrial expansion were followed, after 1914, by virtually three decades of crisis, stagnation and, frequently, falls in production. Only after the Second World War did a new period of continuous economic expansion set in, which lasted into the 1970s. During the Weimar period, and in some respects throughout the inter-war years, production levels at best only equalled those of 1913 and in poor years either remained below pre-war norms or, in times of acute crisis, sank appreciably lower still. The causes and effects of this endemic economic weakness will be discussed in more detail later (see chapters 5 and 13). Suffice it to say for the moment that any verdict on the Weimar Republic must take account of the fundamental social and economic fact of stagnation and crisis.

Economic historians have put forward many different explanations of this phenomenon, and their accounts go hand in hand with different ways of placing the Weimar Republic within the longer span of German history.[16] Writers who postulate that the specific growth trajectory of a nation's economy is basically governed by the conditions prevailing at the start of industrialization have viewed the inter-war period as a short-term, externally induced perturbation which was overcome by the economic expansion that followed the reconstruction after the Second World War. Those, on the other hand, who see capitalist development as a succession of long-term waves of growth and stagnation regard the inter-war period of economic weakness as a phase that was virtually inevitable, and maintain that new expansion could occur only after painful structural adjustments. While this pessimistic account of the period at least acknowledges that renewed expansion was conceivable, economists living at the time were often impelled to even bleaker conclusions. During the depths of the recession between 1929 and 1933, in particular, there were 'right-wing' and 'left-wing' economists alike who maintained that capitalist industrialization had either reached saturation point (for example, Wagenführ) or had even entered its final phase of collapse (Varga).[17]

The responses of ordinary people caught up in economic crisis may not be entirely commensurable with the prognoses of professional economists, but Germans did not merely complain about the trials and tribulations of the moment: they placed the particular events that affected them within the wider framework of their own lives and their future hopes and expectations. These longer-term perceptions of the prospects for everyday life cast events in the twenties in a very bleak light. Conditions were deteriorating yearly: this was certainly the common verdict during the period 1930–33, at any rate, as the brief recovery of 1927–8 gave way to world recession. But earlier, too, the performance of the economy had lagged behind its pre-war levels. The only way in which demands for higher wages could be met was by redistribution from one group to another or by higher deficits. There was never sufficient growth to permit agreement on higher welfare provision, except during the false inflationary boom of 1920–21. To Germans living through these years of crisis, the 'good old days' of the monarchy were bound to take on a nostalgic afterglow.

As if its problems of political legitimacy were not enough, the Weimar Republic was also unable to win popular confidence on the economic front. Whether or not the new republic was actually responsible for the economic misery of the times, the effect on ordinary people of living through unremitting crisis was deeply demoralizing. Long-term economic prospects were grim; there was no chance of higher living standards in the short term; and memories of the Wilhelmine past grew fonder as the realities of life under the Republic grew more austere.

This hankering for the past on the part of many Germans was particularly significant because it was not a nostalgia for a few isolated myths and symbols but rested on real remembered opportunities and hopes from the pre-war period. Increasingly, the dark side of the Wilhelmine world – which, after all, had gone giddily to war in 1914 – was ignored as the shadows descended over the present.

FOUR POLITICAL GENERATIONS

We can get a fuller sense of the longer-term continuities affecting people's lives if we consider the different generations of public figures who played a prominent role during the Weimar Republic. We can broadly distinguish four generations of leading political actors; the figures selected are not meant to constitute a representative sample in every sense, but they are sufficiently representative for our purposes. Births, of course, form a continuum, and to label a particular succession of age-groups as a 'generation' is not to pick out a 'real' objective entity. We can use the notion of a generation, however, as a way of focusing attention on certain specific features which a particular collection of age-groups, in a given context, can be seen to have in common.[18] We can ask when the formative political and social experiences of the leading personalities of the Weimar period took place, and under what circumstances these individuals emerged as figures who, in turn, influenced the politics and society of their own times. This is a difficult task, but a well-defined one. Asking different questions would, of course, lead to the tracing of different generational patterns.

The four generations of public figures who played leading roles during the Weimar Republic can be defined as follows (see also figure 4):

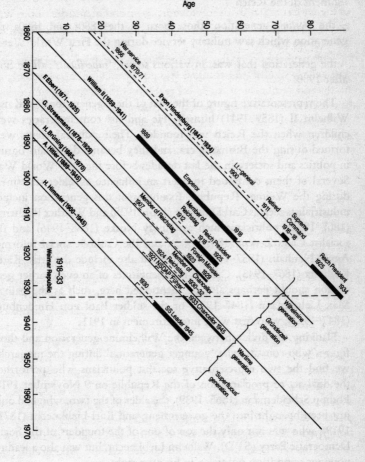

Figure 4. Political generations during the Weimar Republic

– the *Wilhelmine* generation: contemporaries of Wilhelm II

– the *Gründerzeit* generation: those born in the decade of the establishment of the Reich

– the *wartime* generation: those born in the 1880s and 1890s, the generation which saw military service during the First World War

– the generation that was, in various senses, '*superfluous*': those born after 1900.

The representative figure of the first of these generations[19] is Kaiser Wilhelm II (1859–1941) himself. He and his contemporaries were children when the Reich was founded. Their political views were formed during the Bismarck era, and they became dominant figures in politics and society in the last decades before the First World War. Several of them continued to exert an influence as 'elder statesmen' during the Weimar Republic. Examples of this generation include industrialists such as Carl Duisberg (1861–1935) and Walther Rathenau (1867–1922), politicians such as Gustav Noske (1868–1946) and the socialist Clara Zetkin (1857–1933), and the Catholic social reformer Agnes Neuhaus (1857–1933). We might also include the artist Käthe Kollwitz (1867–1945). Certain representatives of an even earlier generation should perhaps also be mentioned here, such as the painter Max Liebermann (1847–1935) or the soldier Paul von Hindenburg (1847–1934), who first went into retirement in 1911.

Flanking the divide between the Wilhelmine generation and those figures who constituted a 'younger generation' during the monarchy we find the two representative socialist politicians who performed the dual act of proclamation of the Republic on 9 November 1918: Philipp Scheidemann (1865–1939), the elder of the two, who had only just been brought into the government, and Karl Liebknecht (1871–1919), who was not only the son of one of the founders of the Social Democratic Party (SPD), Wilhelm Liebknecht, but was also a leading younger opposition politician in his own right.

The figures who made up the younger generation of politicians under the monarchy were born in the decade after the establishment of the Reich. Their political attitudes were shaped, and their careers launched, during the period following Wilhelm II's accession to the throne. These younger, *Gründerzeit* figures did not attain positions of responsibility and influence until after the turn of the century, and most of them had still not reached the very top by the time of the revolution. But this was the generation from which the dominant personalities of the Weimar Republic were drawn: for example, Friedrich Ebert (1871–1925), who became a member of the Reichstag in 1912, and Gustav Stresemann (1878–1929), who had been a member of the Reichstag (apart from one brief hiatus) since 1907. Among the many representatives of this generation there is room to mention only a few: Rosa Luxemburg (1870–1919), Otto Braun (1872–1955) and Konrad Adenauer (1876–1967); the industrialists Fritz Thyssen (1873–1951) and Hugo Stinnes (1870–1924); two important figures in social reform and the women's movement, Alice Salomon (1872–1948) and Gertrud Bäumer (1873–1954); and Albert Einstein (1879–1955) and Thomas Mann (1875–1955). This somewhat arbitrary list of names indicates that much of the achievement we associate with the Weimar era was the work of people who had lived the first forty or so years of their lives under the monarchy.

The image of Weimar, however, also conjures up a distinct, younger generation, mainly born in the 1880s, among whom Heinrich Brüning (1885–1970) may be taken as a representative figure. The members of this group reached adulthood around the turn of the century and experienced both the expansionist euphoria and the anxious forebodings of the years leading up to the First World War. The men in this age-group included many who underwent long and frequent spells of service at the front during the First World War. They can thus be termed the 'front' or wartime generation.[20]

Because of the war, the members of this generation did not gain their political experience, and often did not choose a career or start a family, until after 1918. And with the Weimar political landscape dominated by the *Gründerzeit* generation, they were often obliged to play second fiddle or to project themselves as rivals to their elders. Among them were the leaders of the KPD (the Communist Party), Ernst Thälmann (1886–1944), and of the NSDAP (the National Socialists), Adolf Hitler (1889–1945). This younger generation also included many figures who were prominent in the avant-garde culture of the 1920s, such as Walter Gropius (1883–1969), George Grosz (1893–

1959) and Carl von Ossietzky (1889–1938). Plainly, it was easier to make headway in the world of culture than it was in national politics. It is noteworthy, however, that the leading personalities in the women's movement during the Weimar years belonged either to the *Gründerzeit* generation or even to the preceding Wilhelmine age-group. In this instance the stalwarts from the period of the monarchy do not seem to have had so many successors among those who were in their thirties when the First World War ended.

Although there were tensions between the older, *Gründerzeit* figures who were prominent during the Weimar era and their younger rivals from the wartime generation, the age-group born around the year 1900 had even more reason to assert the claims of a younger generation against the established Weimar gerontocracy.[21] These young men felt 'superfluous' because they were confronted by a stagnant economy and a saturated labour market; their adolescence had been disrupted by war, and yet they had also been deprived of the legitimizing rite of passage of active service at the front. Later this generation was particularly hard hit by the mass unemployment caused by the world slump. It was thus understandable that sizeable numbers from this age-group should attach themselves to the radical extremes of the political spectrum. Representative names here include Heinrich Himmler (1900–1945), the charismatic Communist leader Heinz Neumann (1902–1937) and the philosopher Theodor W. Adorno (1903–1969). At the same time, however, we should not forget those figures whose response to the crises of the time was to forge an identity by submerging themselves in what they regarded as non-political normality. A characteristic example of this sort of member of the 'superfluous' generation, who passed unscathed through fascism and war into the post-war *Wirtschaftswunder*, or economic miracle, of the 1950s, was the film actor Heinz Rühmann, born in 1902 and thus only a little younger than Heinrich Himmler and Martin Bormann.

II. New Directions, 1918–23

===

The war they went to fight was lost. But we ... must remember that this war would still have meant the end of an epoch, revolution and the dawn of a new age, and that afterwards, even if it had ended differently, we should still have found ourselves living in a new and unfamiliar world.

Thomas Mann

III. NEW DIRECTIONS, 1940-55

2. OLD LEGACIES AND A NEW
START, 1918–19

On 10 February 1918 the *Frankfurter Zeitung* made an appeal to the newly elected National Constituent Assembly, which had gathered in Weimar away from the turmoil of civil war in Berlin:

The German National Assembly in Weimar should resolve as a matter of urgency that a large notice be put up in every room used by the politicians and wherever the machinery of party runs. This notice should bear the message, in letters of fire: 'Do not forget: the German people has carried out a revolution!'[1]

Stirring words – and their fiery message still inspires the writings of many modern historians. Yet they should also give us pause: not only because of their disparaging comparison of the 'machinery of party' with the 'people', which reflects a problematical strain in the German political tradition, but because we need to ask what the pressures were in response to which the founding fathers of the new constitution were liable to 'forget' the revolution.

If there was to be a new start in 1918–19, then many problems inherited from the past had to be dealt with first. The National Assembly was faced with the task of drawing up the framework for a new system of government and a new social order, while also having to decide what degree of continuity there should be with the political and social institutions that had gone before. This entailed a confrontation between, on the one hand, those in favour of stability, who had just gained a narrow majority in the elections, and, on the other hand, the forces of counter-revolution and the supporters of the increasingly radical *Räte* movement (soldiers' and workers' councils). Given the magnitude of the burdens imposed by the peace settlement, and the social and political problems created by demobilization, by the switch from a war to a peace economy and by the need to make provision for war victims, the 'revolution' was in reality only one aspect, albeit an important one, of the transition from a monarchy to a republic and from war to peace. The 'German revolution of 1918–19' was part of the process of the establishment of democracy, and as such has rightly been the object of much historical study and controversy;[2] but it can be properly assessed only if it is seen within the larger context of the events of wartime and the post-war period, if its successes and failures are viewed in the light of international comparisons and if the events of the revolution are judged in terms of the strategies and options that were available, or were perceived to be available, at the time.

Above all, we must ask precisely what sort of revolution the German people can be said to have 'carried out'. The fierce controversy that still rages among historians concerning the nature of the revolution of 1918–19 is a reflection of ideological differences among the scholars concerned, but it also indicates the many-faceted character of the revolutionary process itself. It is imperative, therefore, if we are to understand the events that took place, to distinguish the several political strands of the revolutionary movement (indeed, to distinguish the several separate revolutionary movements) and to specify the different chronological phases of which the revolution consisted. The concrete historical events of the revolution, I suggest, were the product of three distinctive movements, and fell into three stages.

It is, of course, always somewhat arbitrary to extract a particular set of phenomena from the inchoate mass of historical events and to highlight them in ideal-type fashion. Alternative explanatory models are quite possible. I think it is useful, however, to suggest that the 'German revolution' was made up of the following three relatively independent ideal-type revolutionary movements:

– the *constitutional revolution* carried out by democratic politicians and their parties and complemented by corporatist co-operation between the leaders of the institutions of labour and capital and the state

– the *peace and social-protest movement*, which was the product of spontaneous action by workers (though not only workers) and found institutional expression in the *Räte* movement

– the *socialist movement*, led by a mixed grouping of left-wing politicians, which became significant only as the revolution gained momentum.

These three movements – which partly reinforced one another and partly obstructed one another, with the balance among them constantly shifting – together passed through three broad chronological phases:

– a period of *hope*, lasting until the revolution was successfully accomplished in Berlin on 9 November 1918

– a period of *decisions*, leading up to the elections for the National Assembly on 19 January 1919

– a period of *disappointment*, which can be said to have ended in the spring of 1919 (if the events leading up to the Kapp putsch and the March revolution of 1920 are left aside).

When did the first phase, the period of hope, begin? Certainly we need at least to go back to before the naval mutiny of late October and early November 1918, to the end of the preceding September, when Germany's leaders decided to face up to imminent defeat on the battlefield by seeking an armistice on the basis of Wilson's Fourteen Points and, on the domestic front, set in train a parliamentary reform of the constitution. But the origins of the three partly complementary, partly conflicting movements that we have identified as fuelling the revolution really went back further still. We need, in fact, to seek the origins of the 'German revolution' in the 'German awakening' (*Deutscher Aufbruch*) of 1914. It is only in the light of the mythology of August 1914 that the drama of November 1918 can be understood.

HOPES

As early as 1915, in a highly prophetic essay which remained unpublished at the time, Max Weber wrote:

Here, too, the prolongation of the war is entirely the result, not of objective political considerations, but of a fear of peace . . . To a far greater extent still, however, people are afraid of the domestic political consequences of the disillusionment that will inevitably set in, given the foolish expectations that have now run riot.[3]

These expectations had 'run riot' in August 1914, as war fever had taken hold in Germany. While the troops mobilized, hopes that the Reich could break out of its self-inflicted international isolation were stirred into a millenarian frenzy. The euphoria gripped mainly the middle class, though not exclusively so. Sections of the working class also hoped for social regeneration under the aegis of a united 'Volksgemeinschaft', or 'national community', but these hopes rapidly faded when the prosaic reality of war set in. It was in this climate that the political movements which, in altered form, were to bring about the revolution of 1918–19 first took shape.

The Kaiser's proclamation of a 'Burgfrieden', or domestic truce, encompassing all the political parties, including the previously ostracized Social Democrats, as well as the trade unions and employers' organizations, seemed to herald a new political era: the prospect of a fresh start which very few political leaders were at first able to resist. The politicians were also carried along by the surging popular sense, extending to the working class, that the 'national community' faced a time of trial both at home and abroad. Here, then, was the origin of the latent mass feeling of expectancy, and disappointment, that subsequently played a decisive part in shaping the revolution. In addition, August 1914 brought about the bewilderment and isolation of the hitherto socialist left, a political blow whose effects remained even after the revolution had broken out. Finally, mass rallying behind the banner of 'Volksgemeinschaft' and the establishment of a 'Burgfrieden' among the dominant social institutions provided the foundations for a political model of chauvinistic integration under the hegemony of the military–conservative complex that was eventually to reach its fatal culmination in the era of totalitarianism.

The unfavourable turn taken by the war increased domestic tensions. The military–conservative complex tightened its hold on power, while disillusionment and dissatisfaction became more widespread among the population. As a result of this polarization, the liberal and democratic forces in society slowly re-established the traditional position that they had temporarily abandoned in August 1914. At the same time, conflicts over the basic issue of wages and living standards stepped up sharply, with groups that had previously been under-represented in the Social Democratic movement, such as women and young people, now playing a larger role. Since action by representative trade union and political bodies was officially in abeyance, social protest often also found expression in new, spontaneous forms.

By 1917–18 a mood of disenchantment had descended on the three movements we have identified, and they were now prepared to break free from the military–conservative hegemony. The Inter-Party Committee representing the 'Burgfrieden', politicians who formed a majority in the Reichstag – the Social Democrats, the liberals and the Centre – provided a platform, albeit a shaky one, for moves towards a negotiated peace and the introduction of parliamentary reform. This alliance set the pattern for the constitutionalist movement that kept its hand on the reins though all the later vicissitudes of the revolution.

The euphoria that had swept through the masses in 1914 had long since given way to disillusionment at the way the war was proceeding and to anger at the authorities' inability to ensure an equal division of the burdens the war imposed. Workers rediscovered the old traditions of class conflict. A large number of strikes took place, culminating in the great January strike of 1918, and there were many other acts of social protest and dissent that pointed to the dissolution of the reigning social and moral order. At the same time, however, the peace and social-protest movement, which had seen its hopes dashed after 1914 and was now demanding that the colossal sacrifices of the war should at least be rewarded by a fundamental change in the post-war social order, was nurturing a new set of exaggerated expectations which would guarantee a new round of disappointment later.

The socialist left also regained some of its influence during the war, but it reorganized itself into a number of splinter groups and embarked on the revolution as a divided force. Furthermore, the main divisions that emerged within what had been the SPD Reichstag group –

between the Majority Socialists (MSPD), the Independents (USPD) and the Left Radicals (Linksradikale, or Spartacus) – did not reflect differences between left and right on matters such as the nature of revolution and the structure of post-revolutionary society, but rather attitudes towards war credits and ways of ending the war. As long as the events of the revolution did not entail the making of clear-cut choices, however, these differences could be glossed over in the common call for 'socialism'. During the crucial weeks of the revolution, at any rate, this meant that almost everyone could appeal to socialist slogans without feeling the need to follow them through to their logical conclusions.

Such was the state of the various movements that determined the course of the revolution when the final death-throes of the monarchy set in on 29 September 1918. Ludendorff, who until now had been the all-powerful head of the Supreme Army Command and had staked everything on victory in the offensives of the previous spring, now foresaw imminent collapse on the western front and demanded that an immediate request for an armistice be made on the basis of Wilson's Fourteen Points. At the same time, he pressed for the formation of a new government, which would have to concede Germany's defeat and accept the likely peace terms that would follow, from the majority parties in Parliament: the Social Democrats, the liberals and the Centre. The eventual effect of this cynical manoeuvre, which absolved the ruling conservative and military leadership from responsibility for the consequences of its own failed war policy, was to inflict on the democratic parties the odium of the notorious *Dolchstoß*, directed by stay-at-home politicians against the fighting soldiers in the trenches.

In the short run, however, Ludendorff's panic move backfired on its author. President Wilson's replies made it clear that an armistice was conditional on Germany's laying down her arms and on the resignation of those who had been responsible for German policy. The result was that the constitutional reforms put before Parliament in October by the new government under the Chancellor, Prince Max von Baden, became quite far-reaching; indeed, if they had been implemented, the Reich would have become a parliamentary democracy. There were also increasingly insistent calls behind the scenes for

Kaiser Wilhelm II to abdicate. At the same time, the people who had panicked in September now tried to change course yet again as events both inside and outside the country threatened their position. Rumours of a coup at the Kaiser's headquarters in Spa and an order to the German fleet to set sail on a last engagement sparked off a naval mutiny in Wilhelmshaven on 28 October and a sailors' insurrection in Kiel on 3 and 4 November. With these events, the mass peace movement had come into play.

Until this point it had looked as though the constitutionalist movement enjoyed sufficient institutional influence and popular support to be able to wind up the war on both the external and domestic fronts along the lines envisaged in October. Yet the uprisings of early November led to a rapid, and largely bloodless, seizure of power by workers' and soldiers' councils in most German cities, culminating in the revolution in Berlin on 9 November. The speed with which the *Räte* movement spread, and the fact that it spontaneously assumed the same form everywhere, demonstrated that the military and civil structures of the monarchy had forfeited all remnants of their legitimacy.

On the other hand, the attitude of the members of the peace and protest movement towards the agents of constitutional reform remained favourable. The *Räte* were quite ready to accept trusted figures in the two workers' parties as their leaders and representatives, and in some regions even liberal and Centre politicians as well. The *Räte* movement and the politicians who represented it in practice fell in behind the traditional methods of the constitutionalist movement; the socialist vocabulary used by the *Räte* had no substantive force. The language of the peace and protest movement did show, nevertheless, that there was a general expectation among its supporters that when the war and the revolution were over a new and just social order would have to be created, to compensate for the sacrifices made during the war and to fulfil the utopian hopes that had been dashed after August 1914. These conflicting attitudes within the *Räte* movement during the revolutionary period explain why the representatives of the radical left, notably the Spartacus group around Liebknecht and Luxemburg, remained so uninfluential. At the same time, however, it could be foreseen that the radicals would increase their influence if the gulf between the socialist aspirations of the *Räte* and the sober pragmatism of the SPD politicians were to widen. The gap between socialist idealism and cautious constitutionalism might conceivably have been bridged if the Social Democratic politicians had addressed themselves to the radical democratic elements in the *Räte* movement's programme and integrated them into the constitutional framework of the revolution. But this was an experiment that was never tried.

DECISIONS

The 'period of decisions' lasted two months: from 9 November 1918 to 19 January 1919. It was during this period that the lasting results of the revolution were achieved. At the same time, the decisions taken by the constitutionalist politicians created the conditions which led inevitably to the collapse of the mass movements that arose during the months that followed. The leading Social Democratic politicians insisted on the paramount importance of pursuing the limited goals of the constitutionalist movement, and with mass support – though this support was becoming increasingly divided against itself – they implemented them. In the process the resilience of the alliance between the constitutionalist and *Räte* movements was tested to the limit, until unity finally gave way and the two movements, one victorious and the other increasingly radicalized, became locked in the bitter confrontation that was to be the key feature of the revolution's final phase.

The revolutionary government that was formed in Berlin on 10 November 1918 from representatives of the two socialist parties rested on this unusual dual legitimacy, the crucial structural fact of this central stage of the revolution. The 'Council of People's Representatives' proclaimed itself an organ of the revolution, deriving its legitimacy from the Berlin workers' and soldiers' councils. At the same time, in its function as the government of the Reich it stood clearly for the tradition of constitutionalism, for the new constitutional system embodied in the October reforms and for continuity in the administration of state. Leading bureaucratic figures remained in positions they had previously occupied, and on 14 and 15 November two prominent liberals, Eugen Schiffer and Hugo Preuß, were appointed to head Reich ministries.

This rigid adherence to administrative continuity on the part of the new Reich leadership, despite its revolutionary mandate, is one of the most striking and distinctive features of the German revolution of 1918–19. For Friedrich Ebert, who rose during these months to become the dominant figure not only within the SPD but within the Reich government, the need for order remained paramount. All government measures had to conform to this requirement, even if they were based on fundamental and hitherto undisputed principles of Social Democracy. If we are to understand the political logic of the men who were now in charge of the revolution – and who, as we have said, could count on the backing of the bulk of the *Räte* movement, at least between November 1918 and January 1919 – we must examine their obsession with order.

There were several reasons, of varying significance, why Friedrich Ebert and his comrades did not question the primacy of order.[4] First and foremost, these men were conscious, as they viewed matters in 1918, of the truly shattering spectacle of events in Russia. The awful warning here was not so much the seizure of power by the Bolsheviks – most observers doubted that the Bolsheviks would last long, and their German imitators in the Spartacus group remained relatively uninfluential – as the breakdown, on both the domestic and international fronts, that had gone hand in hand with it. The Peace of Brest-Litovsk, dictated by the Germans in the spring of 1918, had deprived Russia, defenceless and in chaos, of half of its European territory, while the rest of the country was in a state of economic collapse, starvation and civil war. In addition, the conditions for an armistice imposed on Germany by the Allies were severe, and Ebert wanted to be able to enter the forthcoming peace-treaty negotiations from a position of greater strength. A further reason for wariness was that demobilizing the army and putting the economy back on to a peacetime footing would entail a degree of organizational effort by the state that had never previously been contemplated. These considerations underlay the agreement which was made on 10 November between Ebert and the *de facto* head of the armed forces, Groener, and which formed the basis for the fundamental compromise that conditioned relations between the new republic and the old military. Finally, the preoccupation with order and administrative continuity was also a product of the statist tradition within German Social Democracy. Apart from a few theorists such as Rosa Luxemburg, German socialists had envisaged socialism not as a process of spontaneous self-organization by the masses but as an expansion of public administration designed to promote the general welfare.

The revolution of 1918–19 remained faithful to this conception of the role of the state, and in this sense was a clear continuation of the liberal, parliamentary tradition of the constitutionalist movement. It also reflected the reluctance of the leadership, conscious of its new responsibilities in government, to subject a highly complex industrial society, with an infrastructure essential for the smooth running of daily life, to disturbing experiments in radical reorganization.

But despite the fact that there was considerable support for this concern for order, there were three vital problems which the constitutionalist revolution could not solve and which it merely trusted would go away. First, the hope that the military and the civil service would display a loyal neutrality was soon shown to be misplaced. By then, however, the government had become dependent on them. Secondly, although the new *Räte* movement was an important independent institutional factor in the political situation, the Social Democrats made no attempt to draw on the support of the *Räte* to introduce democratic reforms of the state administration, or to build up an army that might have been politically more compliant than the old monarchical officer class was able or willing to be. It is impossible to tell how such an experiment would have fared, but it was a fatal mistake that it was never tried. Thirdly, the only immediate reforms that the Social Democratic leadership was prepared to countenance were ones which formed part of the process of introducing constitutional democracy. All more ambitious measures, such as the nationalization of heavy industry or the break-up of the East Elbian estates, were referred to the jurisdiction of the future German Parliament. This decision, which had far-reaching consequences, was approved by a Reich Congress of Councils convened in Berlin on 16 December 1918. The same body also confirmed the authority of the Council of People's Representatives led by Ebert and called for the election of a National

Constituent Assembly based on universal proportional suffrage.

It is difficult to say whether or not the deferment of substantive economic and social reforms was a wise move. Certainly, it deprived the young republic of the chance of establishing a clear and distinctive socio-political identity which the adherents of the *Räte* movement might have been more willing to defend. On the other hand, the fact that the Prussian Minister for Education, Culture and Church Affairs, Adolf Hoffmann, failed in his attempt in December 1918 to bring about a permanent separation of schools and the church shows how limited the political options were, even in this early phase. All that Hoffmann achieved was to boost the electoral fortunes of the Centre Party, trading on memories of Bismarck's conflict with the Catholic church, which possibly cost the two socialist parties their electoral majority. It is also debatable whether, say, nationalization of the mining industry would actually have satisfied the expectations of those in the peace and protest movement, since those expectations would later have been dashed anyway by the economic distress of the early post-war period.

In any event, the leaders of the revolution decided to go no further than to call for a constitution to be drafted by a National Assembly. This course of action met with widespread assent, if only because Germans had long been accustomed to the mechanism of political representation through Parliament. Not the least important consequence was that the balance of forces within the National Assembly would bring the non-socialist half of the electorate back into the reckoning and so tone down the constitutional transformation to which the SPD was committed.

In a further development, on 15 November 1918 the leaders of heavy industry and the trade unions concluded an agreement on a *Zentralarbeitsgemeinschaft*, or 'central working association'. The outlines of such an agreement had already been sketched in October during discussions on a joint approach to the impending problem of demobilization. The prospect of a new corporatist socio-economic settlement allowed trade union leaders to feel that they could live with the retention of capitalist forms of ownership.[5] Long-cherished social demands such as the eight-hour day were to be met, and there would be an attempt to establish new ways of dealing with problems of social welfare and collective wage bargaining. This agreement between the representatives of major economic interests reinforced the SPD leadership's reluctance to launch an interventionist attack on property.

Decisions of this sort, clearly signalling that the revolution was to be confined to constitutional and corporatist measures, were bound to place a strain on the alliance with the *Räte* and to rupture the coalition with the USPD (Independent Socialists). There were armed clashes in Berlin over Christmas 1918; at the end of December the USPD representatives left the government; street fighting followed in Berlin between 5 and 11 January 1919. The latter events have since acquired the somewhat inappropriate label of the 'Spartacus uprising'. The Spartacists were, in fact, preoccupied with the internal problems of setting up their party – the KPD (Communist Party) was founded on 1 January 1919 – and had no more of a clear-cut strategy during the confused events of January than did the representatives of the *Räte* and leaders of the USPD who also took part in the 'uprising'. The left's uncertain stance underlined its marginality and fragmentation; its defeat at the hands of pro-government workers' units and Freikorps (free corps) volunteers, whose atrocities culminated in the murder of Rosa Luxemburg and Karl Liebknecht on 15 January, heralded the imminent collapse of the alliance between the constitutionalists and the protest movement. Thwarted in their aspirations, the revolutionary workers turned 'Karl and Rosa' into a unifying symbol of martyrdom that was far more potent than the two leaders themselves had ever been while they were alive.

Gustav Noske's ruthless decision to act as a 'bloodhound' in order to uphold the Social Democrats' version of the revolution, and the unscrupulous drafting of so-called Freikorps fighters, of dubious political coloration, to move against protesting workers, turned the Social Democrats into a party of civil war. The split within the working class that the revolution had hitherto kept largely concealed was now ripped open to view; and the party had also – quite unnecessarily, given the real balance of forces in January – delivered itself into the hands of armed groups for whom the fight against 'Bolshevism' was merely a prelude to the fight against the revolutionary current as a whole.

The final important event in these two decisive months was the election of the National Assembly, held on 19 January 1919. In the polls the workers' parties failed to secure an absolute majority of votes: the SPD won 37.9 per cent and the USPD 7.6 per cent. A full-fledged socialist programme was thus rejected by the electorate. All the same, the parties which had made up the Inter-Party Committee in 1917–18, the nucleus of the constitutionalist movement, did achieve an overall majority. These parties – the 'Weimar Coalition' that was to bring in the new constitution – comprised, in addition to the SPD, the Centre Party, which gained 19.7 per cent of the votes, and the liberal-left German Democratic Party (DDP), which gained 18.5 per cent. To their right were the parties that rejected the Republic, the one hesitantly, the other vehemently: the national-liberal German People's Party (DVP) with 4.4 per cent electoral support, and the German National People's Party (DNVP) with 10.3 per cent, the latter party a mixture of conservative and radical-right elements.

Apart from some changes at the margins, these results display a considerable degree of electoral continuity between the monarchy and the Republic. If it is legitimate to use the election figures for 19 January 1919 as evidence of the state of national opinion in the preceding November and December, then Ebert's policy of caution – his unwillingness to govern against the wishes of the majority – was justified. On the other hand, it is a moot point how far the very cautiousness of the Ebert government may actually have reinforced the resistance to revolutionary change on the part of the German people.

DISAPPOINTMENTS

By 19 January 1919, then, the period of decisions was over. For the time being, the question of the power structure was settled: the shape of the new political order would be the responsibility of the Weimar Coalition, and the new social and economic order would be defined by the *Zentralarbeitsgemeinschaft*. But the social forces that had given rise to the protest movement and the *Räte* had not been broken. On the contrary, in the months ahead the struggle by the working-class masses reached a level of intensity which surpassed that of the revolution proper in November 1918. A clearer action programme also emerged, with its aim the participation of the *Räte* in decision-making at all levels and structural reforms such as the nationalization of the mines. During this phase the more radical politicians in the USPD and in some radical-left groups within the *Räte* movement made increasing headway, and the break with the SPD widened. Yet despite the upswing in revolutionary activity, the period in general can be characterized as one of disappointment, and not only in terms of concrete achievements. The mass strikes and armed conflict that took place in the Ruhr, in Munich (where there was a short-lived *Räte* republic), in Bremen and in central Germany were sparked off by the realization that the hope of establishing 'socialism', in whatever form, had been dashed.

In effect, the months between January and April 1919 saw a repetition, in the different regions of the Reich, of the course of events in the fighting in Berlin at the beginning of the year. The outcome was that the *Räte* movement was, at one and the same time, politicized and robbed of its power, and its adherents retreated into bitterness and disenchantment. This pattern was later to repeat itself in 1920, with the Kapp putsch and the March revolution that followed it.

The overall effects of the upheavals of 1918–19 cannot be assessed until we have dealt with the peace treaty, the creation of the new constitution and Germany's domestic adjustment to peacetime conditions. We can, however, briefly sum up the position in which the three principal movements that had carried out the revolution found themselves at the end of this third phase.

The constitutionalist movement had carried the day on all of the issues, including corporatist reform, which it regarded as vital: in this sense it had had a 'good' revolution. On the other hand, it had bought its victory at the cost of a heavy reliance on the old élites in the military and the bureaucracy, and as early as the Reichstag elections of 6 June 1920 it had to face the fact that majority electoral support for the Weimar Coalition that had brought in the new constitution had already faded away.

The social-protest and peace movement had helped bring the constitutionalists to power in November 1918, but in the two crucial months of the revolution the movement had been unable either to evolve its own independent line of action or to lodge itself within the new political order as a kind of alternative force for democratization. The thwarting of the hopes of the mass movement – which were never likely to be fulfilled in their entirety – led to conflict tantamount to civil war. This conflict was later to make the gulf between the majority Social Democrats and the more radical sections of the working class unbridgeable.

As part of this process of disenchantment, the USPD split, and in 1920 sections of the protest movement allied themselves with the KPD, which, after the failure of the revolution in Germany, became increasingly firmly committed to the apparently more successful Bolshevik model.

Once these processes of transformation were complete, by the summer of 1920, the pattern that was to typify the remaining years of the Weimar Republic was fixed: the forces of democratization were split, and their capacity to act effectively was checked.

THE MAKING OF THE CONSTITUTION: OPENNESS AND COMPROMISE

The victory of the constitutionalist revolution was most clearly apparent in the drafting of the constitution itself. Yet the constitution can scarcely be said to have been the crowning glory of the revolution, as the process of its adoption was fairly unspectacular and was not an event of symbolic importance that imprinted itself on the minds of contemporaries. Besides, the months of 1919 during which the debates on the constitution occurred were overshadowed by far more momentous matters: the third phase of the revolution and the peace conference at Versailles. Largely ignored by people at the time, unloved by almost all strands of political opinion in the later years of the Weimar Republic, severely castigated by historians – the principal document in the history of German democracy has never had a good press. And yet, to be fair to the Weimar constitution, we should not measure it against expectations which the immediate events of the revolution and the later exigencies of the post-war situation were bound to leave unsatisfied; nor should we ascribe to it all the ills that arose when its provisions were implemented, or indeed resisted.[6]

Vital preliminary decisions concerning the basic principles of the new political and social order had already been taken by the time the National Assembly began its work. When Ebert, on 15 November 1918, charged the liberal-left jurist Hugo Preuß with the task of preparing a draft constitution, it was clear that the resulting document would represent a continuation of German constitutional tradition. On the same day, moreover, the trade unions and employers launched their policy of corporatism on the socio-economic front, with the unions acknowledging the principle of capitalist ownership. Since, in addition, the revolution had spread on a regional basis, with separate governments being formed in the various *Länder* (states), it was also apparent that the new Reich would be organized as a federal structure and would have to take account of different political traditions in the provinces. Originally, in fact, Preuß had proposed a restructuring of the *Länder* whereby Prussia, with its position of dominance, would be partitioned, the smaller states would be merged and the sphere of jurisdiction of the central national authority would be considerably enlarged. But by the time a states' conference of Reich and *Länder* representatives had gathered on 25 January 1919, this scheme had already become a dead letter. The influence exercised by the *Länder* over the shape of the constitution was strengthened by being institutionalized in a states' committee which drafted the 'Law Concerning Provisional Authority in the Reich'. Once this law was passed, on 10 February, the basic division of power in the new republic was laid down, even before the formal debate on the constitution in the National Assembly had begun.

The actual drafting of the constitution itself also proceeded in relatively unspectacular fashion because the politicians in the National Assembly, where there were no clear-cut majorities and the balance of forces was always shifting, were constantly driven to agree to compromises. Thus, on questions of property ownership there was a middle-class alliance between liberals and the Centre, whereas on all matters concerning educational and religious policy the Centre stood opposed to the secular-minded liberals and Social Democrats. The *Räte* movement, of course, had been defeated as a political force, and yet some of its ideas on *Mitbestimmung* (co-determination, or participatory decision-making) on economic matters also found their way into the National Assembly's resolutions. In addition, a split between centralists and federalists ran through all parties.

A fully consistent constitution had never been likely, nor would it have been desirable. The only way in which such a constitution might have come about would have been through the fiat of a victorious radical majority, but both the power-political pattern created by the revolution and the party-political verdict delivered by the German electorate amounted to a blend of continuity and change, and the result was an unstable balance of political forces. The inconsistencies of the constitution may have offended political and legal purists, and were indeed frequently deplored. Yet, as an authentic expression of the power balance prevailing in 1919, they were an attempt to get to grips with the basic structural problem confronting any modern constitution: namely, how to accommodate mutually antagonistic social pressures, organized special-interest groups and competing political ideologies and sets of values. Of the two possible ways of dealing with this problem – confining the constitution to being a set of purely structural and administrative statutes, or making it a repository of competing prescriptions, an avowedly pluralist compromise – the founding fathers of Weimar went for the second, more risky, option. The constitution set out an array of provisions, but these were to be given definition and substance only by subsequent legislation and political action.

Historians, like people living at the time, have judged the Weimar constitution in the light of the concrete political uses to which it was put. Certainly, the ways in which a particular constitutional scheme is used or misused are in a sense the responsibility of that scheme. But if we are to judge the Weimar constitution fairly, we should also take into account the alternative outcomes which were inherent in it but which, in the political conditions of the 1920s, had no chance of actually being realized. It is precisely when a constitution explicitly enshrines the principle of openness and compromise, as was the case with the constitution of the first German Republic of 1919, that we should lay stress on the unused potential for democratic innovation which it contains.

As far as the detailed provisions of the constitution are concerned, we shall deal only briefly with some of them here.

The adoption of proportional representation directly bolstered the organizational importance of party lists in the political system, despite the fact that parties were not explicitly named in the text of the constitution. Interestingly, however, the results of the 1919 election were not greatly different from the results of the Reichstag election of 1912 in which each constituency had only one member. The introduction of female suffrage and the lowering of the voting age made little difference either. This relatively high degree of continuity in respect of party politics is evidence against the view, common in older research, that proportional representation contributed significantly to the collapse of the Republic. The fact that the middle-class parties lost votes in the 1920s, first to splinter parties and then to the NSDAP, was not a result of proportional representation; nor could the rise of the NSDAP as a mass party between 1930 and 1932 have been blocked by some different form of voting system.

As we have mentioned, the decision to adopt a federal system had been made during the first days of the revolution. But although certain matters involving, for example, education and religion now came within the jurisdiction of the Reich, as they had not done after 1871, the powers of the national government were tempered by the continuing existence and independent political role of the *Länder*, notably including Prussia. Indeed, it was the Social Democrats, ideologically committed to a centralized republic, who in practice were to rely on the 'Prussian bulwark', governed by an SPD-led Weimar Coalition.[7] Conversely, repeatedly canvassed plans for centralization, which was provided for under the constitution, were eventually (albeit only partially) implemented in 1932–3 by those political groups whose aim was to destroy the last remaining self-defence mechanisms which the Republic possessed.

The centrepiece of the power structure created by the constitution was the much-debated dual system whereby both the Reichstag and the Reich President were elected by direct popular vote. This system, in which the national government was tugged in different directions by Parliament and the head of state, was a perpetuation, for better or worse, of German political tradition, despite the fact that, in contrast to the position under the monarchy, the head of state was now elected and the head of government was subject to the approval of (or at any rate the absence of express rejection by) a parliamentary majority. Since the Republic was destroyed through the active connivance of the second Reich President, Paul von Hindenburg, the dualistic nature of the Weimar constitution has attracted widespread criticism. On the other hand, it can be said that under Ebert the selfsame dual system proved to be a stabilizing force during the crises of the post-war years.

Those political thinkers, such as Max Weber, who helped pave the way for the new constitution had particularly favoured a strong Reich President invested with charismatic legitimacy, on the grounds that such a figure would be able to counteract the political paralysis they feared would result if parliamentary power were monopolized by party bureaucrats. Institutional conflict was thus built into the constitution, in the interest of encouraging political flexibility and innovation. No one foresaw that before long there would actually be too many political crises and that the party system itself would become unstable.

The desire for stability that was felt so strongly in the years after the Second World War was based on historical memories of the crises that had marked the Weimar era. This feeling found particular expression in the strengthened position of the Federal Chancellor under the Basic Law of the Bonn constitution. It would be unhistorical to look for similar sentiments in the constitutional debates of 1919. In any case, the lifetime of the Weimar Republic was far too short for well-tried ground rules governing political activity within the dualistic framework of the constitution to have evolved. It should be remembered, however, that dualistic systems have functioned successfully, and have weathered crises, in the United States and in France under the Fifth Republic.

Ultimately, the success or failure of the Weimar scheme would depend on whether the political forces operating within it were prepared to exercise their rights according to the terms of the constitution or whether they would actively seek to undermine it.

The principal test was to come with the use of emergency powers granted under the notorious Article 48.[8] This article not only allowed the Reich President to override *Länder* which failed to fulfil their constitutional obligations but also gave the President sovereign legislative and executive authority in a state of emergency. The validity of legislation enacted under Article 48 was not restricted to the duration of the state of emergency, although it could be rescinded by Parliament at any time. Despite this democratic safeguard, Article 48 was used in the years 1930–33 to legislate in defiance of the will of Parliament, when the President countered each attempt to terminate his emergency powers by ordering a dissolution. Indeed, in this situation Parliament's right to rescind led the presidential governments into a predicament from which there were only two ways of escape: either constant dissolutions of the Reichstag followed by new elections, or an outright coup. In this sense Article 48 certainly did not offer adequate protection against abuses on the part of a President hostile to the constitution. On the other hand, what provisions would have been adequate?

A directly elected Reich President was only one among various plebiscitary elements which the framers wrote into the constitution. A further ingredient was the institution of the referendum itself. A referendum could be called by the Reich President or by the Reichsrat, if either of these were opposed to a piece of legislation passed by the Reichstag, or by petition on the part of a specific proportion of the electorate. In practice, referendums were used rarely and were never successful, so that the view of earlier historians that plebiscitary elements in the constitution fatally undermined the Republic would not appear to be particularly plausible.

Not only did the Weimar constitution specify the institutional structures and decision-making processes of the political system: these formal, procedural regulations were complemented by a second main section of the constitution containing substantive provisions. Going well beyond a statement of traditional fundamental rights, a total of fifty-six articles spelled out in detail the 'basic rights and obligations of the German people'. The constitution, in fact, was a brave attempt to specify the essential characteristics of a democratic welfare state. The statement of new basic rights guaranteed local self-government and the position of the permanent civil service, protected the rights of religious denominations and defined the basic structure of the system of education and learning; declarations on the family and the protection of children and young people were also included. In the field of social welfare and the economy, the 'regulation of economic activity' was linked to 'principles of justice' and the goal of a 'dignified existence for all people', guaranteeing the 'economic freedom of the individual' (Article 151) 'within these limits'. On these foundations, which reflected both the aspirations of the revolution of 1918 and the class compromise with which the revolution had ended, a series of specific provisions was erected, dealing with nationalization, safety measures for workers, welfare insurance, labour exchanges, unemployment benefit, freedom of association for trade unions and workers' participation in decision-making in *Wirtschaftsräte* (economic councils).

This list of basic rights demonstrates graphically the sense in which the constitution was a compromise document. The demands of different social groups were simply set down in disjointed fashion. Concrete pledges were made which could be delivered only by votes in Parliament, along with formulaic injunctions which, again, could be given content only by subsequent legislation.

While it is easy to enumerate such inconsistencies, it is hard to suggest an alternative constitution that might have been better suited to the conflicts and complexities of a modern industrial class society. Given that the Weimar Republic led such a short and crisis-ridden life, the extent to which it implemented the programme of basic rights was really quite creditable. The successes ranged from the Reich Youth Welfare Law of 1922 to the Labour Exchanges and Unemployment Insurance Law of 1927. Other projects, it is true, such as a Reich School Law and a labour-law code, could not be implemented because of social tensions and lack of parliamentary support.

Any open and avowedly pluralistic constitutional settlement would have had to face the same fundamental problem. The new structure had to pass the practical test of achieving a basic consensus and gaining the co-operation of a working majority from among the political and social groups that had created it. But the open character of the Weimar constitution came into collision with a number of factors that would have been present in Germany in the 1920s under any circumstances:

– in the realm of domestic politics, there was growing segmentation and deadlock among the groups which had established the Republic;

– on the economic front, there was little scope for raising living standards: there was no growth to cushion the effect of, and extend, the initial compromise that had been reached between employers and unions;

– accordingly, in the realm of social policy, too, the scope for compromise and reform became increasingly narrow.

The Weimar constitution, in fact, was simply not given the chance of proving itself: of becoming accepted, through practical day-to-day routine, as the basic legal framework underlying the political and socio-economic life of the Republic. Instead, it was used as the source for a series of stopgap solutions which satisfied no one. Under these circumstances, no sustainable political settlement was possible. Everyone would have been happy to claim credit for success, after the event; but when the Weimar settlement most needed friends, almost everyone was only too happy to disown it.

THE PEACE TREATY AND ITS PROBLEMS

The Paris peace conferences had scarcely been concluded before the Versailles myth became a more potent factor in German attitudes than the actual terms of the peace settlement itself. The nationalist response, transcending party lines, was summed up in the slogan 'the shameful diktat of Versailles',[9] and such thinking continued to prompt many historians after the Second World War to hold the Versailles Treaty responsible for the rise of Hitler. If we are to judge the period dispassionately, however, we need to make a distinction between the psychological burdens which Versailles imposed and the real effects of the peace treaty.[10] At the same time, it must be granted that the German obsession with Versailles played a part, in turn, in influencing subsequent political realities.

Four groups of factors served to determine in advance the nature of the peace treaty that would emerge.

The nationalistic frenzy of 1914, and the subsequent belief that the massive losses caused by the war could be justified only by equally massive eventual victory, at first meant that public opinion in all the combatant nations was bent on inflicting a punitive peace settlement. Although by the end of 1918 the Germans were coming round, reluctantly, to the idea of a negotiated peace, earlier attitudes were still very powerful below the surface, and they provoked a surge of indignation when the peace terms were made public. Conversely, public opinion in the victorious powers was scarcely willing to be fobbed off with a negotiated peace rather than the spoils of triumph. All the politicians concerned were influenced by the strength of public feeling, or at any rate were obliged to take it into account.

In the second place, Germany herself had demonstrated, with the Peace of Brest-Litovsk imposed on Soviet Russia in 1918, the sort of treatment that her own defeated opponents might expect. This, in the eyes of the Allies, undermined the moral force of the case for a lenient treatment of Germany on their part.

Thirdly, the armistice conditions of November 1918 had curtailed German armaments and power to such an extent that it was impossible for Germany to start up the war again. This automatically reduced the political influence of the United States, but in any case Wilson was hesitant in exerting American power in favour of a peace settlement along the lines of his Fourteen Points (to the extent that these were capable of being given a precise interpretation).

Finally, during the Paris peace conference, wars in Turkey, Russia and elsewhere were still going on. While the debate over the Versailles 'diktat' continued to fuel Germany's long-standing preoccupation with her own problems, the Allies' attention was shifting to wider questions of world peace. For the Allies, the new pattern of states in large areas of eastern, central and southern Europe, the 'red peril' threatened by Soviet Russia and by Communist uprisings in other countries and problems of demobilization and reconstruction of the world economy were matters just as pressing as the German question.

Given these prior conditions, it was inevitable that the process of peace-making at Versailles should have been marked by inconsistencies. On the purely procedural level, the Allies presented the Germans with a completed draft of the treaty for signature. Note was taken of only a few of the objections raised by the German delegation and, more important, no formal negotiations with the losing side were conducted. In a formal sense, indeed, the victors imposed a diktat. On the other hand, the Allies' action was not so much an arrogant exercise of power as a symptom of their disguised internal disunity. The Allies were only able to reach compromises among themselves behind closed doors. The form of the Versailles process, which was so humiliating to the Germans, actually reflected divisions among the western powers which if anything worked to Germany's material advantage.

There was a similar ambivalence about the actual content of the Versailles terms themselves, which were a blend of harsh, symbolic and immediate penalties and milder structural conditions, with possibilities of revision and conciliation in the longer term. Germany's economic and demographic superiority over her neighbours, particularly France, was not erased by Versailles. France did not achieve her war aims and was only partially protected by the new League of Nations and a projected British–French–American security pact (which never in fact materialized). Some of the symbolic gestures were actually worse than useless. They may have satisfied public opinion in the victorious states in the short run, but in German eyes they discredited the treaty as a whole. The war-guilt clause, for example, which was included in order to justify the demand for reparations, was turned into a powerful weapon of agitation by German counter-propaganda.

The substantive conditions imposed by the peace settlement were severe, but they were bearable.

The territories that Germany lost – leaving aside the colonies, which were valueless anyway – either had majorities of non-German speakers (in the case of cessions to Poland and Denmark) or, as in Alsace-Lorraine, had a German-speaking population which had never been fully integrated into the Reich after 1871. The creation of non-viable German-speaking mini-states in Danzig, Memel and the Saar was certainly ill-conceived; only the last of these was given the prospect of determining its future in a plebiscite. The drawing of the boundary with Poland caused particular indignation among Germans. Given the mixed national pattern of settlement over a wide area of contiguous territory, any German–Polish frontier was bound to leave a sizeable minority on the 'wrong' side, but whereas this fact had worked in the Germans' favour under the frontiers of 1815 to 1918, this time the Poles were the beneficiaries. But the widespread feeling in Germany that an amputation had been performed on the eastern frontier did not spring merely from local absurdities in the way the new border was drawn; it was a response to the fundamental alteration in the position of nationalities that had taken place in central, eastern and southern Europe. Three multinational empires had been replaced by a dozen small and medium-sized states. Of these, only the states which were successors of the powers that had lost the war (Germany, Austria and Hungary) had become fairly homogeneous in terms of national make-up (although they were forced to accept that sizeable minorities of their own nationals now lived outside their own borders). The other new states had boundaries that were contentious according to criteria of nationality, and all contained substantial national minorities within their territory. Whereas the great international peace treaties between 1648 and 1815 had led to the creation of a balanced group of federal structures out of this jumble of nationalities, the Paris peace treaties were based entirely on the principle of national self-determination; any resulting problems would be resolved through the League of Nations and by legislation protecting minorities. In practice, however, these new states were too weak to project a clear national identity and they became breeding-grounds for mutually conflicting irredentist claims and for experiments in enforced nationalist regimentation. But the German reaction to the impossibility of drawing satisfactory frontiers in eastern Europe also remained caught in the same nation-state mentality that had given rise to these problems. The Germans argued for a revision of frontiers in their own favour, but this would merely have transposed the problem of minorities back within their own territory.

Indeed, by succumbing to the nationalistic obsession with revising her eastern frontier, Germany deprived herself of the opportunity of playing the real trump card which the Paris peace settlement had dealt her. The repulse of Russia and the division of central, eastern and southern Europe into a handful of small and medium-sized states, temporarily dependent on France but not likely to remain so in the longer term, gave Germany the chance to establish an informal hegemony in the region by expanding her economic and cultural influence through a policy of accommodation and co-operation with the new nations. The Germans' fixation on the myth of the 'shameful diktat' of Versailles blinded them to the medium-term strategic advantage which the new realities created by Versailles and the other Paris treaties had given them.

long-term sense, Germany's geographical position and
strength were only slightly weakened, or perhaps even
by Versailles, onerous disarmament conditions certainly
made up for this in the short term. These conditions included the
restriction of the Reichswehr to a professional army of 100,000 men
and massive limitations on weapons and defensive fortifications; the
Allies were given comprehensive rights of inspection and disarmament
control within Germany; and the Rhineland was to be occupied for
fifteen years. All of this was bound to be seen as particularly humiliating
by a nation whose conception of itself, during the war and the pre-
war era, had been founded on military strength and a militarist posture.
In the longer run, however, the treaty itself provided Germany with
a strong case for revision on this point. German disarmament had been
proclaimed as the prelude to general disarmament, but if other nations
were not going to be made to comply, then Germany's right to rebuild
her own weaponry would be given moral legitimacy.

Reparations provoked a national outcry, not least because of the
war-guilt clause that was invoked to justify them, but, although they
proved to be a serious burden on the post-war German economy, they
were by no means the obstacle to future economic recovery that
nationalistic propaganda painted them to be. In any case, the level of
reparations and the size of the payment burden did not become a
central matter for controversy until the period 1920–24.

To sum up, we can characterize the Versailles Treaty as a document
which, while not without its shortcomings on matters of detail, sought
overall to provide a balanced solution to the problem of establishing
peace both in Europe and in the world as a whole. Despite the Allies'
triumphalist behaviour in the moment of victory and the angry,
nationalistic response of the Germans, Germany's long-run position as
a great power was not only maintained but enhanced. From the point
of view of *Realpolitik*, practicable routes to possible future revision
were left open. At the same time, the treaty had created a psychological
barrier, in the form of the nationalist notion of the 'diktat', which
would not make revision easy to achieve.

*

WINDING UP THE WAR ON THE DOMESTIC FRONT

For all those in positions of political responsibility, the main worry at the end of 1918 and the beginning of 1919 was that of winding up the war on the domestic front. Millions of soldiers had to be brought back home and found work; millions of war victims had to be cared for. A highly complex economy geared to war had to be transformed into a peace economy. Not least, mechanisms of supply, transport and law and order had to be kept going at a time of defeat and revolution.[11]

Of course, those in charge of the economy had already given thought during the war itself to the eventuality of demobilization. But their plans to use the bureaucratic controls of 'war socialism' as a basis for establishing a state-capitalist planned economy in peacetime found little support. It was not only employers who wanted to return to a 'free economy'. Economic direction had existed to deal with short-ages, and it was discredited among the population generally, workers included. The group of industrialists led by Hugo Stinnes and trade union leaders headed by Carl Legien encountered relatively little resistance when, at the time of the October reforms of 1918, it drew up the outlines of an agreement providing for co-operation between trade union and employers' leaders to complement the measures being taken by the state Demobilization Office. The revolution delayed the conclusion of this *Zentralarbeitsgemeinschaft* agreement only by a few days, and it was signed on 15 November 1918. The new director of the state Demobilization Office, Josef Koeth, fitted into the picture well: he had already resisted all proposals for a system of state-capitalist economic planning, and had spelled out his own position *vis-à-vis* the unions and industry by saying that 'on questions affecting the workers he was more in the Social Democratic camp, whereas on economic questions he was on the side of the employers'.[12]

The first phase of demobilization went through astonishingly smoothly. There was sufficient administrative continuity to sustain transport and the infrastructure, and co-operation among employers and trade unionists enabled the most pressing problems of reintegration to be handled flexibly. Above all, the measures that were taken accorded with what people were doing anyway: the soldiers simply wanted to get home as quickly as possible and, once home, to re-establish their 'normal' pre-war way of life. Another successful aspect of the transition to a peacetime economy was that the maximum use was made of the free market, but state intervention was retained to deal with severe problems and a corporatist agreement was used to safeguard employees' welfare. By contrast, most of the longer-term plans of the Demobilization Office came to naught: the principal feature of the second phase was that the peacetime economy was consolidated and stimulated by means of open-handed inflationary financial measures. On the other hand, this inflationary policy of 1919–20 undoubtedly kept the unemployment figures relatively low and protected Germany from the effects of the world economic crisis of 1920–21. We shall discuss later the longer-term significance of the inflationary decade 1914–24 (see chapter 3).

It is only if we compare the demobilization after the war of 1914–18 with the chaos that followed the Second World War that we can measure the scale of the earlier achievement – an achievement that was not grasped by contemporaries precisely because it happened with such apparent ease. The comparative success of the Demobilization Office, the *Zentralarbeitsgemeinschaft* and the revolutionary government cheated these institutions of the credit they deserved. At the same time, the smooth transition to a peacetime economy kept expectations high, pegged to nostalgic memories of pre-war standards rather than the plight the country actually now faced. The effort put into providing for war victims, for example, was substantial, and yet was taken for granted, whereas there was perpetual criticism of the bureaucratic procedures involved and of the generally fairly modest levels of benefit that were all that the state of the post-war economy permitted.[13]

All told, the Republic did not gain recognition for its achievements precisely because it succeeded in re-establishing a peacetime economy in a relatively trouble-free fashion. This did not, however, prevent the blame for the generally poor performance of the post-war economy from being laid at its door.

*

A REVOLUTION THAT FAILED, OR A
COMPROMISE THAT WOULD SURVIVE?

Seen as a social revolution, the establishment of a new order in Germany in 1918–19 was a revolution that failed. But the revolution was only one part, albeit an important and spectacular one, of a wider process: the winding up of the war on both the domestic and external fronts. If the German situation is considered in its entirety and is compared with post-war developments in other European countries, it is possible to deliver a more favourable verdict. Certainly, events did not proceed in a clear, simple sweep: the recourse to compromise merely put off the day when conflicts would have to be resolved, while also depriving the new state of a glamorous focus of identity in the form of a symbolic revolutionary act comparable with the storming of the Bastille. Compromises can be lived with, but hardly loved. Yet the new constitutional structure stood up well in a comparison with the preceding Wilhelmine dispensation, and particularly so in view of one of the potential alternatives, namely the sort of chauvinistic mass integration that had flared up in August 1914.

The effects of the euphoria of August 1914 should not, of course, be exaggerated. Nevertheless, although mass sentiment had become more friable, towards the end of the war it rallied once again as hopes for victory were aroused by the installation of the Hindenburg–Ludendorff Supreme Command in 1916, the diktat of Brest-Litovsk and the noisy propaganda put out by the 'German Fatherland Party'. The options at the end of the war, in other words, were not limited merely to left-wing socialism and moderate Social Democracy. Some form of mass totalitarian integration, riding on a wave of aggressive nationalism, remained a long-term threat even after the Supreme Command had forfeited its credibility through military defeat in the autumn of 1918. The temporary crippling of the right gave the November revolution an easy victory: perhaps too easy a victory. The orderly departure of the old power groupings and the conciliatory behaviour of those members of the old élites who remained encouraged the illusion among the constitutionalist politicians that they could count on the loyalty of the armed and unarmed 'servants of the state'. Because there seemed to be no present danger of counter-revolution, the wind was also taken out of the sails of the social-protest movement and the left during the decisive revolutionary months. And by the time the threat posed by the Freikorps and the citizens' militias became apparent, the new power relationships had already stabilized.

From a longer-term perspective, it is clear that the proto-totalitarianism that flared up in 1917 was the truly significant alternative to the fundamental constitutional compromises of 1918. And it was this strain in the German political tradition that reasserted itself, in radicalized form, when the National Socialists seized power in 1933.

The achievements of Weimar constitutionalism, then, need to be judged against the totalitarian potential that existed on the right, and not just in light of the failure to institute a full range of democratic or socialist reforms. Despite its imperfections, the Weimar Reich constitution provided an open framework for an experiment in democracy which would have been quite capable of further refinement under more favourable external circumstances. It brought different groups into the new order: enduringly so in the case of the old 'enemies of the Reich' (*Reichsfeinde*) in the Social Democratic labour movement and Catholic political groups, temporarily so in the case of sections of the middle class. It offered new corporatist ways of attempting to reconcile basic social divisions, and it laid down the foundations for an expansion of the welfare state. Finally, it was signally successful, by international standards, in helping make possible the transition to a peacetime economy.

So much for the positive achievements of the immediate post-war years. There were, however, a number of important elements in the situation which did not bode well for the future. These included the burdens imposed by the peace treaty; the fact that the hopes of the social-protest movement had been frustrated; the continued existence of élites with anti-republican attitudes, notably in the higher echelons of state where their influence might be critical; the dearth of republican commitment, both social and symbolic, on the part of a growing number of members of the middle class who were among the losers in the decade of inflation; and, aggravating all these factors, the lack of governmental freedom of manoeuvre in policy-making, caused by the stagnation of the post-war economy.

Given all these problems, the openness and reliance on compromise which characterized the new order in Germany made the future of the democratic experiment highly uncertain. The experiment would turn out to have been justified only if it produced concrete political and social results. It was not yet clear whether the scope for implementing reforms, consolidating the welfare state and providing ɹ financial underpinning for the settlement of 1918–19 actually existed, or whether, instead, the conflicts and social divisions that had not been resolved would flare up even more fiercely. Would the old élites exact unceremonious revenge for the revolution? Would a surge of nationalist resentment even sweep away the unglamorous compromise of 1918–19 altogether and reinstate the model of society that had prevailed during the war?

We can agree with Heinrich August Winkler's conclusion that German society was already too 'advanced' for a revolution of either the classical or the Bolshevik type.[14] The existence of a democratic tradition in Germany and the complexity of Germany's industrial and social structure meant that any radical break with the past was impossible; what was needed was a delicate balancing act among different groups in society and a constant trade-off between continuity and reform. At the same time, it was her very modernity that made Germany susceptible to the temptation to avoid resolving her internal conflicts within a social-liberal constitutional and political system, and instead to displace the pressure externally, resorting to an aggressive, authoritarian, nationalistic system dominated by a military–industrial complex. This danger had been provisionally warded off in 1918–19, thanks to military defeat and the establishment of the new republican order. The survival of the new settlement would depend on whether or not the constitutional and class compromises on which the Republic was founded would prove a sufficient basis for its legitimacy, and whether the Republic's openness could be mobilized to protect and consolidate them. But this meant that the success of the republican experiment would depend critically on the amount of freedom of manoeuvre, notably in an economic sense, that it was given during the years which lay immediately ahead.

3. The Post-War Crisis,
1920–23

The years 1920–23 were among the most hectic and eventful of the Weimar Republic. There was a headlong succession of dramatic developments in domestic, economic and foreign policy, either combining in their impact or severally constraining the government's ability to act. Since, therefore, a strictly chronological account of events would be confusing, we shall discuss separately the most important groups of problems on the foreign, economic and domestic fronts.

It should, though, be borne in mind that a schematic approach of this sort runs the risk of distorting the historical picture in an opposite sense, since the broad shape of events during the years of post-war crisis was, after all, obscure to people living at the time; indeed, the very confusion felt by contemporaries and the interdependence of the problems in which they were caught up were perhaps the most decisive factors of the post-war era.

FULFILMENT AND DEFIANCE

The Treaty of Versailles came into force on 10 January 1920, but anyone who supposed that German foreign policy was embarking on a period of calm was due for a disappointment. It was only now that the real problems began to make themselves felt. In the first place, the Allies had postponed making final decisions on reparations at Versailles. Instead, the total sum which Germany would have to find was to be fixed in later negotiations; so was the method of payment, a question which would have vital consequences for financial policy. Secondly, the actual conclusion of the treaty caused international relations to slide into outright confrontation as all the parties, victors and vanquished alike, now suddenly discovered a pressing need to try to revise the treaty's provisions. Wrangles over the way in which the terms of the treaty should be applied in detail went cheek by jowl with attempts, veiled and overt, to start up a second round of the struggle for the post-war European order.

Although questions of reparations and treaty revision overlapped, we shall discuss first the broad aspects of the reparations issue.[1] The central problem was that Germany was to pay compensation not merely for the war damage that she herself had directly caused, but also for the costs of the war as a whole. This reflected the fact that the First World War had turned into a total war – a war in which, in each country, the entire national economy and the 'home front' had been mobilized, and not just the military machine. But the resulting assessments for reparations were so colossal as virtually to defy imagination, and they were far in excess of anything that past financial experience and techniques could cope with.

Nevertheless, in January 1921 the Paris conference fixed on an overall figure of reparations of 269 thousand million gold marks. This figure was reduced to 132 thousand million at the London conference held in the spring of the same year, but the amount still seemed no less incredible. The main reason for the size of the reparations bill was that the immediate beneficiaries – Belgium and France, and also Britain – were in turn in debt to the United States, whose loans had played a large part in financing the European war. As long as the Americans insisted on full and speedy repayment of these war loans, the west Europeans were forced to attempt to recoup by insisting on reparations from Germany.

The vast size of these sums not only defied the imagination but, not surprisingly, aroused the indignation of the Germans, who felt that a generation yet unborn would be forced to grow up in 'debt slavery'. If we examine, however, the financial burden which Germany actually carried during the period of a little over ten years during which reparations were being paid, a much less dramatic picture emerges. The main reason for this lay in the old financial principle that a debtor's real burden is determined not by the overall size of his debt, but by the method of repayment.

From this point of view, the reparations plan that was finally presented to Germany in the London ultimatum and accepted on 10 May 1921 was more realistic than the high total sum implied. The overall amount of reparations was first divided into three separate sets of bonds – so-called A, B and C Bonds – only the first two of which would initially give rise to annual payments (at different levels). Even contemporary experts could scarcely make head or tail of the arcane minutiae of the regulations that determined the actual quantities of annual instalments. It is not surprising that modern historians also still argue over the real size of the burden which reparations placed on the Germany economy. Opinions range from the traditional verdict that the national budget and economy were intolerably squeezed to the opposite view that the burden was scarcely larger than present-day aid to developing countries. For once, the truth really seems to lie somewhere midway between these positions. It is certainly true that the flexibility of the German economy, already constrained by the low post-war level of economic activity in any case, was further restricted by the need to pay reparations. On the other hand, the actual payments that had to be made were perfectly manageable. Reparations were not, therefore, an utterly intolerable burden, especially since any clear-sighted politician could reckon that after a few years of uninterrupted payment and reduced international tension there was a reasonable chance that the overall size of the debt would be cut down.

Nevertheless, the heated disputes over reparations during the 1920s cannot be dismissed as mere shadow-boxing. Three groups of factors caused the question of reparations to cast a dark shadow over international relations during this period, especially up to 1924 and later from 1929 to 1932 (between the production of the Young Plan and the cessation of reparations payments).

First, the fact that the overall sum of reparations was so high and that the terms and procedures for calculating the payments were so complex and opaque was bound to breed fierce resistance on the German side, for obvious psychological reasons. This root-and-branch hostility to reparations inevitably meant that any attempt to settle for a workable compromise would be condemned as a sell-out.

Secondly, the actual provisions regulating payments, and hence the real burden on Germany, emerged only in the course of bitterly contentious dealings among the parties concerned. More sober counsels did not prevail until after the disastrous confrontation of 1923; before then, realistic approaches had made little headway.

Above all, in 1919 and 1920 no one had had any previous experience of financial transactions of such magnitude and duration. Some economists who were opposed to reparations, such as J. M. Keynes, predicted serious consequences for the world economy, but doubts were easily stilled and these warnings dismissed. With the post-war reconstruction of the international economy proving a serious challenge in any case, the economic and financial effects of reparations served as an additional constraint on recovery, rather than as a stimulus to growth (as had been the case with the boom after 1871, financed by French war indemnities to Germany). Transfer problems were especially acute. If Germany was going to make payments in cash as well as in kind, she would first have to obtain the necessary currency reserves. The western powers, however, had little to gain from a German export drive. Since, in addition, a proportion of the German payments had to be passed on again in repayment of Allied war debts to America, the payments would do little to stimulate European demand. On top of all this, the fixing of the level of German reparations required a reliable basis of assessment, but rising inflation in Germany made this increasingly difficult to achieve and, after 1922–3, quite impossible. The question of reparations eventually became inseparably entwined with the domestic and foreign impasses of 1923.

Further conflict over the administration of reparations was bound to happen anyway, because the reparations issue became one of the counters in the wider struggle over the revision of Versailles. France exploited the issue by pressing for political, especially territorial, sanctions each time there was a German default; Germany exploited her payments problems to demonstrate that the real trouble lay with the peace treaty.

This brings us back, then, to the general question of foreign policy.[2] The important fact here was that practically all the signatories of the Versailles Treaty dissociated themselves from its provisions. In effect, all were revisionists, victors and vanquished alike.

It is true that in Germany there was a certain measure of rivalry between the two strategies of 'Erfüllungspolitik' and 'Katastrophenpolitik' – fulfilment of the terms of the treaty, and defiance to the point of confrontation. But on closer inspection, the line between these strategies appears a fluid one, and the goal of a speedy revision of Versailles was common to both camps. Those in favour of a policy of fulfilment wanted to demonstrate their good will towards the Allies while making it clear that the provisions of the treaty could not, in fact, be fulfilled and were thus in urgent need of revision on that account. Their hope was that the United States' interest in a calm European market and British unwillingness to countenance French hegemony in Europe would work to Germany's advantage. Such thinking came into its own between 1923 and 1929, when Gustav Stresemann was in charge of the Foreign Ministry, but before 1923 'Erfüllungspolitik' had little chance of making headway since its aim was too obviously to fan differences among the Allies and to isolate the French. Moreover, the policy failed to yield rapid results because it needed to be projected as a superior form of revisionism in the eyes of the German people, once its exponents had also embraced the nationalist interpretation of the 'diktat of Versailles' and exploited this line in order to strengthen their own popular support.

'Katastrophenpolitik', like the policy of fulfilment, was based on an inflamed nationalist sense of outrage and had the same revisionist goals, but it was simpler and more straightforward inasmuch as its proponents assumed that a German revival would come only from a new escalation of international conflict. There were three strands of thinking here, not always voiced simultaneously. There was a belief that the war which was still smouldering in the east, and which in 1920 had brought the Red Army to the edges of Warsaw, might lead to the dismemberment of the newly formed state of Poland and might conceivably even lead to some kind of national revolutionary war of liberation against France. It was also thought – rather more plausibly – that the prospect of war, economic chaos and civil disturbance in central Europe would arouse other countries' fears of Bolshevism and be perceived as a threat to their national interests, particularly on the part of the United States, and hence prompt the Americans to push for a renegotiation of the Versailles terms. Above all, there was speculation, again as in the case of 'Erfüllungspolitik', that the Allied coalition would split – a view which ignored the fact that an escalation of conflict would inevitably strengthen British and American solidarity with France, as the events of 1923 proved.

To a certain extent the United States was also seeking a revision of the Versailles settlement, despite having emerged from the war as the true victor in global terms. Whereas in the Far East, after the Washington conference of 1921–2, America assumed both a dominant economic function and a responsible political role, in Europe she initially withdrew from political commitment. The USA did not ratify the Versailles Treaty, did not join the League of Nations and refused to sign the promised security pact with France. On the other hand, she did not renounce her crucial economic and financial influence in Europe. Her position, therefore, was 'isolationist' only to a limited extent. Nevertheless, it took the upheavals of the years 1920–22 and the crisis of 1923 to bring the United States to the point where she was finally ready to play a role in the stabilization of post-war Europe that was commensurate with her true importance.

Great Britain had the greatest interest in defending the new power balance created at Versailles, whereby Germany was weakened, though not permanently, and France was granted a fragile post-war hegemony that was likely to come to an end in the not too distant future. Accordingly, the British simultaneously championed both the upholding of the treaty and its revision. At the same time, they were so preoccupied with maintaining and restructuring their overseas empire that they were anxious to avoid becoming embroiled in European crises. They could not favour French dominance, but they did not want a cessation of their French alliance either. This meant that Britain, like the USA, could do business with the Germans in the sense of making pragmatic arrangements within the general framework of German fulfilment of the treaty, while remaining loyal allies of France, at least outwardly, when the Franco-German conflict escalated.

The only reason why France had been deflected from taking an extreme punitive line on Germany at Versailles – that is, from insisting on the dismemberment of the country and using control of the left bank of the Rhine to create a permanent shift of balance between the two powers in her own favour – was that Britain and America, who were opposed to such an outcome, instead proposed a three-power security pact and collective guarantees under the League of Nations.

When this promised protection failed to materialize because of the change in posture of the Americans, France pressed for a second round of international conflict to secure for herself the territorial guarantees from Germany that she had not been granted in 1919. This version of revisionism received extra impetus after the victory of the right wing *Bloc national* in the French elections of November 1919 and the entry into office of the aggressive nationalist Poincaré in January 1922.

By 1922 and more especially in 1923, after various attempts at international agreement had failed, France and Germany – the two main antagonists from the First World War – were thus once again involved in a confrontation that brought them to the edge of war. Victor and vanquished alike seemed set on a second round of conflict designed to rectify the results of the first.

The hectic sequence of disputes, conferences, agreements and confrontations that characterized the years between 1920 and 1923 took place against this background of the main world powers' broad interests and strategies. It is not possible here to do more than give a somewhat schematic outline of the most important of these events.

The acceptance of the London ultimatum by the Wirth cabinet and by the Reichstag in May 1921 marked the beginning of a period in which, by and large, 'Erfüllungspolitik' prevailed in Germany. The policy led to German participation on equal terms in the world economic conference in Genoa in April and May 1922, where the consolidation of the European economies and a common economic policy towards Soviet Russia were discussed. Yet the policy of fulfilment proved unfruitful, in the sense that it did not deliver rapid results which might have satisfied nationalistic expectations in Germany: the Allies at Genoa were not yet prepared to grant the Germans an equal, untrammelled role as a co-operative partner.

In this uncertain situation, the decision of the two outsiders, Germany and Soviet Russia, to conclude a treaty in nearby Rapallo made a sensational impact.[3] But the treaty's specific provisions concerning the waiver of war indemnities and the establishment of economic and diplomatic relations were not unduly alarming. There was a great deal of discussion on the significance of Rapallo at the time, as there has been in the academic literature since. The following points are fairly generally agreed.

1. For some German politicians (such as von Maltzan) and military figures (such as von Seeckt), the treaty was part and parcel of more ambitious plans for a possible German–Soviet axis designed to revise the Versailles Treaty.

2. For the Foreign Minister Rathenau, however, and most of the others involved, the treaty was an additional trump card in the continuing strategy of developing co-operation and dialogue with the western powers.

3. Rapallo produced few positive short-term results. As far as the so-called 'eastern orientation' was concerned, it led merely to some secret co-operation between the Reichswehr and the Red Army and some modest economic initiatives. At the other end of Europe, it failed to persuade the western powers into adopting a gentler line towards Germany.

4. Indeed, France saw herself as thrust back into the front line against Germany – a Germany which had destroyed plans for a united economic and political front against Soviet Russia and had thereby demonstrated once again that she would not fall in with a French-led design for Europe. Furthermore, France could not fail to be aware of the 'eastern orientation' on which some German politicians were secretly placing their hopes: this was also bound to seem to pose a threat.

5. But in British eyes, too, the German proponents of a policy of fulfilment, having only just begun to make some headway, now appeared to have turned out to be unreliable customers after all. Britain would therefore adopt a restrained but loyal attitude towards the coming offensive mounted by her French ally, as long as the Germans continued to insist on an open-ended revision of Versailles.

At the end of 1922 France used a German delay in some reparations shipments and an accompanying request for a moratorium of several years (that is, a temporary suspension of reparations payments) as a pretext for marching into the Ruhr. The official reason given was to secure 'productive guarantees'; the unstated aim was finally to split off the Rhineland and the Ruhr from the rest of the Reich.[4]

The German response was a great upsurge of nationalist outrage, which was sanctioned, inflamed and exploited by the Reich government's declaration of a policy of 'passive resistance'. This policy called for all Germans in the occupied region, from railway workers to miners, to refrain from co-operating with the occupying forces, in an attempt to ensure that the 'productive guarantees' would remain unproductive. An unlimited general strike was officially called, which the Reich government financed by paying the wages and salaries of workers and public employees. Political tensions in the occupied region increased, and there were separatist disorders and acts of terrorism.

By the summer of 1923 it had become apparent that the campaign of 'passive resistance' was going to fail. It was being financed by the printing of money, which sent inflation into an ever-ascending spiral; the rest of the Reich economy was struggling under the strain; by ruthlessly bringing in outside workers the French were succeeding in making the 'guarantees' productive after all; and it was clear that a prolongation of the confrontation would indeed bring about the separation of the Rhineland from the Reich which the French had been hoping for.

In the autumn, therefore, the newly formed Great Coalition under Stresemann attempted a wholesale change of course on the political, economic and external fronts. Although there was at first a hope that the ending of the policy of 'passive resistance' on 26 September 1923 would lead to an international agreement paving the way to negotiations, Stresemann was soon forced to acknowledge that there was no option other than full capitulation to France. And yet France's total victory in the struggle in the Ruhr was to be turned, over the next months, into an unexpected yet clear gain for Germany as general exhaustion set in and more sober counsels began to prevail.

On 30 November 1923 the Reparation Commission set up a committee of experts chaired by the American financial specialist Charles Dawes to make a realistic assessment of Germany's ability to pay and, on this basis, to work out a feasible new programme of payments.[5] The Dawes Plan, published in April 1924 and accepted by the Reichstag in August, granted Germany a reasonable scale of annual payments and also made American credits available, though at the same time German economic and financial administration of the plan was placed under the supervision of Allied commissioners and an Agent for Reparations Payments. This supervised stabilization coincided with the currency reform that ended the inflation.

Once international agreement to establish a more viable system of reparations payments had been secured, the argument about 'productive guarantees', which had hitherto provided the French with the pretext for their presence in the Rhineland, now rebounded against its proponents. Under pressure from her own allies, France was forced to announce the end of her occupation of the Ruhr when the Dawes Plan was accepted, and the withdrawal began in August 1925.

It took the crisis of 1923, then, to induce both sides, victors as well as vanquished, finally to face up to the fact of the Versailles settlement. After four years of obdurate wrangling over revision of the treaty, the Versailles terms proved to constitute a by no means impracticable basis for inaugurating a new post-war era in Europe. In a sense the world war of 1914–18 did not end until 1923.

The weariness and the chastened mood that descended in 1923 helped to make possible a stabilization of the situation on both sides. Germany and, in a different fashion, France were each given a much needed breathing-space. Nevertheless, only time would tell whether this new-found stability would lead to a permanent strengthening of the balance of power in Europe and, with it, to a new solidity in German foreign policy.

THE INFLATIONARY DECADE, 1914–24

While events on the international stage obeyed one kind of rhythm, economic developments in Germany, and with them the pattern of change in society, followed a different rhythm of their own. As in the case of foreign affairs, however, the economic and social changes that had begun in 1914 had not come to a halt by the end of the war in 1918; a provisional equilibrium was not reached until late 1923 and early 1924. Stabilization was preceded by acute crisis.

The constant factor throughout the decade 1914–24 was inflation.[6] It had a profound bearing on social structures, and these in turn helped to stimulate inflation. But before we attempt an assessment of the social significance of the inflationary decade, we must first outline the different stages of inflation through which the economy passed during the period. Three principal phases can be distinguished: the period of war inflation from 1914 to 1918; the demobilization inflation of 1919 to 1921; and the catastrophic hyperinflation that built up during 1922 and led to the complete collapse of the German currency in 1923.

Before 1914 inflation had been an unfamiliar phenomenon, to German economists and the German public alike. People were thus at a loss, during the war and the early post-war period, to know how to respond to the unmistakable fall in the mark's domestic purchasing power and its decline on foreign-exchange markets. The wholesale price index had risen from 1 in 1913 to 2.17 in 1918: by the end of the war, in other words, the mark was worth only half of its pre-war value. This was a substantial reduction in the value of money holdings and a drain on the purchasing power of people dependent on fixed incomes.

The causes of this inflation became apparent only gradually. The imperial government had decided against financing the war by imposing special new taxes or even by increasing the taxes of the more wealthy. Instead it employed two measures that had inflationary consequences. It raised war loans, which would be repaid with interest after the 'final victory'; and, skating close to the limits of financial probity, it increased the volume of money in circulation, progressively abandoning the link between paper money and gold reserves that had been maintained before the war. Shortages of consumer goods and unscrupulous profiteering on armaments also generated price rises, which the increasing quantity of money served only to exacerbate. The defeat of 1918 shattered any surviving illusions that the government would clear away this mountain of debts and paper money by imposing reparations on Germany's opponents. Only a radical currency reform would have rectified the situation.

The republican governments, however, were hardly likely to impose a painful remedy of this sort: it would have amounted to an expropriation of war-loan subscribers and people on fixed incomes, and the odium would have been incurred by the new state, not by the Wilhelmine authorities which had actually created the problem. In addition, a rigorous dose of austerity would have deprived the government of funds it needed to tackle the urgent tasks of post-war recon-struction. Accordingly, a cheap-money policy was deliberately pursued during the period of demobilization, which meant that com-pensation could be paid to war victims, to resettled ethnic Germans and to anyone who had owned property in lands that had now been detached from the Reich. It also meant that despite low tax yields in the first months after the end of the war, all the state's regular financial commitments, from civil servants' salaries to welfare benefits, could still be met. Furthermore, the economy needed to be bolstered by subsidies and cheap credits as the switch to peacetime production took place. Last but not least, the danger of unemployment among demobilized soldiers had to be averted. The combined effect of these policies, financed by inflationary means, was to halve the value of the mark within a year of the end of the war and to reduce it further the following year. The wholesale price index (again taking 1913 as 1) rose to 4.15 in 1919 and to 14.86 in 1920. The inflationary boost to the economy was certainly successful in the short run in promoting expansion and easing the process of demobilization. While the Allied powers became caught up in a world economic crisis, Germany was assured full employment and economic recovery. But there was no avoiding the fact that a solution to the underlying currency problems had merely been postponed.

In 1921 the German currency stabilized somewhat, in comparison with the previous year (the wholesale price index remaining at 19.11), but in the following year inflation accelerated dramatically: the index for 1922 reached 341.82. There were several reasons for this increase, involving both domestic policy (over half of government spending was financed by printing notes) and foreign policy (the dispute over reparations). The Reich government also tried to exploit the growing monetary chaos so as to win support for its 'Erfüllungspolitik', the tactic of using short-term compliance with the Versailles terms to demonstrate that they could not, in fact, be fulfilled.

The moment of truth came in 1923. On the foreign front 'Kata-strophenpolitik' won the upper hand, with the crisis in the Ruhr; the printing presses became overheated, turning out money to finance the campaign of passive resistance; and the economy began to falter. There was a complete loss of confidence on the foreign-exchange market.

At the same time, there was a first real increase in unemployment, and hunger riots took place. The hyperinflation that had begun in 1922 now became a currency collapse of astronomical proportions. During 1923 the paper mark gradually lost its function as a medium of payment, and firms and local authorities resorted to issuing substitute forms of currency. In January 1923 the wholesale price index was already 2,783 times higher than its 1913 level; by December 1923 it was 1,261 thousand million times higher.

The hyperinflationary excesses of 1922–3 have left a profound imprint on the German psyche, although in the interests of historical accuracy the common view needs to be modified on two counts. In the first place, it must be remembered that the inflation began as early as 1914 and received its decisive boost from the methods the Wilhelmine government used to finance the war. Secondly, the inflation of the immediate post-war period had beneficial effects in the short run, both for the economy and for social policy. Nevertheless, the dramatic image of breakdown in 1923 was significant, not only because it left a long-lasting psychological scar but also because the complete collapse of the currency actually made the ensuing currency reform more acceptable. Certainly, when a new bank of issue was established on 15 November, with German property assets providing security for its Rentenmark, the new parallel currency was accepted relatively rapidly both at home and abroad. In 1924, following the adjustments to reparations agreed in the Dawes Plan, the German currency was stabilized permanently when the new Reichsmark was tied once again to the gold exchange standard.

So the inflationary decade ended. It remains to be seen, though, whether the terms on which stability was achieved in 1924 were of long-term benefit or disadvantage to the German economy.[7]

The social effects of the decade of inflation are not easy to assess.[8] On the one hand, substantial and deep-seated processes of change clearly took place. On the other hand, when examined closely these changes cannot be described exclusively in terms of the relative economic positions of the social classes: there are too many inconsistencies of detail, and too many variations between regions and over time. The general account that follows must be accompanied by the proviso that it is a rough one which needs to be modified on various specific points.

The social groups that gained included, first, the entrepreneurs. They obtained cheap credits and were able to undertake sizeable investment projects and to build up big commercial empires. (Hugo Stinnes was the most notable case in point.)[9] The decline of the mark gave them a price advantage on world markets, while the rises in costs that had been brought about by new social policies after the revolution could always be passed on in inflated prices.

Gainers also included farmers and anyone else with mortgaged property who was able to pay off debts in valueless money, as well as possessors of foreign exchange or tangible assets, provided that they were not obliged to dispose of their real assets simply in order to meet the costs of day-to-day living.

For workers the effects were less straightforwardly beneficial,[10] even if we separate the dramatic fall in living standards that occurred in 1923 from the easier years of inflation that had gone before. Broadly speaking, the demobilization inflation of 1919 to 1921 served to finance state welfare benefits and the agreements on hours and other industrial questions that had been negotiated by the unions and employers; real wages also rose, though not back to their pre-war levels. Above all, until the year 1923 there was no unemployment to speak of, apart from a brief spell, quickly overcome, immediately after the war. On the debit side, however, standards of living remained low. Only unskilled workers saw any real improvement in their position, unlike skilled workers, white-collar workers and public officials.

The losers from inflation included all those who had previously lived on long-term investment interest: that was a substantial section of the pre-war middle class, and included many intellectuals. The position of the salaried middle class – white-collar workers and *Beamten* (public employees) – also deteriorated. Pensioners and recipients of welfare benefits were hit as inflation increased, since their incomes were adjusted to price rises only partially and after delay. Small shopkeepers and craftsmen were able to profit financially from the inflation if they operated on the black market, but this left them socially marginalized: targets of criminal investigation by the state and of the resentment of outraged consumers.

This, as we have said, is a generalized picture of the effects of inflation on different social groups, and we should remember that the effects on individuals were far more confused and confusing. Two individuals from the same broad social class might be affected very differently, depending on the precise period in question, the part of the country in which they lived and their exact role within the fabric of the economy. Indeed, it was precisely through the confusion experienced by individuals and their fears for their social status that the real psychological impact of the inflation made itself felt. A profiteering ethic became common among people who had previously prided themselves on their rectitude. Others turned to crime out of sheer hardship, justifying their action on the grounds that it was the only way they could survive. Both phenomena, profiteering and poverty-induced crime, showed that the rather rigid social and moral code of the age of the monarchy had at last begun to work loose. Many social thinkers had predicted that this would occur as a result of the spread of industrialization, but it was only now that the process became irreversible and began to happen on a mass scale. (See figure 7, p. 149.)

In a sense, there had been an inversion of values. Money and success were now seen as goals that justified breaking the law, while honesty was stigmatized because it flew in the face of the rules of a dog-eat-dog inflationary society. The shifts in the relative standing of the different social groups that we have described not only made individuals uncertain about their social status but also helped foster a widespread new relativism in social morality.

THE REPUBLIC ON THE DEFENSIVE

Kurt Tucholsky wrote in the *Weltbühne* on 8 May 1918: 'We have not had a revolution in Germany – but we are certainly having a counter-revolution.'[11] He was referring to the fact that so many 'Prussian students' had been pouring into the Freikorps that university lecture courses had been disrupted. The Freikorps were fighting against 'Bol-shevists' in the Baltic region, against Poles in Silesia and West Prussia and against alleged 'Spartacists' in the big cities of the Reich;[12] they had as many as several hundred thousand members, although the numbers fluctuated. But the counter-revolution was not confined to the

Freikorps. Neighbourhood civilian militia organizations, student fraternities and middle-class clubs and societies were also centres of reaction, and anti-republicanism was common in the formal and informal networks linking peasant farmers and large landowners in the provinces. The Freikorps had been called out by the republican politicians, but their attitude towards democracy was lukewarm at best. For the most part they despised and hated the Republic.

The counter-revolution drew on a tradition of thought and action that went back much earlier than the tumultuous events of 1918. Its attitudes and expectations owed much to the militant nationalism of the 'Pan-Germans', to imperialist dreams of world power, to Germany's colonialist propaganda and colonial adventures. Extreme right-wing views on domestic issues – anti-Semitism, anti-liberalism, anti-Marxism – had also become more prevalent in the late-Wilhelmine period, and the years immediately before the war saw attempts to build up new forms of authoritarian political mass movement.[13]

The 'spirit of 1914' was the product of these symptoms of late-Wilhelmine crisis and the illusions of 'Volksgemeinschaft', or 'national community' – notions of 'Burgfriedenspolitik', 'Frontkameradschaft' and 'Kriegssozialismus' (political 'truce' at home, the 'comradeship' of the trenches and 'war socialism'). The mixture was a potentially explosive one, its aim the belligerent mobilization of the masses and a militarist reactionary leadership. It came most clearly into political focus in the dictatorship of the Supreme Army Command under Ludendorff and Hindenburg, and for a period during 1917–18 it generated a highly effective mass organizational apparatus in the shape of the 'German Fatherland Party'. This new form of mass party (whose leaders included Wolfgang Kapp and Tirpitz) claimed to have recruited over a million people opposed to the conciliatory policies advocated by the majority Reichstag grouping of the SPD, Centre and left liberals. Its influence was at its greatest between the Brest-Litovsk negotiations of late 1917 and the spring offensives of 1918, which inspired a last illusory hope of outright victory. When Germany had to acknowledge defeat in the autumn of 1918, the movement broke apart, but the beliefs and goals that had fuelled it did not thereby cease to exist. The fact that the monarchy collapsed so rapidly and with so little bloodshed in November 1918 led the Social Democrats to underestimate the potential for counter-revolution that remained: a misjudgement that was to have fateful consequences.

Even before the end of 1918, and especially during the first months of 1919, as the *Räte* movement was being bloodily put down, the forces of counter-revolution began to regroup, taking up arms as Freikorps and neighbourhood militias. In the course of 1919 the *Dolch-stoßlegende* and the revanchist campaign against the 'shame of Versailles' crystallized as the key articles of faith – along with hatred of the revolution – of the movement's ideology, embraced not only by counter-revolutionary activists but by a very large body of sympathizers. The *Dolchstoßlegende*, the myth that the Social Democratic, liberal and Catholic Centre politicians and the *Räte* movement had betrayed the 'unvanquished' front-line army, was given additional ideological respectability by inflammatory statements from Hindenburg and Ludendorff, despite the fact that it was the two generals themselves who had told the democratic politicians, virtually overnight, to sue for peace in 1918.

The politicians of the Weimar Coalition did not make a good job of dealing with the counter-revolution. In part this was because they were obsessed with stemming the impending chaos on the left; in part, because they relied naïvely on the supposedly non-political civic loyalty of public officials and soldiers. And when it was no longer possible to ignore the signs of a radical right-wing insurrectionary threat to the Republic itself, they had neither the means nor the energy to take action against it. In the event, the disarmament conditions of the Versailles Treaty came to the Reich government's rescue by breaking up the dangerous concentration of radical right-wing forces in the Freikorps.

These moves to disband the Freikorps provoked the so-called Kapp putsch of 13 March 1920, led by Wolfgang Kapp (a leading figure from the 'German Fatherland Party') and General von Lüttwitz, who was the commander of the armed forces in eastern and central Germany.[14] Ludendorff, who had not abandoned his political ambitions from the wartime days of the Supreme Command, was also behind the attempted coup.

Those units of the Reichswehr which did not support the putsch nevertheless refused to use arms against its perpetrators, obeying a decision by General von Seeckt (and defying the orders of the head of the Army Command, Walther Reinhardt, who remained loyal to the government). The Reich government fled to Dresden and thence to Stuttgart. Social Democratic members of the government issued a call for a general strike, which was backed by the central trade union organization, the leaders of the two socialist parties and, after some hesitation, the Communist Party. The call was obeyed in all parts of the Reich except Bavaria. This display of mass resistance was so impressive that public officials and the military units, which had at first stood on the sidelines, declined to give their support to the putsch. The organizers of the coup were isolated, and they threw in the towel on 17 March.

For the time being the general strike continued, as the trade unions and working-class parties pressed for a 'workers' government' that would carry out a thorough purge of the power structure, introduce new measures of democratization and nationalize key industries. This time there would be no repetition of the half-measures of 1919; with the working class primed for militant action once more, the Republic would be put on a solid class foundation. But the campaign came to nothing. The proponents of a 'workers' government' were lacking in political firepower, and the selfsame polarization of the labour movement that had led to civil war in 1919 reasserted itself.

In the Ruhr the striking workers had armed themselves, beaten off several Freikorps attacks and gradually occupied the whole of the industrial region up to the Lippe with 'Red Army' units that had formed spontaneously under the leadership of representatives of the various workers' organizations. Although the Bielefeld Agreement of 24 March succeeded in combining the dissolution of the 'Red Army' with a policy programme that met the unions' demands, some of the armed workers' units did not immediately comply with the agreement and the newly formed Weimar Coalition government sent Reichswehr troops and Freikorps into the Ruhr: troops that had only just been engaged in support of the putsch, or had at least not acted against it. There followed a campaign of terror in the industrial areas, which alienated large sections of the working class from Social Democracy and the Republic.

As far as the working-class mass movement was concerned, March

1920 was a repetition of the decisive events of the months of revolution of 1919; indeed, it was a repetition on an even greater scale. But the episode can scarcely be regarded as a continuation of the German revolution. In March 1920 the forces of counter-revolution held the initiative, as was conclusively demonstrated by the entry of the Reichswehr into the Ruhr in April. Rather, the events of March were symptoms of a basic political impasse that was of crucial importance throughout the remaining years of the Weimar Republic:

1. The forces of counter-revolution were too weak and disorganized to topple democracy completely, but they still had to be reckoned with even after the Kapp putsch had failed.

2. The constitutionalist parties of the Weimar Coalition remained in power, but they were forced to manoeuvre within a space bound by a counter-revolutionary right that had gained in strength and a working-class left that had become more radical.

3. The *Räte* movement, with its base in sections of the working class, had been the vehicle of the third phase of the revolution in 1919 and of the general strike in 1920, but it was now beaten. Its embittered supporters either withdrew into political passivity or transferred their allegiance to the Communist Party, which now gained the mass support it had previously lacked.

The new balance of political forces was reflected in the Reichstag elections that were held on 6 June 1920, when the radical parties of the left (the USPD and KPD) and the right (the DNVP) and the national-liberal DVP increased their strength, while the Weimar Coalition of the SPD, Centre and DDP lost its majority.

From this time onwards, the process of forming governments and securing parliamentary backing for legislation became chronically unstable. Even though the DVP now threw in its lot with the Republic (albeit with some reservations), the only possible combinations of parties that could form a government, between this time and 1930, were the following:

– a centre–left combination (the Weimar Coalition), which was never able to constitute more than a minority government

– a centre–right government, also a minority coalition, incorporating the parties from the Centre to the DVP

– the latter grouping could combine with the Social Democrats to form a Great Coalition (as under Stresemann in 1923)

– alternatively, the centre–right coalition could seek overt or covert support from the far-right DNVP to form a *Bürgerblock* (Bourgeois Coalition) majority.

Governments, in other words, either had no clear majority in Parliament, or were based on such wide and conflict-prone party combinations that it was only a matter of time before they collapsed. For this, the 'inflexible' and 'ideological' parties have often been held responsible. But the political impasse went deeper, and even if the party leaders had been more ready to make compromises, they would have been unlikely to surmount it. The impasse was the result of a power division that had been created by armed struggle, and it was an accurate reflection of the fact that a majority of voters had become disenchanted with the constitutionalist parties. It also reflected the sense of utter alienation felt on the reactionary right and within the revolutionary ghettos on the left, now led by the Communists. Perhaps the miracle of Weimar is that the Republic – despite such obstacles, despite a never-ending series of greater and lesser crises – actually survived as long as it did.

Superficially, domestic politics between 1920 and 1923 were marked by a rapid sequence of changes of governing coalition, but beneath the surface there were two crucial processes at work: the left became marginalized, though its retreat was punctuated by occasional Communist attempts to stage a putsch; and the counter-revolutionary movement on the right, though rebuffed, transferred its attentions to building up support in the murky area where underground terrorism shaded into political subversion.

On the left, the USPD at first seemed to have profited from the loss of support for the Social Democrats, receiving almost as many votes as the SPD in the election in June 1920. But the USPD had been a heterogeneous grouping from the time of its formation, and was fated to split over future tactics after the revolutionary workers had been roundly defeated. A majority of party officials and roughly half of the members voted in favour of the brand of revolution that seemed to have been so successful in Soviet Russia. At the end of 1920 the KPD thus acquired a mass organization and body of voters for the first time.[15]

The KPD owed this gain in strength to its unswerving adherence to the winning formula of the Bolsheviks; to seal its legitimacy, therefore, it would have to stage a German version of the October revolution. Mass revolutionary sentiment began to wane, however, and even the critical events of 1923 produced only splintered social protest rather than a unified movement to overthrow the political system. KPD tactics were correspondingly divided between, on the one hand, the issuing of demands for 'immediate action' and proposals for workers' 'united fronts' and, on the other, the channelling of all expressions of protest into the Bolshevik 'offensive'. Altogether, the manifestations of class conflict in which the Communists played a part in the post-war period had a somewhat schizoid character. Conflict was as much the product of the radicalization and embitterment of sections of the working class as it was of the KPD leaders' and Comintern's strategy to stage a German coup. The Communists' policy proved a failure, first in an attempted insurrection in Saxony in March 1921, and then again in Thuringia and Saxony in 1923, when, despite the fact that they had become participants in government and the workers were armed, a 'German October' failed to ignite. An ill-timed 'revolt' by a handful of Communists in Hamburg-Barmbek in October 1923 was also suppressed.

These events testified to a profound division within the German working class, with regard both to political and trade union organization and to attitudes towards the Weimar social order. Roughly one-tenth of all German voters, and one-third of organized workers, had decisively turned their backs on Social Democracy and installed themselves in the ghetto of the far left. They were too few in number to sweep the whole of the labour movement into revolution, but they were also too many to enable the reformist left, which wanted to operate within the framework of the Republic, to ignore them.

As far as the right was concerned, the disbanding of the Freikorps had the effect of removing any immediate threat of violence against the Republic from that quarter; but there was a price to be paid. The Reichswehr, under General von Seeckt, acquired a position of autonomy within the state, and the Republic was powerless to prevent conservative and radical right-wing forces from coming to power in Bavaria.

The political topography of the far right was highly intricate. There was a host of *vaterländisch*, *völkisch* and anti-Semitic associations and parties, which operated legally; there were anti-revolutionary bodies which had a considerable degree of autonomy, such as the Reichswehr and the Bavarian government; and, operating in the shadows, there were secret terrorist groups which carried on the violent traditions of the Freikorps and now raised them to new levels of violence.[16] Two sensational murders of prominent republican figures took place: Matthias Erzberger was assassinated in 1921, for the crime of signing the armistice agreement in 1918, and Walther Rathenau was murdered in 1922, having incurred the odium of the far right for being a Jew, an intellectual and a signatory of the Rapallo Treaty with the Soviets.

There were impassioned protests against the murder of Rathenau. The centre and left mobilized briefly in the cause of democracy, and a Law for the Protection of the Republic was passed, but this response was not sufficient to stem the continuing rise of the radical right as it capitalized on the nationalistic mood stirred up during the Ruhr crisis of 1923. Although the far right – in contrast to the position in the early 1930s – had no unified structure or ideology, and indeed was notable for the limitless variety of its modes of organization and ideological idiosyncrasies, the different parts of the movement had certain basic features in common.[17]

In the first place, the right's ideology was a highly combustible mixture of anti-Marxism, anti-liberalism and anti-Semitism, the cardinal points of which were its chauvinistic interpretation of the events of the war, its support for the actions of the Freikorps and its ambition to efface the 'shame of Versailles' and smash the Republic of the 'November criminals'.

As far as organization was concerned, the experience of those who had fought in the war or joined the Freikorps was exploited to promote a *Landsknecht*-like version of the militarist ideal, which would inspire the individual as well as serve as a political rallying principle. The public face and internal structure of the radical right were also characterized by a cult of youth, glamorized with *völkisch* ingredients, and a cult of leadership.

In social terms, the typical supporter of the far right was the young officer back from the front, unable and unwilling to adapt to the constricting conditions of daily post-war life. Other characteristic groups were students, middle-class people frightened by revolutionary disorder and embittered by inflation, and young people from the provinces who had been uprooted from parish-pump politics by the war.

This new resentful nationalism had begun to detach itself from traditional conservatism as early as the Freikorps period of 1919; certainly by the time of the collapse of the Kapp putsch of 1920 (although contact with the established right was not entirely broken). The younger people on the far right differed from the old-school members of the DNVP, not just because they were younger and more radical, but, above all, because they did not set great store by a restoration of the monarchy and a return to the halcyon days before the war. The hated Weimar 'system' had to be smashed to make way for something that was new but as yet unspecified, something fundamentally different from what had gone before, a form of 'socialism' that would somehow also be 'national', with a strong state and a martial ruling ethic. Although the inchoate fantasies of 'Volksgemeinschaft' which dominated the thinking of the radical right were not unconnected with the 'spirit of 1914' and the goals of the 'Siegfrieden' Party of 1917–18, they represented a 'revolutionary' advance on these earlier ideas, and were explicitly articulated as such.

It was in the grey area between the established far right and the revolutionary rhetorical politics of nationalist resentment that the National Socialist German Workers' Party (NSDAP) of Adolf Hitler began to make a name for itself, winning support outside its Bavarian base in the crisis of 1923. On 8 and 9 November 1923 Hitler led an amateurish putsch in Munich, hoping to bounce the radical-right Bavarian government into a march on Berlin; the attempt failed.

The beer-hall putsch took place at a time of very considerable domestic unrest in Germany generally: there were separatist uprisings in the Rhineland, and Communist plans for uprisings in central Germany and Hamburg. But it also occurred at a moment when conditions on the domestic and international fronts were poised for a new period of consolidation. Gustav Stresemann, first as Chancellor of the Great Coalition, then (when the Social Democrats withdrew because the government was not prepared to act against the reactionary Bavarian regime) as Chancellor of a minority government and finally as Foreign Minister, had begun the hard task of conciliation after the campaign of passive resistance in the Ruhr had been called off. His move against Communist participation in government in Saxony and Thuringia, and the conferment of executive power on General von Seeckt on 9 November following an emergency decree by the Reich President Ebert, led to an unexpectedly rapid stabilization of the internal political situation.

The currency reform also played its part, although the immediate effect of the after-shock of the events of 1923 and of the rigours of the initial measures introduced to bring about economic stability was actually to produce further gains for the radicals in the Reichstag elections of 4 May 1924. At these elections the DNVP received 19.5 per cent of the votes and the National Socialists won 6.5 per cent, while on the left the KPD won 12.6 per cent. Further elections on 7 December, however, showed that the new stability was beginning to make itself felt, as the SPD made a strong recovery and the Centre, DDP and DVP all recorded slight improvements in their standing. After the 'show-down' of 1923, the Republic was about to enter on a short spell of relative calm, despite the fact that the conflicts that were to arise during the coming five years would demonstrate that the crippling structural problems which had dominated the immediate post-war years had not really been solved.

Nevertheless, the degree of calm that arrived in 1924, after the dramas of the preceding year, is very striking. Why, then, did the Republic survive in 1923, when it collapsed ten years later? There is no clear or simple answer to this question. And yet the very absence of such an answer suggests that we should perhaps not ascribe too much inevitability to the events of 1933 themselves. That there are no entirely hopeless situations in history was shown by 1923. By the same token, 1933 showed what can happen when the actors in a specific historical situation choose one not entirely inevitable course of action rather than another.

The difference between 1923 and 1933, though, does not boil down merely to the fact that, in comparable conditions of structural crisis, the politicians in the former case opted for the more favourable alternative. Paradoxically, indeed, the very depth of the national and international crisis in 1923 served to bring about a move towards stabilization. There were several contributory reasons for this.

First, it was only because confrontation on the international stage had led to a complete impasse and because hyperinflation had led to a similar sense of hopelessness on the domestic front that Germans were brought to accept the true scale of their defeat abroad and of economic distress at home, after having refused to face up to these facts in the years since 1918. The crisis of 1923 was a nadir, but for that very reason it was capable of providing the starting-point for a new and more sober process of consolidation.

Secondly, that the Republic, in the last resort, survived all the crises of the years 1920–23 was due less to its strength than to its weakness. Even the specific stabilization measures adopted in 1923 looked at first all too much like stopgap concessions. There was no strong, concerted drive towards a clear and agreed solution, and it was only afterwards that events proved to have conspired to lead to a successful outcome. Finally, the Republic also survived because it had not been challenged by a convincing, full-dress alternative. The left had not yet recovered from its defeats of 1919 and 1920. The right was divided and pre-occupied with short-term campaigns of action: the ignominy of the failure of the Kapp putsch still clung to it, and although the Ruhr crisis of 1923 had furnished the revanchists with some martyrs, it had also shown up Germany's weakness in the international arena and thereby demonstrated the complete impracticability of the right's strategy in foreign policy.

By 1924 the Republic had survived these crises and had entered a new phase of stability. There was time to draw breath.[18] Whether the breathing-space would be an extended one would depend on how willing the Germans were to embrace policies of realism, moderation and social compromise, and on how much economic freedom of manoeuvre there would be to enable such policies to succeed. Unfortunately, the very factors which had given rise to the new calm of 1924 offered a less than hopeful prognosis.

III. MODERNIZATION AND ITS TENSIONS

———

It's a Polyhymnia ... German make, I might say. We're the best in the field, by a long way. The true spirit of music, in the mechanized form of the modern age. The German soul, 'up to date'.

Hofrat Behrens, in Thomas Mann, *Der Zauberberg*

The history of the Weimar Republic does not lend itself to purely chronological exposition. If, as I wish to argue, Germany's first experiment in democracy was crucially influenced, and ultimately defeated, by the fact that the political system forfeited its legitimacy and ceased to function when it was faced by deep-seated crises of economic, social and cultural modernization, then we must study this process of modernization in its own right, and the trends and tensions inherent in it, before we can decide how far these tensions contributed to the undermining of the Republic. At the same time, of course, we must not make such an explanation otiose by playing down the political dimension.

'Modernization' is a vague term, embracing a variety of shades of meaning; its usefulness as an explanatory tool in history has been much debated. Modernization theories, which were first put forward by English-speaking authors and only later taken up by German social historians, have commonly been claimed to provide a systematic account of the evolution of all industrialized societies.[1] They have also been a means of importing blatant value judgements into historical analysis, since they have tended to incorporate an idealized notion of 'western' social evolution, set against which the course of German social history has seemed to constitute an exception: a 'Sonderweg', or 'special path of development'.[2]

Whatever one's view of the complexities of modernization theory – and it must be said that there is growing scepticism about its explanatory value – it may be useful to work with a more empirical, descriptive concept of 'modernity' and 'modernization'. Let us, therefore, take the term 'modernity' to refer to the form of fully fledged industrialized society that has been with us from the turn of the century until the present day. In an economic sense, modernity is characterized by highly rationalized industrial production, complex technological infrastructures and a substantial degree of bureaucratized administrative and service activity; food production is carried out by an increasingly small, but productive, agricultural sector. Socially speaking, its typical features include the division of labour, wage and salary discipline, an urbanized environment, extensive educational opportunities and a demand for skills and training. As far as culture is concerned, media products dominate; continuity with traditional aesthetic principles and practices in architecture and the visual and other creative arts is broken, and is replaced by unrestricted formal experimentation. In intellectual terms, modernity marks the triumph of western rationality, whether in social planning, the expansion of the sciences or the self-replicating dynamism of technology, although this optimism is accompanied by sceptical doubts from social thinkers and cultural critics.

If this admittedly schematic and incomplete account gives a recognizable picture of what we think of as 'modernity', then the complex interwoven set of historical changes that have given rise to it can be termed the process of 'modernization'. In other words, leaving out of account earlier stages of development, the central thrust of modernization may be seen as consisting in the process of industrialization that took off on a large scale around the middle of the nineteenth century, the urbanization that followed in the closing decades of the century and the social and cultural transformations that occurred as the nineteenth century was succeeded by the twentieth.

This means that without falling into the normative mode of earlier modernization theories, we can nevertheless still ask how the political system, the economic system, the mechanism of social relations, social attitudes and beliefs, cultural expression and patterns of everyday behaviour all function and interact within the overall framework of the process of modernization.[3] If abrupt changes and sectoral imbalances can be expected to occur as the complex set of modernization processes unfolds, then the crucial factor governing a society's stability and survival is going to be the way in which that society deals with these broadly inevitable tensions. Hence, although we may no longer be convinced that there is such a thing as a royal road to modernization, the Weimar Republic's attempts to deal with the conflicts caused by modernization are of special interest precisely, though not only, because the Republic ultimately fell victim to these conflicts.

We shall analyse the tensions generated by the impact of modernization on society, culture and the political system in Weimar Germany by selecting six areas which caused particularly conspicuous problems. First, upheavals in the *demographic structure* led to conflicts between the generations and struggles for emancipation. Secondly, within the *economy*, attempts to create a new order in industry and industrial relations foundered because the 'sick economy' lacked the capacity to sustain it. Very much the same thing happened in the area of *social policy*, where ambitious schemes and crisis-induced retrenchments threw the contradictions of a modern welfare state into stark relief. There were similarly far-reaching, and highly indicative, changes in the *public domain*, as old social milieux broke up and were replaced by totalitarian formations dominated by the new mass media. This shift towards a *mass culture* and mass consumption was also reflected in the visual, literary and performing arts, which have played such an important role in defining our prevailing notions of the 'modernity' and avant-gardism of the 1920s. Finally, linked with these modern cultural forms, and closely bound up with the social processes of rationalization, what were felt to be 'modern' *life-styles* became the centre of debate – new ways of living that were either celebrated, or anathematized, as 'Americanism'.

No one who was aware of these manifestations of modernization in the twenties and who felt their impact personally and on society in general could remain neutral about them. The pressure of the changes, and the anxieties which the economic and political crises of the era were also causing, generated a sense of bewilderment. Since crisis and modernization seemed to be going hand in hand, modernity itself became the issue.

Social change does not follow a unitary time-scale. Separate processes of change may occur simultaneously, or in sequence, or may indeed conflict with one another; and the rates of change of these separate processes need in no way be consistent. We can distinguish three different temporal levels of social change that are relevant to the history of Weimar Germany (leaving aside sheer inertia or absence of change). At the broadest level there were *secular trends* whose roots went back into the nineteenth century. At a lower level we can isolate *patterns specific to the period itself*, as when, for example, we earlier compared the distinctive features of the economy in the inter-war period with the longer-term trajectory of economic growth. Thirdly, in social history as well as in political history, *specific events* may be significant at the time, and may indeed also have longer-term effects: an example would be the hyperinflation of 1923.

It should not be forgotten that, although it is important to pick out separate temporal dimensions of social change in order to place historical phenomena in their proper context, to do this is to use an analytical device that draws distinctions which contemporaries did not draw. It may, for example, be historically accurate to locate the roots of a particular aspect of modernity, which the German middle class found disturbing in the 1920s, in the period around the turn of the century, when contemporaries were first exercised by it. But that does not mean that the phenomenon was not a central defining element in the world of the 1920s as people perceived it at that time. What then has to be shown is the particular circumstances that gave rise to this sense of unease in the later period. Accordingly, when analysing the processes of modernization during the Weimar Republic we shall often hark back to the imperial era, when our purpose is actually to establish what was distinctive about the period between the end of the First World War and the onset of the Great Depression.

Underlying these considerations is a more general fact of German social history. Research in a number of separate fields suggests that the 1890s and the turn of the century marked an important threshold in the modernization of German society. This was the period in which the new industrial and urban society became established on a wide scale; it saw the first emergence of many of the problems that have continued to characterize modern life, and of first attempts to solve them. The Wilhelmine period, in other words, was the start of what has been called the age of 'classical modernity'. Although this term is taken from the history of the arts, it can also be used to characterize the state of society and culture in general. What made modernity possible was a prolonged and largely unbroken spell of economic expansion, which held out the promise of a wide range of social reforms while also generating sufficient material capacity to mitigate many of the stresses and strains that rapid social change would cause.

War, however, led to economic stagnation and crisis. At the same time, the revolution in Germany suddenly created the opportunity for what had hitherto been theories and experiments to be put into practice on a grand scale. Society and culture during the Weimar Republic were thus faced with two momentous new challenges: mass social change was to be introduced, and it was to be introduced at the very time when economic and political crisis made success most doubtful. Classical modernity had entered a crisis of its own.

4. Generation Gaps and Emancipatory Struggles

Although the subject of social history is the lives of individual human beings, we may need to take our bearings on the experience of the individual in history by using generalized demographic statistics. Indeed, abstract aggregate data on the structure of the population can provide vital background information on social life and on the factors that shape and sustain the lives of individual people.[1]

THE DEMOGRAPHIC TRANSFORMATION

If we compare the age make-up of the German population in 1910 with that in 1925 (see figure 5), it is immediately apparent that some dramatic changes took place in the span of a mere fifteen years.

First, all age-groups from 12 upwards had become larger in 1925 than they were in 1910. The total population, in other words, had continued to grow.

Secondly, within the 25- to 50-year-old age-group – that is, people in the most active years of their lives – the effect of war losses among men was clearly apparent. In the age-ranges most heavily affected, 30- to 35-year-olds, the number of surviving men was actually below the level of 1910. (In fact, to bring out the full impact of the destruction wrought by the war we should need to supplement the figures reflecting male deaths with the figures for war wounded, not shown in figure 5, which were roughly similar.)

Thirdly, the same age-group, born between 1875 and 1900, shows a corresponding surplus of women. A large number of women of marriageable age were thus forced to remain single. This created a

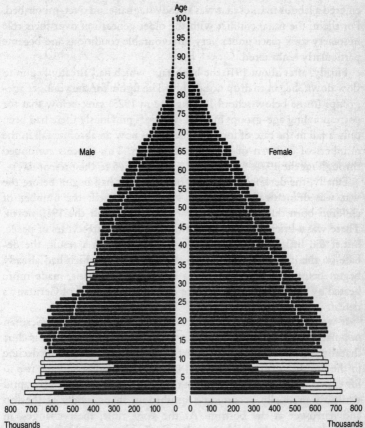

Figure 5 Age structure of the German population, 1910 (white bars) and 1925 (black bars)

Source: B. Mewes, *Die erwerbstätige Jugend*, Berlin, 1929, p. 8

large pool of working women, many of whom were unable, even if they wanted, to switch to the role of housewife supported by a husband.

Fourthly, the 15- to 25-year-old age-group in 1925 was the product of a particular peak in the birth rate. These young people, born between 1900 and 1910, left school during the Weimar years and entered a labour market that was already stagnant and over-subscribed. For them, the usual conflict with the older generation over their rôle in society took place under very unfavourable conditions and became particularly embittered.

Fifthly, after about 1910 the birth rate, which had already begun to slow down, began to drop noticeably. The figure for the younger age-groups (those below school-leaving age in 1925) sank below that for corresponding age-groups in 1910. Whereas previously there had been only a fall in the rate of increase, there was now an absolute fall in the numbers of children of corresponding ages. This process continued throughout the 1920s (and indeed has continued to the present day).

Finally, the decline in numbers of births that had begun before the war was dramatically magnified by the war itself: the number of children born during the war years was about half the 1910 norm. There was a brief catching-up period in the first three years of peace, but it did little to alter the longer-term trend. As a result, the debate on the impending decline in the population, which had already begun before the war, took on a sharp new emphasis, made more heated by the traumatic experience of the war itself and of Germany's defeat.

If we now set this comparison of the age make-up of the German population in 1910 and 1925 into a wider historical context, it is clear that the salient changes formed part of a long-term trend. The decline in the number of births, the ideal of the small family and the rise in life expectancy together meant that the previous demographic pyramid was now gradually becoming a mushroom shape, wider at the top and narrower at the bottom. At the same time, these changes, in themselves a novelty, had been alarmingly accentuated by the short-term demographic effects of the war. The structure of the population had been relatively stable: it was now radically transformed, with a much sharper segmentation based on age and sex.

It was not only professional demographers who were aware of the change. The new divisions within the population were a central and obvious fact of life even to the unsophisticated. They inspired anxieties and new conflicts which had an enormous influence over people's states of mind during the Weimar period. There were conflicts over the position of the younger generation and the role of youth as such;

there were changes in the position of women, and even greater changes in women's (and men's) perceptions and definitions of women's status; and changes in reproductive patterns set off debates about the role of sexuality, the family and the bringing up of children. To these changes we now turn.

THE 'SUPERFLUOUS' YOUNGER GENERATION

The mystique of 'youth' was a more pervasive part of public consciousness in the Weimar Republic than it was in other contemporary societies or than it had been in other periods of German history.[2] Yet all the essential aspects of both the mystique and the actual problems of 'youth' were already in existence before the end of the nineteenth century. Even the principal institutions and policies for dealing with the problem of the younger generation had taken shape before the First World War.[3]

The rise of urbanized industrial society had assigned younger age-groups a special pioneering role. They were represented in disproportionate numbers in industry, in the big cities, in the centres of population influx and at the flashpoints of social change. Young people were becoming conspicuous; *Jugend* (youth) was becoming a code-word, implying the breakdown of traditional ties and social controls. Indeed, the noun *der Jugendliche* (young person) had entered the language only in the 1880s: previously there had been only the terms *die Jugend* (youth in the sense of the condition of being young, applying to both sexes) and *der Jüngling* (youth in the sense of young man). Problem groups, personified as the 'young worker' (*jugendliche Arbeiter*) or 'young criminal' (*jugendliche Kriminelle*), were now generalized into the problem case of the *Jugendliche*. These linguistic facts indicate the sensitive areas of social change on which the public concern about youth was focused. There was a debate about the ways in which educational and training facilities could be extended, overhauled and refined in order to meet the demands of industrial society; there was the problem of how the new generation was to be socialized into adopting traditional moral values at a time of rapid social change; and, more specifically, there was the problem of the hiatus between 'school bench and barracks gate', the spell between school and military service when adolescent boys were thought to be in danger of enjoying too much freedom from social supervision.

These three perceived groups of problems remained uppermost in people's minds during the Weimar period. Similarly, the strategies for solving, or at least mitigating, them which had been evolved under the monarchy also remained paramount. The 'youth problem' was still seen as a problem of control. The Weimar constitution gave the Reich government legislative responsibility over various areas involving education and culture that had previously belonged to the *Länder* alone, so that the plethora of fragmented institutions dealing with education and young people was now integrated and reformed,[4] at any rate to the extent that the philosophical aims of the Social Democrats and the Centre Party could be reconciled. The Reich Youth Welfare Law of 1922 separated the functions of the institutions into two broad categories: youth welfare (*Jugendfürsorge*) for 'deviant' young people and youth service (*Jugendpflege*) for the 'normal' majority. Its first article, citing the constitution, proclaimed: 'Every German child has the right to an upbringing that will ensure physical, intellectual and social fitness' (or proficiency; *Tüchtigkeit*). This broad-minded-sounding formulation may seem child-centred, but it was certainly not a guarantee of the child's right to develop his or her own personality: rather, it gave the child the right, which public institutions would actually implement, to be brought up to achieve a form of 'fitness' defined in terms of the needs of society.

Thus under the Weimar Republic the organization of young people, as regards both its aims and the way in which it was run, was largely controlled from outside. Weimar youth policy was certainly effective in the sense that by 1926 (using statistics of the Reich Board of German Youth Associations), out of over 9 million young people, 4.3 million belonged to a youth club or organization: rather more than one boy in two and slightly fewer than one girl in two. Of these, however, 1.6 million belonged to sports clubs and another 1.2 million to church youth organizations. By contrast, the workers' youth movement had 368,000 members (to which another few thousand Young Communists should be added), while the youth movement based on the ideal of the *Bund* – the quasi-spiritual notion of a German (male) élite – though it has received most attention in the historical literature, numbered only 51,000.

To the extent that there was an autonomous youth movement, these last two groups were its leading representatives. Both also had their roots in the period before the First World War, and both developed by being, for different reasons, ignored by the rapidly growing public youth service. The *Wandervögel* (literally birds of passage), in origin hiking groups consisting mainly of secondary-school pupils and reform-minded teachers, emerged after about 1900. The workers' youth movement took shape in the last decade before the war, when Social Democrats, as 'enemies of the Reich', found themselves excluded from public youth organizations.

Both movements underwent a transformation during the war and the revolution. The *Wandervögel* evolved into the *Bündischen*; the war had made them more nationalistic, their organization was now more rigorously committed to the command principle and the youth mystique was blown up into a diffuse ideology of mission. Within the workers' youth movement, the political splits on the left became highly visible, and there was also a clash between the generations, fought in organizational terms, as the younger members became more radicalized.

The influence of the socialist and *bündisch* youth movements was certainly greater than their relatively low levels of membership implied. They made their voices heard through their own publications and in the broader public media. Spokesmen for the two movements played a prominent part in shaping the image and cult of youth in the twenties. The youth movements recruited many younger members of the educational professions and political organizations and gave them a chance to prove themselves, though it was also during the Weimar period that tensions were exacerbated between older figures in established positions and the young rank and file claiming the 'right of youth' to determine the shape of future policy. In addition, both the *bündisch* and socialist youth movements were milieux in which, within limits, new ways of living and new kinds of personal relationships could be tried out. They attracted their fair share of enthusiasts for educational reform, sexual reform, alternative life-styles and avant-garde culture.

Despite all this, it is doubtful how much direct impact the explicit goals of any of the various youth movements had on the mass of young people – either those in the numerically dominant organizations for public youth service or those in the other smaller but more highly publicized youth movements. None of these organizations, after all, played more than a marginal role in the everyday lives of the young.

Young people's lives did undergo a number of fundamental changes, however.[5] These changes were not universal and did not all occur together, but they could scarcely escape attention at the time. There were the beginnings, for example, of a debate on new patterns of socialization. During the war many children and young people had grown up without fathers, and there had been considerable hardship in the last winters before the armistice; juvenile delinquency had shown an alarming increase. Anxious educationists believed that there had been a general loss of authority on the part of parents and that the younger generation – notably many children in middle-class and lower-middle-class families – was rejecting previously accepted social and moral norms. The material position and social status of the middle classes had indeed been hit by the years of war and inflation, and this now created a more receptive audience for the sorts of attack on the ossified values of the adult world that had been mounted by spokesmen for the young since the turn of the century.

Similar disputes over authority probably took place within the working class, where there had also been traditional patriarchal family structures among skilled workers, for example. But here, on the whole, another trend was more significant: the growing role of the family in everyday life, as numbers of children in the family fell and leisure activities were centred more on the family. Many working-class children now received greater care and attention from their parents, and more expense could be devoted to education and training. This was certainly the long-term trend, though of course it was periodically interrupted as stagnating incomes and rising unemployment caused economic hardship.

Although living standards were generally constrained, young people in the Weimar Republic nevertheless began to experiment with new forms of leisure activity.[6] The eight-hour day, collective wage bargaining and the Republic's new social policies explicitly established for the first time the principles of free time on working days, of weekends and, in a preliminary way, of holidays. Leisure opportunities were, of course, taken up by all age-groups, but young people were very much the pioneers in the field, and in the popular mind the notions of leisure and youth were virtually inextricable. The young spent their free time among friends, availed themselves of commercial leisure opportunities such as the radio, the gramophone and the cinema, and went out to fun-fairs and dance-halls or to eat and drink; hiking and youth hostelling provided a foretaste of the new culture of tourism. There were also the youth clubs, further-education courses, sports clubs and other offerings of the organized leisure and youth associations. And, in rivalry with all these commercial and organized providers, so-called *wilde Cliquen* sprang up: nonconformist, marginal groups, mainly of working-class young people, who alarmed middle-class society and the guardians of authority by flouting the 'official' rules.

The youth organizations, youth subcultures and youth mystique that define our image of youth during the Weimar Republic were undoubtedly male-dominated. Sports clubs and the various youth movements admitted girls as members, and older boys would take out their girlfriends to entertainments in their free time, but there were no independent forms of leisure for girls, let alone a distinctive girls' leisure subculture. Girls still spent most of their free time in the semi-private realm of the family or in small groups of female friends, and if they went out, it was usually 'in company'.

As the new forms of leisure activity came into being, many young people were quicker than adults to adopt the new values of an urban and industrial mass culture. The models for the young of both sexes were 'American'. At the same time, however, other groups of young people became fanatical ideological opponents of the 'corrupting' and 'un-German' effects of modernization. It is not very helpful to try to analyse the gulf between advocates and enemies of modernity in terms of social class: the clash of values was resolved by each individual in a different way. What is clear is that the dilemmas facing young people were formidable. Unlike their parents, who had already safely made the crucial decisions of their lives – decisions about a career, a home, a marriage partner, a life-style – young people had to work out how they wanted to live, and what goals to set themselves, amidst all the upheaval and disorientation of the post-war years.

Whether working-class or academically trained, young people had to undergo these rites of passage at a time of exceptionally high structural and short-term cyclical unemployment.[7] We have already discussed the demographic disadvantages faced by age-groups born in the pre-war years of high birth rates. Youth unemployment was particularly serious because the crisis in welfare provision led to cuts in benefits to the young, who then had to be supported by their families, which were often affected by unemployment in their turn. Unemployment was even higher among skilled workers aged between 18 and 30 than among young apprentices and the unskilled, and the sense of frustration and hopelessness in this group was particularly acute.

In the academic world, there was a cycle of expansion and surplus, first in the educational system and then on the academic job market, the effects of which were especially severe in the 1920s. There had been a phase of expansion around the turn of the century and a further increase in jobs as public employment, welfare services and the educational system were built up and reorganized during the war and the period of the establishment of the Republic. But the new generation found the doors to employment barred. A crisis mentality spread among young university-educated people, and the language of political and cultural debate became more extreme. There was much talk about 'élites' and 'talent', and about ways of separating those of 'lesser value' ('Minderwertige') from those of 'high value' ('Hochwertige'); the shortcomings of the educational system engendered *Kulturkritik* and hostility to the Weimar 'system' as a whole; a self-styled 'younger generation' declared war on a 'senile' republic that was unable to cater for its needs; and a generation without jobs found a new identity by joining the chauvinistic campaign to liberate the 'Volk ohne Raum' from international 'debt slavery' and the yoke of the 'Versailles diktat'. It was no accident that the NSDAP made many of its recruits among this 'superfluous' younger generation. At an early stage the National Socialists became the most popular party at universities, especially among students.[8]

Opposition to the capitalist 'system' and the bourgeois Republic also became more extreme among the young unemployed. Radicals within the organized labour movement, whose lives had been shaped by struggle on the streets, tended to find their way into the KPD, the only other clearly 'young' party in the Weimar era apart from the National Socialists.[9] A sense that personal aspirations would not be fulfilled and that society as currently constituted had no future encouraged the belief that a socialist revolution was imminent. The young unemployed, unable to give structure to their daily lives through work, found meaning instead in the social cohesion of the working-class districts and in the activism of the Communist paramilitary organizations. Their sense of impotence could be assuaged by a resort to force. Some of this youthful working-class radicalism was also channelled into Hitler's SA, especially in areas where socialist organization had traditionally been weak.

The Weimar years, then, gave young people new prominence, but at the same time threatened them with marginalization. The cult of youth was a symptom of the unprecedented significance that was now attached to being young, and yet commerce, youth organizations and the educational system were all busy enlisting young people to their own ends. The young had greater opportunities of emancipation than ever before, and yet they were also seeking release from rootlessness and lack of hope by joining totalitarian movements. The story of young people in this period, therefore, is not simply one of liberation, or simply one of being controlled by others. Rather, the central fact was the clear tension that existed between competing, indeed mutually exclusive, conceptions of youth itself. The young, in typical cases, were torn back and forth between these competing alternatives – or, to put it more positively, were driven to make a choice between them.

THE 'NEW WOMAN'

There were similar conflicts and controversies, both in the real world and in public perceptions of the real world, with regard to the role of women. The questions here included the position of women in employment, the political significance of the women's movement and the vexed matter of the 'new woman'.[10]

The proportion of women in employment in Germany (the ratio of women in employment to the total female population) remained broadly constant at about one-third, rising slightly from 31.2 per cent in 1907 to 35.6 per cent in 1925, after the establishment of the Republic. More important, however, were changes in the internal make-up of the female workforce. Over the same period (1907–25) the proportion of female domestic servants and other domestic employees fell from 16.1 to 11.4 per cent, and that of farm workers from 14.5 to 9.2 per cent. Conversely, the proportion of female industrial workers rose slightly from 18.3 to 23 per cent, and that of white-collar workers and women in public employment increased markedly from 6.5 to 12.6 per cent. At the same time, the single largest category of working women, namely women helping in family businesses, remained virtually unchanged at 36 per cent.

These statistically quantifiable changes are scarcely sufficient on their own to explain why the question of women's employment was so passionately debated in the Weimar Republic. The truly shattering change was the emergence of certain clear shifts within the gender-based division of labour, which in turn affected the perceived image and social role of women.

What was novel was the concentration of women in the modern sectors of industry, commerce, public employment and private services. New categories of 'typical' women's jobs were being created which had not previously existed, and others were now being increasingly vacated by men: jobs such as those of shorthand typist, assembly-line worker, shop assistant, primary-school teacher and social worker.[11] The general perception was that these new female jobs were appropriate either for young single women or for older unmarried or widowed women. A married woman with a job, on the other hand, could be sure of attracting vociferous criticism for being a 'Doppelverdiener' (bringing home a second wage-packet). This fact and the relative long-term stability of the total proportion of women in work show that the pattern of female employment continued to be governed by the wife-and-mother principle, even though the actual areas in which women were now working had expanded. Even the role played by women workers during the First World War, which was seen as a dramatic departure at the time, turned out in the longer run to be the exception that proved the rule. Although the overall proportion of women in employment was changing only gradually, wartime public opinion was much intrigued by the fact that women were taking over typical 'men's jobs' in, say, transportation or heavy industry. But as soon as the men came back from the war, these particular roles were reversed once again. It was the female influx into administrative, welfare and educational work that proved permanent. The women's movement had earlier paved the way here, with its slogan of 'soziale Mütterlichkeit' (social motherliness), calling for the recognition of specifically feminine qualities and qualifications.

Even within these areas, however, it remained the case throughout the Weimar period that women generally performed the lower-paid, subordinate tasks, while the proportion of better-paid and more responsible jobs held by men increased. And if women did perform the same work as men, they received lower rates of pay, even under collective-bargaining agreements. Ironically, the result was that during the employers' 'rationalization' drive between 1924 and 1929, and later during the 1929–33 world recession, women workers, because they were cheaper, were laid off less often than men. Nevertheless, women workers were also badly hit by unemployment, especially if they were single or the sole bread-winner in the family and their job was thus a vital necessity.[12]

The economic crisis also deepened popular resentment of married women who were 'Doppelverdiener'. It was in 1932, and not under the National Socialists, that a 'Law Governing the Legal Status of Female Civil Servants and Public Officials' was passed which made it possible for women who were second earners to be dismissed from public service. Measures of this sort particularly injured the job prospects of female graduates. After the turn of the century women had begun to struggle for admission to higher education, and under the Weimar Republic the proportion of women students rose, reaching 16 per cent in the winter semester of 1931–2. This represented a total of 20,000 female students; in addition, before 1933 there were over 12,000 women in employment who had completed university studies. None the less, even before restrictive measures were introduced during the world recession and later under the National Socialists, the rise in

the number of women in higher education and the professions had by
no means been an unmixed success story.

The universities were still dominated by centuries-old traditions of
male exclusionism. Student fraternities and university teachers alike
made life difficult for women students by practising conscious and,
more especially, thoughtless discrimination.

The struggle against such discrimination in universities and in the
workplace generally was made more difficult because women themselves were very much influenced by the traditional argument of the
German women's movement that 'female' virtues had a distinctive
part to play in culture and society. As a result it was difficult for
women to draw the line between discrimination and legitimate
treatment based on gender difference. In industrial employment, too,
the majority of women – to say nothing of men – identified with the
gender-specific notion of the woman as a temporary member of the
workforce, taking a job between leaving school and getting married
or having children, or, once married, at most working on a stopgap
or temporary basis. Single women might have to work, but only out
of economic necessity. It should not be forgotten, furthermore, that
women occupying traditional roles in households, on farms or in
family businesses were still the dominant group in the female workforce. In addition, very many women were engaged in casual or
temporary work as cleaners, dressmakers, children's nurses and the
like – jobs which were not included in the official statistics but which
served to perpetuate traditional attitudes towards female roles.

The organized women's movement had developed under the monarchy, campaigning for greater participation by women in society
while also, as we have said, preaching an ideal of femininity and
motherly virtues.[13] This was, in fact, the great period of the women's
movement. It was rounded off in somewhat equivocal fashion by the
mobilization of women during the First World War, on a wave of
nationalistic fervour and amid much rhetoric of female self-sacrifice.
The 'nation' and the women's movement, it seemed, had come
together. Women certainly made a significant contribution to the
social services during the war, doing far more than just charitable
work, and the women's movement – within which pacifists formed a
small and declining minority – looked forward to suitable recognition

and recompense after military victory. Defeat and revolution brought, at least, the right to vote and to stand for office, so that women who had spent long years campaigning in the women's movement or working in social fields could now pursue their aims through the ballot box and Parliament. After the war opportunities for doing social and educational work were also expanded, enabling more women to devote themselves to the ideal of 'soziale Mütterlichkeit'.

And yet despite, or because of, these achievements, the organized women's movement declined in importance during the Weimar Republic. Most of its leading figures belonged to the generation which had already risen to prominence during the monarchy. Its political demands seemed to have been met, at least in a formal sense, while the model of femininity promoted by these older feminists was not exactly appropriate to new notions of female emancipation.

Two counter-currents were at work in the second half of the Weimar period. The widely propagated image of the modern young female white-collar worker – non-political, consumption-oriented, enamoured of the products of the mass media – came under fire from the older feminists. At the same time, there were a number of symptoms of a new hankering, among women as well as among many reactionary men, for the idealized role of the wife and mother, safe on her pedestal within the happy family. This escapist fantasy was itself, in part, a reflection of the additional burdens which the image of the 'new woman' was imposing on women in their daily lives.

The most challenging version of this image, and the one most closely linked with the 'American' syndrome, was the male-generated fantasy of the 'vamp': the glamour girl, a bit too independent to be true, armed with bobbed hair and made-up face, fashionable clothes and cigarette, working by day in a typing pool or behind the sales counter in some dreamland of consumerism, frittering away the night dancing the Charleston or watching UFA and Hollywood films. This caricature bore little resemblance even to the young female white-collar workers from whose lives it had borrowed certain props. This did not, however, prevent the mythology of the 'new woman' from being promoted by the media and taking on a life of its own. The worlds conjured up by the illustrated magazines, serials and hospital romances, by romantic films and musical comedies and by advertising and the new consumerism made their mark on the attitudes and daydreams of many young women in the white-collar class. In reality, unfortunately, their incomes were so low that the most they could hope for was to make an occasional hard-earned outing into this brave new world on a night off or at the weekend.

Another facet of the 'new woman' phenomenon that became common was the image of the efficient housewife. There was a flood of information and advice about hygiene, nutrition and new ways of organizing the kitchen and the home. Technological advances meant that many labour-saving devices were available. But even in the middle class purchasing power was not strong enough to sustain a mass market for refrigerators, vacuum cleaners and washing machines; that did not come until the 1950s. In compensation, advice on efficient home management was all the more ingenious. A typical example was the campaign for the kitchenette, hailed as the successor to the old, big kitchen-cum-living-room. Tiny model kitchens were commonly incorporated in the design of new flats on public housing estates, partly as a way of cutting costs by reducing living-space.

On the face of it, these new efficient methods of household management were time-saving, but the result was not necessarily to make women's work easier. Women were either still stuck with the double burden of housework and a job, or they were expected to spend more time on housework and child care in order to meet the norms of modern family life that were being promoted. Conforming to new standards of hygiene or interior decoration similarly took more time, not less.

All told, then, greater expectations were being placed on women in many areas of social and private life. Women had new opportunities in politics and in the world of work; they had new role models with which to identify. But the old assumptions about women's roles had not been abandoned, and the tensions created by the new demands on women had not been resolved, with the result that the traditional double burden borne by women was simply made heavier still by new chores and anxieties. Enemies of female emancipation, as well as many women who were victims of these ostensibly liberating changes, reacted by looking for alternatives to the modernity which they were being urged to embrace. This may help to explain why the ideological images of women promoted by reactionaries and by the Nazis found a ready reception among many women, as well as men, during the last years of the Republic.

RATIONALISM AND SEXUALITY

Feelings on the 'sexual question' ran high. There were disputes about the roles of the sexes and about attitudes towards marriage, the family and child-rearing, and these disputes were bound up with arguments about social policy and demographic trends. Since the turn of the century there had been much prophesying of the reproductive decline of the German nation. From about the same time onward, attempts had also been made to devise a new scientific discourse for describing and explaining psychological and instinctual processes.[14]

Although there were several different sources for new, more rationalistic attitudes towards sexuality, such attitudes were highly controversial, because they confronted a Victorian prudery that was still very widespread. Rationalism was a struggle against old taboos. At the same time, the ideas and methods of the new sexual enlightenment were themselves still very much the offspring of the nineteenth century, particularly of its faith in science and its technocratic utilitarianism.

Broadly speaking, two separate strands of thought had inspired the movement for sexual liberalization during the Wilhelmine era, and, while overlapping considerably, they remained distinct during the Weimar period.

On the one hand, a movement for health and hygiene campaigned for 'sensible' and 'natural' sex. It sought to disseminate clear, precise information about the physical aspects of sexuality, placing special emphasis on warnings against venereal disease; proper methods of contraception were also sometimes explained. Sexual behaviour was to be guided by scientific knowledge and to take place under optimal conditions – usually, therefore, within marriage. People were to be encouraged to 'keep a clear head' as far as their feelings and instincts were concerned, to abjure the evils of prostitution and perversion and to halt the spread of sexually transmitted diseases.

By contrast, the movement for sexual reform that was associated with the proponents of *Bevölkerungspolitik* (population policy) was propelled by two main anxieties. There was fear that a further decline in the birth rate would lead to 'Volkstod', the extinction of the German people; and there was alarm that state welfare measures, by mitigating the effects of 'natural selection', would cause the 'gesunde Volkskörper' (the healthy 'body' of the nation) to be overrun by the weak, the ill, the less gifted and the 'asocial', who would now survive and be able to reproduce. There were calls, accordingly, for campaigns to be directed at the 'healthy' and 'gifted' sections of the population, urging them to start families, teaching them how to bring up their children and encouraging the use of preventive medicine; at the same time, eugenic measures should be employed to prevent reproduction by those who were 'minderwertig' (of lesser value) or 'erbkrank' (congenitally ill). The demand for eugenic measures as a part of 'social hygiene' was by no means confined to the political right, though the right was more prone to use *völkisch* phraseology in support of stronger state intervention. Left-wing public-health reformers, who included Social Democrats and Communists, were also receptive to ideas of 'biologically' based 'Erbgutpflege' (protection of the national genetic stock), favouring eugenic marriage counselling in conjunction with positive policies of assistance to families.

These two main strands of the movement for sexual reform had in common the aim of combating prejudice, ignorance and baseless fears in the field of sexual behaviour. Both were also attempts to talk about things that previously could not be talked about (or could be talked about only in the specialized languages of poetry, theology and gutter slang), and to do so in rational and scientific terms. But they also reflected new sets of anxieties – about venereal and hereditary diseases, for example. And the new codes of sexual mores were just as rigid as the old norms and taboos, albeit in a different way. Rules about what was natural, normal and healthy in the most intimate areas of life now came stamped with the legitimizing authority of science. People were to be told how to behave in order to have a happy marriage and to uphold the interests of the community.

Two diametrically opposed views of human nature and of social and psychological inquiry had similarly been in competition with one another since the turn of the century, and now acquired a greater public resonance in the 1920s.

One camp took a biologistic approach, viewing human behaviour in accordance with scientific explanations of physiological processes. Theories and concepts from empirical medicine were extrapolated to give 'scientific' explanations of social behaviour, with the help of analogies from zoology and botany, particularly selective breeding. Medicine had begun to conquer epidemic diseases and was making a first truly important contribution to social advance; its prestige was enlisted in support of the utopian biologistic programme of establishing the 'scientific' laws governing the human species and producing 'improved' kinds of human beings. Cholera and tuberculosis had been defeated; now it was time to eradicate hereditary diseases and, with them, 'asocial' behaviour. Rational, 'biologically' guided sexual behaviour would thus play a key part in the creation of the new human being. The initial task was to classify all sexual behaviour, especially deviant behaviour, into well-defined scientific categories. Informed, rational intervention could then follow.

Ranged against such views was psychoanalysis, in which the primary focus was on the individual and on a technique of hermeneutic dialogue intended to unlock the unconscious. Although psychoanalytical theory partly borrowed from the methodology of the natural sciences, its central concepts – as far as the work of Freud was concerned, at any rate – retained a clearly metaphorical character (as did the borrowings from mythology in the Jungian theory of archetypes). Psychoanalytical method itself always led back to the individual personality; each interpretative reconstruction of the unconscious was unique. It is proof, however, of the dominant influence of the scientific, biological outlook that many psychoanalysts (such as Wilhelm Reich), as well as the general public, treated Freud's account of the psyche and the unconscious as a form of factual, instrumental description based on mechanistic biology. Only in cases where ideas from psychoanalysis and humanistic educational reform came together – as, say, in the works of Siegfried Bernfeld – did the two kinds of theoretical approach to the human mind and sexuality that we have discussed display their full liberalizing potential.

Given this intellectual background, it is interesting that attitudes towards sexuality during the Weimar Republic were marked by ambivalence towards the process of liberalization and the dropping of taboos. The new thinking reached a mass audience for the first time. Traditionalist institutions, such as the churches, the middle classes and provincial society, were offended, but where new ideas gained a hearing – leaving aside Bohemian circles, in which promiscuity might even be a mark of ideological soundness – they helped promote a more rational approach to sexuality. Technical advice was given on sexual relations in marriage, and platonic companionship between the sexes in the youth movements was encouraged. There was also a degree of cautious liberalization in social mores and the law: the homosexual subculture was granted a certain measure of tolerance, for example, particularly in Berlin. On the other hand, the law dealing with sexual matters was not overhauled, and the statute book remained dominated by old norms. There was talk, as part of a projected reform of the penal code, of abolishing Article 175, which made homosexuality an offence, but in view of the alliance between the churches and the *Bevölkerungspolitiker*, there was no chance of obtaining a majority in favour of abolishing Article 218, which outlawed abortion. When parliamentary government was suspended during the world recession, the reform process was halted, and once the National Socialists had come to power, the moment for reform had passed altogether.

To sum up, moves towards sexual emancipation were impeded both by powerful conservative misgivings and by anxieties aroused by the new 'scientific' approaches to sexual behaviour.

MOTHER'S DAY AND MALE FANTASIES

A mere glance at the compartmentalized nature of the age structure of the population in Germany suggests that in the controversies about youth and inter-generational conflict, about women's roles, about the upbringing of the young and about sexuality, more was involved than a process of emancipation of the individual personality. The dominant fact was the existence of ambivalences and contradictions. There was traditional-minded resistance to change, and there were new pressures and anxieties. These tensions, in turn, were sharpened by being played

out against the background of a general crisis of socio-cultural legitimacy and a deep-seated crisis in the economy.

In response to the crisis over modern roles and images, many people
sought refuge in ostensibly undamaged traditional notions. There was
much nostalgia for the 'ideal home' – father secure in his authority,
loving mother and obedient children – even though this ideal had
never actually been realized in middle-class society. Cultural pessimists
painted correspondingly demonized pictures of the break-up of the
modern family, the decline of morals and the destructive influence of
the concrete jungle of the cities.

Another, less unpromising tactic of the Weimar era, similar in its
goals to the retreat into an idyllic past but different in its methods, was
to accept modernity, at least in an instrumental sense, but to attempt
to head off new demands and expectations about social roles by calling
for large-scale public institutional intervention and the enlistment of
the modern mass media. Under this heading came campaigns for the
moral protection of the young, which reached a woeful culmination
in a Harmful and Obscene Publications Law of 1926,[15] and the defence
of social work and family welfare services on the grounds that they
were 'strengthening for the nation'. Modern advertising was enlisted
to promote 'Mother's Day', an American import which was introduced after mass lobbying by florists' organizations but which rapidly
became a wider public-relations exercise.[16]

Yet another sort of response to the tensions generated by new images
and roles was the genre of the aggressive apologia for the masterful
warrior male. Ernst Jünger voiced a disturbing post-war mood in his
Der Kampf als inneres Erlebnis of 1922, an account of the intensity of
the experience of combat during the First World War:

When the blood courses through the brain and arteries as before a long-
desired night of love, but much more hotly, more madly ... The baptism
of fire! The air was charged to overflowing with manliness, so that every
breath was an intoxication; one might have wept without knowing why. O
the hearts of men who can feel this![17]

The marked strain of aggressive masculine imagery in nationalistic
writing by former soldiers, which reflected the attitude to violence
prevalent in the virulently militaristic fighting organizations that

sprang up in the early and late days of the Republic, was matched by the presence of even more violence-ridden images of women in these 'male fantasies'.[18] Women in such fantasies were either portrayed as sterilized, bloodless 'white women' – mothers, for example, or nurses – or took on the ghastly shape of proletarian, Bolshevik harpies, Red in tooth and claw, whom the Freikorps fighter was called upon, and willing, to beat into a 'bleeding pulp'. Fantasies of violence – which were, of course, frequently acted out – were a means by which the 'soldierly man', insecure within the body armour in which his rigid upbringing had wrapped him, could find release. Actions that according to criteria of professional military discipline would have been seen as weakness or a surrender to instinct were given moral legitimacy.

The fascist counter-revolution was more than an invocation of tradition and the past: it was an attempt literally to smash the threat to male 'soldierliness' and to lay down rules for a new world order born of violence. Under the new order, life would be simple enough; as Mussolini put it: 'War is to man as motherhood is to woman.'[19]

5. THE POST-WAR ECONOMY: RATIONALIZATION AND STRUCTURAL CRISIS

If we compare the economic recovery of the Federal Republic after the Second World War with that of the Weimar Republic after the First, we find a combination of the familiar and the unfamiliar.[1] The rapid succession of crises that overtook the Weimar Republic, the short-windedness of the recovery and the bitterness of the battles over the distribution of national resources imply an economy so different from the *Wirtschaftswunder* economy of the 1950s as to merit the description 'abnormal'. On the other hand, all sorts of innovative features of the Weimar economic order – 'concerted action' by trade unions and employers' associations, co–determination or participatory decision-making in the workplace, rationalized methods of production and improved welfare benefits for employees – were re-established and extended under the Federal Republic and have been regarded as vital ingredients of its economic stability and growth. But more is involved than a simple contrast between the 'modernity' of the struc- ture of the Weimar economy and the 'abnormality' of the economy's growth performance. These two aspects of the economy were causally interrelated; indeed, it can be argued that it was, precisely, the modern features of the Weimar economy, the welfare state and the wage- bargaining system, that were responsible for the failure of growth during the period of recovery.[2] This implies, however, that the new democratic welfare state was destroyed not (or not only) by external factors, but by itself – by its inability to bring about social reform and economic recovery simultaneously, in the conditions that prevailed after the war.

*

A TRIAL RUN FOR CORPORATISM[3]

From the day when I saw that the [wartime] cabinet system had collapsed, I wholeheartedly welcomed the change to the parliamentary system; and today, on the matter which I regard as paramount – namely, our country – I stand behind the democratic government and, as far as is possible, shall proceed hand in hand with the trade unions and shall seek to salvage whatever can be salvaged. As you can see, I am an opportunist: I adapt to circumstances.

These words are taken from a private letter written on 31 October 1918 by Carl Duisberg, the chemicals industrialist, in which he gave his reasons for supporting not only the adoption of a parliamentary constitution for the Reich but the reform of the national economy on the basis of co-operation between the employers and the trade unions.[4] They demonstrate the changes that had already taken place before the revolution, as a result of the war and military defeat. The old notion of the entrepreneur as master in his own house, not recognizing trade unionists as bargaining partners, had had to take a back seat, at least temporarily, at the time of the 'Burgfrieden' of 1914 and the establishment of a war economy bringing together the bureaucracy, the military, employers and unions. The Auxiliary Service Law of 1916 had secured trade union consent to the centralized registration and direction of labour by conceding the right for elected workers' committees in larger firms to have a say in decisions on matters affecting employees' interests.

Any hopes entrepreneurs might have had that a combination of the Supreme Command dictatorship under Hindenburg and Ludendorff and a crushing peace settlement modelled on the Brest-Litovsk Treaty would allow these concessions to be rescinded and replaced by authoritarian, 'Volksgemeinschaft'-inspired industrial and social policies were dashed by the military collapse of 1918. Defeat made institutionalized co-operation between trade unions and employers as unavoidable in the transition to a peacetime economy as it had been in war. The negotiations that led to the Stinnes–Legien agreement establishing a *Zentralarbeitsgemeinschaft* (see p. 31 above) were the immediate result. The outbreak of the revolution delayed the signing of the agreement for a few days, but the delay served only to underline its urgency in the eyes of the new negotiating partners. The agreement was finally concluded on 15 November 1918. In addition to its corporatist prospectus, it constituted an insurance policy for employers against nationalization and gave the unions a guarantee that the leaderships would not have to surrender control over social and economic issues to the mass rank and file whom they distrusted.[5]

The baptism of German corporatism concealed a deeper structural contradiction. On the one hand, the maturity of German industrial society and the severe pressures it faced as it began to deal with the effects of the war together pointed clearly to the adoption of a corporatist model in the long run. On the other hand, the circumstances of 1918 had forced the employers to make concessions which they would later be loath to uphold when the political situation became more favourable. Only the actual outcome of events in the economy and the welfare state would determine whether this short-term tactical pact was to become a long-term strategic alliance.

The specific terms of the *Arbeitsgemeinschaft* agreement were likewise a mixture of *ad hoc* deal and more long-sighted thinking. The trade unions were recognized as the organized representatives of workers' interests, and support for pro-employer 'yellow unions' was withdrawn. In firms with over fifty employees, elected workers' committees would ensure participatory decision-making in the implementation of wage settlements. Labour exchanges, arbitration boards and a central committee were filled on the basis of parity. These measures created an immediate institutional framework for co-operation during the process of demobilization. At the same time, the introduction of the eight-hour day indicated a willingness on the part of employers to offer concessions of substance, and not just new procedural arrangements.

The economic foundation on which the *Arbeitsgemeinschaft* rested was inflation. Inflation allowed employers to pass on higher costs as higher prices, and it was the easy way in which the state could finance its social policies. When the stabilization of the currency in late 1923 and early 1924 took away the leverage that inflation had created, the basis for the *Arbeitsgemeinschaft* deal also disappeared. Wage disputes became more acrimonious; employers tried to shift international price pressures on to the workers and sought to extend working hours beyond the eight-hour day. As confrontation began to replace co-operation, the formal abrogation of the *Arbeitsgemeinschaft* became inevitable.

Corporatism's trial run came to an end at the moment when it became clear, after the illusions of inflation had been dispelled, how restricted the scope for higher living standards in the post-war German economy really was. The hopes invested in the *Arbeitsgemeinschaft* were shattered by the realities of class conflict. Nevertheless, the restructuring of industrial relations that had occurred during the inflationary period survived. Trade unions were recognized as parties in collective wage bargaining, workers had representation in plant decision-making and compulsory state arbitration had been instituted.

Betriebsräte[6] (works councils) had been foreshadowed by the workers' committees of the Auxiliary Service Law of 1916, but they did not become enshrined in law until the *Räte* movement (soldiers' and workers' councils) had been tamed. During the revolution, particularly in its third phase in early 1919, *Betriebsräte* functioned as units of political power, not merely as grass-roots bodies representing workers' interests, and the trade unions at first viewed them, somewhat warily, as potential competitors. But they rapidly became a focus for mobilizing action at the level of the firm and hence a significant means whereby the unions might increase their influence. The Works Councils Law of 4 February 1920 called for workers' co-determination through a hierarchical system of councils, giving concrete expression, at the level of the firm, to Article 165 of the Reich constitution. The law was not popular with employers, nor with those on the left who had been active in the *Räte* movement. For the former, it gave workers too much say; for the latter, not nearly enough. In the event, it did not do an enormous amount for workers' rights. Workers' representatives were required to act in the interest of the enterprise and of industrial harmony. They were entitled to lodge appeals against dismissal and to participate in decisions affecting terms and conditions, but other rights – to inspect balance sheets and to nominate up to two delegates to the board of directors – while constituting a symbolic challenge to the principle of unfettered managerial control, did not amount to a great deal in practice.

The annual elections to the *Betriebsräte*, though, fulfilled an important function, soon becoming a closely watched political test of the relative strengths of the different strands of political opinion in the unions. At the same time, these regular industrial election campaigns led to a hardening of union attitudes and actually caused workplace disputes over terms and conditions to become very highly politicized. Communist opposition groups, particularly, sought to exploit workers' demands as part of their campaign to 'expose' the Social Democratic union leadership.[7]

The new system of conciliation and arbitration[8] came to play a decisive role in wage disputes during the Weimar Republic, but it was certainly not originally envisaged as a permanent institution. It should be remembered that the institutional mechanisms for dealing with wage disputes which the *Arbeitsgemeinschaft* agreement created had never previously been put to the test. The idea in 1919, in view of the problems caused by demobilization, was to try to resolve disputes through conciliation boards on which the two sides had equal representation and, if this failed to secure agreement, through a final and binding state arbitration award. This system survived the period of inflation, and indeed the exacerbation of wage conflict that followed the stabilization of the currency positively strengthened it. Decrees on arbitration and conciliation procedures and on working hours, designed to prevent strikes and to deter employers from undermining the eight-hour day respectively, were issued on 30 October and 21 November 1923 and put the system on to a permanent basis.

The practical effect of compulsory state arbitration, however, was to leave the negotiating parties entrenched in irreconcilable positions, since the task of reaching a compromise now fell, in the last instance, to the state. Unions and employers felt compelled to hold out for their full demands in order to secure as favourable a ruling as possible, and the position of maximalists within either camp was strengthened. Since an arbitration award was the result of political calculation, rather than of a gruelling trial of strength between the two sides, no one felt obliged to make the best of a bad job. Wage disputes accordingly became politicized, and the state arbitration authorities, which automatically got caught in the political crossfire, forfeited their legitimacy.

Neither the establishment of the original *Arbeitsgemeinschaft* nor the wider framework of conflict management created by the Weimar

Republic was conducive to the forging of compromises. On the contrary, they made conflict more acute, particularly since the state of the economy did not provide sufficient leeway for conflicts of interest to be resolved, however incompletely.

THE IRRATIONAL CONSEQUENCES OF RATIONALIZATION

The year in which stability was achieved, 1924, saw the death of many illusions, though there was still hope that the way was now clear for a rapid upturn in the economy. Not only was the stabilization crisis itself rapidly dealt with, but there was an inflow of foreign, especially American, capital, and there was considerable optimism that the German economy would be comprehensively modernized.[9] Nevertheless, as can be seen on closer inspection, views about the form that rationalization should take differed widely.

The trade unions and Social Democrats had always been in favour of technological progress, seeing it as the vehicle for the achievement of social reform. Increased productivity would lead to higher wages and shorter working hours and would make for easier and safer working practices. The unions also accepted, at least in principle, that rationalization would create new short-term pressures and temporary hardships; these, they envisaged, would be offset by welfare measures. Behind this altogether co-operative attitude lay a vision of a step-by-step rational restructuring of society as a whole, a vision that was articulated, for example, in Rudolf Hilferding's diagnosis of 'organized capitalism' and his strategy of 'economic democracy'.

In the eyes of business entrepreneurs, on the other hand, the increases in production and reductions in costs that would result from modernization were seen as means to an essentially revanchist end, namely recapturing the position they had lost as a result of the war and the revolution, both on world markets and at home. They meant to be masters again. This was particularly true of the 'hardliners' in heavy industry, whereas figures from the up-and-coming sectors such as the chemicals and electrical industries saw the possibility of using rationalization as a way of integrating workers economically and securing the co-operation of workers' organizations. Either way, the actual effect on firms would be intensified pressure to increase output, utilization of spare capacity and close control over working practices. Both variants of the entrepreneurial rationalization strategy, the revanchist and the integrationist, owed much to a vision of society in which workers would be tightly regimented within the *Werksgemeinschaft* (works community).

This schematic account of employers' and trade unions' attitudes towards 'rationalization' shows that there were considerable differences over what the term meant and, more important, what purposes the process itself might serve. Like every catchword that becomes attached to a particular period of history, 'rationalization' was tantalizing in its ambiguity. Rather than try to provide a single simplistic definition, we need to distinguish the varying connotations the term held for contemporaries.

Central to the notion of 'rationalization' were the managerial principles of Taylorism, which had been discussed and, to a degree, tried out before the First World War but which were now beginning to be implemented on a broad scale. Working processes were analysed scientifically, subdivided into separate operations and subjected to time checks, so that wages could be calculated by reference to the most efficient performance of standardized tasks.

'Rationalization' also referred to new labour- or time-saving forms of investment: the introduction of new manufacturing methods based on high technology, as in the chemical industry; the replacement of manual operations by machine tools; and assembly-line mass production, in which work processes were subdivided into separate tasks performed at a determined speed.

In a broader sense, the term 'rationalization' connoted a commitment to a thoroughgoing modernization of the structure of production in general, especially through investment in new, progressive industries. This notion received a great deal of publicity; it was heavily influenced by the model of the dynamic, prosperous American economy, and there was much talk of importing 'Americanism' into Germany. Yet little of this actually happened. Even in the 'golden twenties', German bankers and entrepreneurs clung to familiar, cautious and, in this respect, utterly un-'American' forms of investment.[10]

For entrepreneurs and unions alike, the concept of rationalization was bound up with a vision of a more 'rational' economy generally. An enhanced degree of 'rational' control, however, was partly the result of other processes whose effects were not so desirable. First, there was the spread of industrial monopolies, which continued even after the collapse of the inflation-swollen Stinnes empire in 1924, with the formation of IG Farben in 1925 and of the Vereinigte Stahlwerke. Secondly, there was the growing use of price agreements and production quotas to create cartels on domestic and international markets. Thirdly, and linked with this, there was an increase in state intervention, which, although less extensive in the peacetime economy than it had been under the *dirigiste* conditions of the war, was repeatedly called for during the inflation and the period of stabilization in the form of special subsidies and protectionist measures to encourage particular types of production. The level of government expenditure, expressed as a proportion of Gross National Product, had been approximately 17.7 per cent in the last year before the war, but it reached about 25 per cent in 1925 and actually rose to 30.6 per cent in 1929.[11] This form of 'organized capitalism', which had to some extent been prefigured in the Wilhelmine era, reinforced the rigidity of the German economy in the post-war period, encouraged bureaucratic mechanisms of resource allocation and made for a concentration of the power of cartels and vested interests. In general, it was not conducive to innovation and was poorly suited to dealing with the new conditions on post-war international markets. 'Organized capitalism' is in fact an incomplete description: it was an over- and ill-organized form of capitalism.[12]

Rationalization and the spread of 'Fordism', however, held out more than merely the deceptive prospect of a new macro-economic order: they were also bound up with grand ambitions in social engineering.[13] Scientific management and the integration of workers into the *Werksgemeinschaft* would dissolve class conflict; pragmatic supervision by social engineers would reconcile competing special interests. This utilitarian faith in the power of science to solve social problems was evident in all areas of society. At one extreme was the pro-business propaganda put out by the German Institute for Technical Work Training; at another was Ernst Jünger's literary invocation of the dawning technological world of 'the worker', or the vision of the unification of heart, brain and hand within the 'great machine' in Fritz Lang's film *Metropolis*. But these fantasies of socio-technological omnipotence were dispelled even before the onset of the great world depression. The divisions within social reality saw to that: persisting conflicts of interest could not be simply wished away. And it was the dashing of these hopes of technocratic social reform based on *Werksgemeinschaft* and *Volksgemeinschaft* that bred a willingness to countenance the National Socialists' solution, in which the contradictions of industrial society would be resolved by force.

As far as the actual impact of rationalization during the 'golden twenties' is concerned, it is difficult to offer a comprehensive summary, both because much detailed research still needs to be done and because changes in working processes and in the structure of employment varied very considerably from one workplace to another and also between different sectors of the economy.

Let us therefore take the mining industry in the Ruhr as a representative example.[14] Until the mid-1920s there was a clear disparity in mining between the advanced technology and high degree of organization that had been established at plant level and the autonomous craft-based pattern of work at the coal-face itself. The surge of rationalization that began after 1925 changed this dramatically and in short order. In 1913 extraction by hand and pick-axe, with or without the preliminary use of explosives, had accounted for 97.8 per cent of coal extraction; the figure was still 52 per cent in 1925, but by 1929 it had fallen to a mere 7 per cent. The proportion of coal extracted by pneumatic pick, by contrast, which was insignificant in 1913, rose to 36.5 per cent in 1925 and had reached 87.37 per cent by 1929. At the same time, face operations were reorganized, so that in place of largely autonomous, small co-operative groups of miners, larger working units were established in which individual coal-getters worked in a line between the seam and a mechanized conveyer belt which carried away the extracted coal. This more individualistic pattern of work meant that the system of group piece rates, which had been the inevitable consequence of the old technology, was gradually replaced by a system of individual piece work. The number of working faces fell from 16,706 in 1927 to 12,500 in 1929 and 5,111 in 1932. In the same five years, the average daily output per working face rose from 23 to 59 tons. Annual output per employee hence rose from 255 tons in 1925 to 350 tons in 1929 and 386 tons in 1932. It is not surprising that these figures were accompanied by a massive fall in the total number of men employed. There had been 400,243 workers in the Ruhr coal industry in 1913, and the figure reached a peak of 544,961 in 1922; numbers fell to 409,404 in 1925, to 352,966 in 1929 and, during the Great Depression, to a low point of 190,009 in 1932.

The effects of rationalization may not always have been as clear as they were in the mining industry, but mining was certainly not an isolated case. Rationalization in the coalfields meant the introduction of more productive machinery, but also caused increased damage to health. It meant the replacement of traditional co-operative forms of working by individual piece work. Productivity rose sharply but, since demand did not increase, the numbers of workers employed had to be drastically reduced. Even before the depression, one miner out of four had lost his job, and in the depths of the crisis over half were out of work. It should also be said that in the longer term some new types of mining job, requiring higher qualifications – fitters and electricians, for example – gained in importance. In the short run, however, many more miners were conscious of the fact that automation had led to de-skilling, greater stress and higher unemployment.

Structural unemployment gave a new edge to the unions' traditional radicalism. Until the early 1920s radical attitudes had been a spontaneous by-product of the solidarity that arose because men were working and living in the same community. Later, the division of the mining workforce into employed and unemployed became more acute, and the unemployed, as they became increasingly marginalized, provided an important source of support for the KPD.[15]

We can sum up the contrasting effects of rationalization on workers in different sectors of the economy as follows.[16]

First, the old structures of job qualifications were altered. Types of work which had previously been performed by members of skilled trades were now de-skilled, while new types of skilled job, calling for specialized technical qualifications, were created. The net effect varied from industry to industry. There might be an increase in the number of unskilled jobs (and assembly-line work, for example, might also lead to a shift in the distribution of specific types of job between the sexes); alternatively, new training opportunities might be opened up, and new types of skilled and white-collar job might be created, as in the expanding fields of management and administration.

Secondly, the fact that rationalization was occurring within the context of a stagnant economy gave rise, in other industries besides mining, to a more pronounced segmentation of the labour force: between the skilled and the unskilled; between those in regular work and those only casually employed or unemployed; between older workers and the younger workers who were pressing hard on their heels. Rationalization militated against solidarity.

Thirdly, there was a growing pool of structural unemployment, which did not disappear even in the brief spells of economic expansion that occurred in 1925 and 1927–8. A category that had been virtually unknown before the First World War now appeared, concentrated especially in certain industries and regions: the long-term unemployed. When the economy went into crisis, as in 1926 and from 1930 to 1933, the unemployment figures reached previously undreamt-of levels. Rationalization, in other words, marginalized a growing section of the German working class.

Rationalization in no sense ushered in a well-ordered world of high productivity and social engineering. Automated methods of production and the pursuit of higher profits often led to a more rapid rate of human attrition. Higher productivity created higher unemployment and a consequent waste of human resources. Vistas of rational micro- and macro-economic control dimmed as the insistent realities of bureaucratic market mechanisms and irreconcilable social conflicts of interest asserted themselves. But as the innovative dreams of the technocrats faded, a new form of salvation arose to take their place: a violent and far from rational 'final solution' to the problems of society. Rational visions were transmuted into the embodiment of irrationality.

*

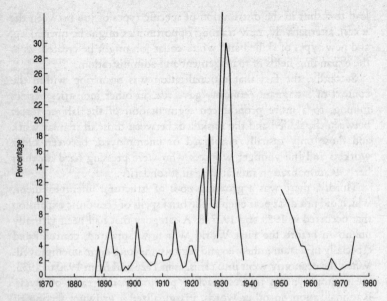

Figure 6 Unemployment rates in Germany, 1887–1975

Source: K. Borchardt, 'Zwangslagen und Handlungsspielräume in der großen Wirtschaftskrise der frühen dreißiger Jahre', in M. Stürmer (ed.), *Die Weimarer Republik. Belagerte Civitas*, Königstein, 1980, p. 330

THE 'SICK ECONOMY' OF WEIMAR

Structural mass unemployment (see figure 6) and poor economic growth (see figure 3, p. 12) are the two most visible symptoms of Weimar's 'sick economy'. Historians, however, differ in their identifications of the full range of symptoms of the crisis and their diagnoses of its causes, and the debate will not readily be resolved, since it concerns not only the collapse of Germany's first experiment in democracy but also, more fundamentally, the whole question of the interconnections between the welfare state, capitalism and economic growth.[17]

Germany's post-war economic weakness was not merely homegrown. Problems in the world economy affected all the European industrial nations, albeit with differing degrees of severity.[18] The war forced the European economies to surrender something of their dominance to nations outside Europe. In 1925 Germany's industrial production (making adjustments for boundary changes) had returned to only 95 per cent of its 1913 level; Britain had to be content with 86 per cent, and France's position, at 114 per cent, showed only a small improvement. The figures for Japan and the United States, on the other hand, were 222 and 148 per cent respectively, and Australia, India and Canada had also undergone more rapid growth than the three European nations that had earlier led the field. In parallel, Germany's share of world exports fell from 13.2 per cent in 1913 to 9.1 per cent in 1927–9, while Britain's fell from 13.9 to 11 per cent and France's from 7.2 to 6.5 per cent. France, therefore, was broadly holding her own, though even her position in the post-war world economy had weakened somewhat. Great Britain was undergoing a long-term structural crisis, which manifested itself in a sluggish industrial recovery, but thanks to her colonial empire she was able to retain a healthier position than Germany in international trade.

These changes in the world economy were the product of three sets of factors.

First, long-term capitalist economic development had entered an entirely new phase. After decades of expansion and industrial innovation, there now followed decades of crisis and limited growth. The reasons for this change in economic tempo have been much debated by economic historians. What is certain is that the pre-war pattern of growth had reached its limits, without creating the conditions for a new pattern of industrial development to emerge in its place. There were some attempts to bring this about in the 1930s, by means of Keynesian expansionary measures, but the new methods did not really come into their own until after the Second World War.

Secondly, as the statistics of world export shares indicate, the old international division of labour was disappearing. The established industrial nations were faced with new competitors; traditional markets were being lost. The pressures on industrial exporters were exacerbated by structural problems on world agricultural markets, where, even before the Great Depression, vast surpluses of foods and agricultural raw materials had built up.

Thirdly, these international structural imbalances could not be converted into a world boom, if for no other reason than that the world's financial system was undergoing great upheaval. The British pound had been unable to sustain its role as the leading world currency, and the dollar had taken on some of its important functions. Paris also remained a rival international financial centre in the 1920s. The gold standard had been abandoned during the war, and in the reconstruction period it was replaced by the gold exchange standard, which was less well equipped for weathering crises. On top of this, the syndrome of war debts and reparations created quite unprecedented problems of procuring foreign exchange and organizing credits and transfers. And while the scale of international financial indebtedness was great enough in itself, the inexperience and uncertainty of those who had to operate the world's financial machinery was even greater.

The effect of this combination of factors was that post-war international markets, painfully rebuilt between 1922 and 1924, broke down again between 1929 and 1931, and the world capitalist system entered on the deepest crisis it had ever known.[19]

Germany's international economic problems, then, were serious. They were augmented, furthermore, by internal difficulties. Economic historians disagree, as we have said, about how the different causes of the German economic crisis should be weighted; what is clear is that, as in controversies about other crises, or indeed about complex historical phenomena generally, all monocausal explanations are inadequate. But merely to list the considerable number of causal factors whose relevance is not in contention is itself sobering enough, and demonstrates how heavily the cards were stacked in favour of economic collapse.

In the first place, German industrial production in 1919 (when German territory had, of course, become smaller) stood at only 38 per cent of the level it had reached in 1913. Boosted by inflation, it rose steadily until 1922 (1920, 55 per cent; 1921, 66 per cent; 1922, 72 per cent), but in the crisis year of 1923 it fell again to 47 per cent of the 1913 level. In the first year of stabilization, 1924, it rose again to 70 per cent, and to 83 per cent in 1925. The small international recession of 1926 brought a fall in the production index, to 80 per cent, but this was followed by three years of growth during which the pre-war level of production was first equalled and then marginally surpassed (1927, 100 per cent; 1928, 103 per cent; 1929, 104 per cent).

This last period, however, saw a falling-off in the rate of growth, despite the fact that the boom had not yet fully run its course. Symptoms of crisis began to multiply in 1928, and these culminated in the full-scale international catastrophe ushered in by the Wall Street crash in late 1929. In 1930 German industrial production fell to 91 per cent of its 1913 level, and it collapsed even more dramatically over the next two years.

These global indices of industrial production are sufficient to demonstrate how the growth of the post-war economy was repeatedly braked and put into reverse. Yet the full picture of the causes and effects of the German economic crisis was even more sombre than these figures imply.

Secondly, industrial stagnation was paralleled by agricultural depression, a world-wide phenomenon that had devastating effects on East Elbian farming, which suffered from structural weaknesses, as well as in many regions of small and medium-sized peasant holdings. The position of the large East Elbian landowners, in particular, had been weakened because they had lost the backing they had traditionally enjoyed from the Hohenzollern monarchy, because the legal prerogatives they had exercised over agricultural workers had been, at least on paper, nullified by the November revolution and because the war had deprived them of their traditional export markets. To sell their products on world markets, or compete with inexpensive imports, they needed to modernize; instead, lack of profitability drove them deeper into debt. They were caught in a vicious circle from which, despite receiving considerable *Osthilfe* (eastern aid) from the government throughout the Weimar period, they were unable to escape. The agricultural crisis affected not only farmers, who quickly became radicalized, but, indirectly, the whole population of the rural provinces and small towns. The provincial revolt against the Weimar 'system' occurred for a number of distinctive socio-cultural and political reasons, but the roots of it lay in the agrarian crisis.[20]

Thirdly, as an industrial nation which had always been active in international trade, Germany suffered particularly from the problems of the world economy because military defeat and the provisions of the Versailles Treaty added extra burdens to her already worsened position. These measures included the seizure of her foreign assets and merchant ships, territorial losses and financial liabilities. They were politically motivated penalties, and they inflamed German nationalistic passions: Germans felt that their country had not only been crippled and humiliated but had been made the victim of economic enslavement and spoliation. The more sober verdict of history may rate the burdens of Versailles less harshly than this, but at the same time it was all too easy for Germans to blame their economic ills on 'foreigners'.

Fourthly, however, Germany's frustrations in external trade were not relieved by any real degree of domestic expansion. The progress of the boom from 1927 to 1929 showed just how sluggish the home market was. While capital-goods production in 1929 was 2 per cent higher than a year earlier, consumer-goods production fell by 3 per cent between 1927 and 1928 and by a similar amount in the following year.

Fifthly, after the inflation-led boom in the capital sector, and more especially as a result of investment in automation in the mid-1920s, shortfalls in demand on both domestic and export markets led to a growth of industrial excess capacity.

This in turn led to a general reluctance to undertake new investment. The national net investment ratio declined from 16 per cent in the years immediately preceding the First World War to an average of only 10.5 per cent in the period 1925–9. There has been much discussion of the reasons for this reluctance to invest on the part of German entrepreneurs; several factors were evidently involved. A study of the areas in which investment was made shows that modern, forward-looking and hence risky forms of economic activity were the very ones that were not selected: traditional activities, and supposedly safe returns, were preferred. These attitudes went hand in hand with an obstinate attachment to cartels and subsidies within heavy industry. In addition, high government spending created a double brake on investment: to the extent that it was financed by taxation, it added to costs, while higher borrowing made credit for industrial projects more expensive.

A further factor was that the role of the state in the economy had expanded. There were higher levels of public spending because of the expansion of welfare benefits, housing and local services, and also as a result of a rise in the number of civil servants and other public employees; on top of this came welfare contributions, fixed by law. Given the faltering growth of the economy in the post-war period, the result was bound to be noticeably redistributive, and this served to undermine employers' cost calculations. More important, disputes about whether the tax burden should be raised or lowered went to the core of Weimar's identity as a state, raising the issue of the constitutional requirement that it be a welfare state as well as the question of the parallel corporatist structure of industrial relations. Any dispute over state expenditure and welfare contributions automatically posed a challenge to the state's legitimacy.

Finally, the same applied, even more forcibly, to those wage disputes that brought employers and trade unionists into head-on confrontation.[21] It was often argued at the time that the relatively high share of the economy taken by wages acted as a check on growth, and the question has recently been much debated by historians. It seems clear that the rise in the proportion of wage income to income from wealth and capital was partly attributable to the fact that inflation devalued people's cash assets; the proportion of better-paid public employees and white-collar workers among wage and salary earners also increased. Against this, an average working-class family had little more money to spend on living costs, even in the best years of the 'golden twenties', than it had had before the war. Certainly, the introduction of the eight-hour day initially led to rises in costs, and these had an extra impact because other countries did not follow suit. Until 1923 employers were able to soften the effect of these cost increases because of inflation, but after the currency was stabilized they sought to deflect cost pressures by lengthening working hours, increasing productivity, extending automation and making a direct attack on wages. These attempts were not, however, successful, though it is debatable how far workers, for their part, managed to improve their position during the years 1924–8 either. As employers saw it, the system of compulsory state arbitration played a crucial role here, establishing 'political wages' which would win the approval of the electorate. From the point of view of workers and their representatives, on the other hand, the situation appeared very different from that painted in big-business propaganda. While employers were concerned about the problem of rising costs caused by shorter working hours, welfare contributions and 'political wages', workers were concerned about family living standards. The eight-hour day, the expansion of welfare benefits and the protection of real wages were seen as the central tangible achievements of the November revolution. The poor general state of the economy ensured that real living standards were little better than they had been before the war, when economic growth had reached its high point; and during the war and immediate post-war years, as in the Great Depression, they actually fell considerably.

In an adversarial economic system there was scarcely room for an 'objective' standpoint on questions affecting the distribution of national wealth. Collisions between employers and workers, with each group pursuing its perceived sectional interest, therefore inevitably became more drastic as the scope for higher living standards was squeezed by poor economic performance. Only economic growth could have mitigated these antagonisms. But since growth on both the domestic and world markets was so hampered during the post-war period, wage disputes were fated to escalate into a full-scale battle for income redistribution. And this battle was incapable of being resolved within the existing system. It is far from certain that a reduction in the share taken by wages would have increased entrepreneurs' propensity to invest, but such a reduction was certainly central to business's lurid scenario of 'Aufstieg oder Niedergang' – advance or decline. As a result, however, it was not only the trade unions that came under fire: so did the Weimar state itself, in its capacity both as the constitutional guarantor of the welfare system and as an interested party within it, determining social policy and providing industrial arbitration.

*

THE ATTACK ON THE 'TRADE UNION STATE'

When the employers responded to the new stability of 1924 by finally jettisoning the consensus with the trade unions that had held during the period of inflation, they did so for a number of different tactical reasons. Many industrialists, especially in more modern sectors of the economy, were keen to retain a basic degree of co-operation with the unions and to preserve an institutional framework in industrial relations that would help to integrate the workers. Their goal was a policy of contained conflict, giving business more flexibility but not foreclosing the possibility of a return to the post-war *Arbeitsgemeinschaft*. In 1926 and 1930, however, their attempts to achieve this goal were thwarted by the resistance of the captains of heavy industry. These men had not abandoned the hope of rescinding entirely the concessions to the workers that had been made under duress in 1918. They were looking for free and unfettered control of their own empires once again.

Yet wage disputes between 1924 and 1928 saw the workers not only halt the entrepreneurial offensive but actually make a series of territorial gains. These gains, in the employers' eyes, were primarily a result of the system of compulsory state arbitration. The unions, too, now began to draw more general conclusions from their experience of wage disputes and state intervention within the framework of a democratic welfare-state constitution. A strategy of 'economic democracy' seemed to offer a way of transforming property relations, step by step, in the direction of democratic socialism. For employers, such talk was bound to sound more dangerous than revolutionary Communist propaganda, given that Communist ideas did not command majority support.[22]

In the mid-1920s, accordingly, the stage was set for bitter conflict, with no prospect of peaceful reconciliation. The economy was too weak to allow room for wage rises. The future of the welfare-state system itself was at stake. The employers were bent on regaining their freedom of action, not only by reducing the share of wages in the economy, but by removing the obstacles constituted by welfare benefits and guarantees, compulsory arbitration and trade union bargaining rights. Any 'purely economic' argument about costs, in other words, took on a wider dimension and became part of a general struggle against the 'trade union state' as such.

A key test for the employers' anti-Weimar strategy came with the Ruhr iron and steel dispute of 1928.[23] In the autumn of that year a wage dispute in the Ruhr and Rhine metal industry had been settled by arbitration after the two sides had failed to reach a compromise. The arbitration award called for a small wage increase, but this was still too big for the employers. The Reichstag elections of the summer of 1928 had seen a swing to the left, and a Great Coalition, led by the Social Democrats, was in office. The employers' rejection of the specific terms of the arbitration award thus became linked with an open campaign of sabotage against the whole system of compulsory arbitration and an outright challenge to the welfare state which the SPD symbolized. In November 1928 the iron and steel employers locked out about 220,000 metal workers. During the four-week lock-out positions hardened further, as even members of the bourgeois parties in the Reichstag condemned the employers' unlawful action. The workers who had been locked out received financial assistance from the state.

For the employers – who eventually said that they were prepared to accept fresh arbitration, but with even lower wage terms – the support given to the locked-out workers by the majority group in the Reichstag, by the government and by local authorities was a further vindication of their fundamental opposition to the system. If they could not get the 'freedom of action' they wanted in the field of wage bargaining, then not only did the system of settling wage disputes have to be dismantled, but so did the system of parliamentary government itself.

The Great Coalition survived until new regulations governing reparations, in conformity with the Young Plan, were approved by the Reichstag in late 1929 and early 1930. But immediately afterwards conflict between employers and trade unions sharpened again over the question of unemployment insurance, now exacerbated by the economic crisis. While the immediate argument within the coalition was about raising contributions or lowering benefits, the employers' ultimate aim was, once again, for the entire welfare apparatus to be dismantled and the system's guarantee by Parliament to be abolished.[24]

Because it lacked the economic resources to meet its commitments, the democratic welfare state was under threat.

Altogether, the survival of the Weimar system depended on whether the social and political settlement that had underlain the creation of the constitution in 1918–19 could be defended and elaborated. Poor economic growth had made this increasingly questionable; the world-wide depression now made it virtually impossible. The twin crises affecting the economy and the political legitimacy of the state show that the basic tenet of an optimistic theory of modernization – namely that economic development and political and social progress go hand in hand – is true only on the assumption of an extended period of economic expansion, such as occurred in the Wilhelmine and Adenauer eras (though neither of these periods was unmitigatedly 'progressive' in a political sense). The 1920s and early 1930s, however, exemplified a different brand of the process of modernization.

1. Forward-looking schemes of participatory decision-making and methods of resolving conflict in the public interest were drawn up, but these proved fragile since economic conditions were too straitened to allow compromises to be struck. Corporatism might perhaps be only a fair-weather solution.

2. Changes in methods of production and, more generally, in social relations gave rise to visions of all-embracing 'rationalization' in the 1920s, but these visions, when translated into concrete terms, led if anything to new and greater irrationalities.

3. The 'golden twenties' saw the first glimmerings of a modern consumer society and of comprehensive welfare provision, but even these modest improvements in living standards unleashed bitter conflict over income distribution, and the public welfare system came under fire from employers, whose aim was to surmount the structural crisis in the economy by smashing the freshly laid foundations of the welfare state.

All of these patterns of conflict were present, in less virulent form, in every capitalist economy during this period. What was unique in Germany between the wars was that the contradictions became so inflamed and so inextricably bound up with the deadly crisis of the legitimacy of the democratic system that no situation that might have preserved the system was feasible. Faced with a Gordian knot, the industrialists resorted to the sword. The victim was the experiment in constitutionalism, democracy and a welfare state.

6. THE WELFARE STATE: EXPANSION AND CRISIS

In the Weimar Republic, the welfare state was enshrined within the constitution. The new republic owed much of its prestige to its promise to extend the compass and impact of social policy. But by the same token, people's experience of the in-built contradictions in social policy and of the cuts in welfare provision that resulted from the economic crisis played a crucial part in undermining the Republic's legitimacy. Economic difficulties loomed large here, making it impossible to implement reforms which were desired and which had been promised, but they were not the only factor. More deep-seated structural tensions in social policy also came dramatically to the fore amid the general problems of the moment – tensions, indeed, that have remained with us to the present day.

Stated briefly, the trouble was that the very success of the expansion of publicly guaranteed welfare provision gave rise to new problems. State welfare services became bureaucratized and subject to norms, and this made for increased social disciplinary pressure and caused the provision of assistance to become more depersonalized. On top of this, the world economic crisis exposed the fatal dependence of the state system on cyclical factors. Boom years generated the resources to permit an expansion of benefits, but made demands for benefits relatively slight. Conversely, in times of crisis, when the need for enhanced social provision was most urgent, the state was also most anxious to save money and reduce benefits.

*

THE CREATION OF THE WELFARE STATE

Like many areas of society, social policy in the Weimar Republic owed much to the achievements of the Wilhelmine era and was a continuation of the reformist impulses of that period.[1]

Once it had become clear that the conflicts and tensions created by industrialization could no longer be damped down simply by liberal *laissez-faire* methods and that the 'social question' could no longer be dealt with only by private charity, a series of social-insurance laws was passed from 1881 onwards which created a basic system of social security. This system, while harking back to older notions of state relief, was also genuinely forward-looking. Under the new model the state was committed to setting up and guaranteeing the social-security framework, the possibility of public subsidy was established and recipients of benefits were required to join collectively organized insurance schemes. Although at first the actual levels of benefit arising from the sickness, invalidity, old-age and accident insurance schemes were modest, the new system took shape without opposition in the years before the turn of the century and continued to be amended until the Reich Insurance Order of 1911.[2]

There was a similar evolution as far as traditional poor relief and charitable work were concerned, which became transformed into modern welfare assistance and social work under the monarchy, although these areas had always been highly fragmented and did not become as integrated and as thoroughly regulated by legislation as did the social-insurance system. Nevertheless, by the time of the First World War a set of new principles and procedures had been worked out and put to the test: individual means-testing and assessment of benefits had been introduced, and legal norms had been established; welfare provision had been bureaucratized and professionalized; the scope for possible state intervention and regulation in private life had increased; and social work and special education had become professional disciplines.[3]

The Weimar Republic thus did little that was intrinsically new in the fields of social insurance and welfare assistance. All the same, it represented a quantum leap in the evolution of the welfare state in Germany – and not only in Germany. The principle of a welfare state and its most important concrete institutional manifestations were enshrined in the Weimar constitution, and entitlement to the services of the welfare state was declared a basic right of German citizens.

At the same time, the serious social problems created by the war and, especially, the war's aftermath brought about a significant expansion and improvement of specific services. In addition, the new constitution defined further areas of future state legislation, and various unfinished reforms were subsequently carried through into law and given institutional form. These reforms included the Reich Youth Welfare Law of 1922; the Reich Juvenile Court Law of 1923, which established the principle of educational rehabilitation for juvenile offenders; legislative regulations governing social welfare brought in by emergency decrees on 13 February and 4 December 1924;[4] and, not least important, the introduction of unemployment insurance in 1927.

The catalogue of basic rights embodied in the Weimar constitution did not merely refer to the provision of welfare services: it amounted, despite schematic formulas and ambiguities that would have to be resolved by later negotiation, to a broad outline of the actual content of the welfare state that was to be created.[5] Marriage was singled out as the 'foundation both of family life and of the nation's preservation and growth'. From these desiderata – at once, goals both of social morality and *Bevölkerungspolitik* – flowed various other social aims and principles: provision through state and local authorities for the 'equality of the sexes', the 'protection' of 'motherhood', the 'maintenance of the purity and health of the family' and public support for the family (Article 119); the responsibility of parents, under state supervision, to bring up the younger generation to achieve 'physical, mental and social fitness' (*Tüchtigkeit*; Article 120); equality of status for illegitimate children (Article 121); and the protection of young people from 'exploitation and moral, intellectual or physical neglect' (Article 122).

Conditions governing the special status of *Beamten* were laid down (in Articles 128–31).

The guarantee of religious freedom was also linked to provisions that were part of social policy in a wider sense: regulations laying down the public and legal status of religious communities, church taxes and Sunday and holiday observance (Articles 135–41).

Most of the provisions relevant to social policy were contained in the section of basic rights dealing with 'economic life' (Articles 151–65). These articles covered the freedom to own property, together with public obligations in respect of property; public commitments concerning land use; a projected movement to build new housing estates, especially for large families and ex-servicemen (Article 155); and the promotion of co-operatives and the possibility of nationalization (Article 156). *Mitbestimmung* (co-determination) by means of works councils and economic councils (Article 165), support for the *Mittelstand*, or middle class, (Article 164) and the protection of intellectual property (Article 158) also had clear connections with social policy.

The articles most immediately relevant to social policy in the strict sense were Article 157, which provided for the protection of employees and promised the 'unification' of labour law; Article 162, which looked ahead to international labour-law reforms; and Articles 161 and 163, the first of which gave a pledge that the existing system of social insurance would be preserved, and laid down the direction to be taken by new developments:

In order to maintain public health and the ability to work, to protect motherhood and to make provision against the economic consequences of old age, infirmity and the vicissitudes of life, the Reich will provide a comprehensive system of insurance, in which those insured will make a vital contribution.

Article 163 entered new territory:

Every German has the moral obligation, his personal freedom notwithstanding, to exercise his mental and physical powers in a manner required by the welfare of all.

Every German shall be given the opportunity to earn his living through productive work. If no suitable opportunity for work can be found, the means necessary for his livelihood will be provided. Further particulars will be given in subsequent legislation.

Hitherto, only Soviet Russia had declared that the meeting of citizens' basic social needs was a goal of the state. The Weimar Reich constitution was the first attempt to base the legitimacy of the state simultaneously on democratic decision-making, constitutionality and a welfare system. Its specific provisions were certainly a mixed bag, and many of them were schematic or couched in terminology that soon became dated. Furthermore, even if political and economic conditions had been more favourable than they were in the 1920s, the gap between what the constitution promised and what it might have delivered could never have been bridged at once. Nevertheless, we should not undervalue the boldness and progressivism of the Weimar vision of the welfare state simply because, in the precariousness of the times, it was implemented piecemeal and then so soon revoked.

In both its framing and its demise, the Weimar welfare state brought to the forefront various problems that are central to modern social policy generally, though the crises that beset German society after the First World War made these problems particularly acute.

1. The commendable principle of equality of social rights led, in practice, to a growing subjection of the individual to criteria of 'normality', as the welfare system became increasingly regulated by legislation and as the conceptions of normality held by legislators and administrative officials were thereby brought to bear.

2. Since the only way in which a citizen's entitlement to social benefits could be met was by the growing bureaucratization of the welfare system, the welfare institutions became more anonymous as the numbers of professional social-service bureaucrats expanded.

3. A principle of last resort operated, limiting state intervention to those cases in which assistance from private individuals, the welfare associations and the local authorities was not forthcoming. Rather than protecting individual autonomy, however, this tended to inflate the role of the religious and non-religious welfare associations and to make them gear their efforts to the prescribed levels of support provided by the state.

4. Since the values enshrined in the Weimar constitution were based on a pluralist compromise, many of its social aims were schematic and empty of content. Where it was specific, it was often negative, as in its references to social deprivation and threats to morality.

5. An unforeseen consequence was that as the general welfare-state principles proclaimed in the constitution were translated into detailed legislation, actual social policy always fell short of these lofty long-term objectives. Although specific services might be expanded, the public tended to judge social policies by the extent to which they failed to live up to promises and expectations.

6. The programme of social policy promised in the constitution had been drawn up without thought for the financial resources that would be needed to implement it. There was a constant tug-of-war between what was desirable and what was affordable. The problem became more acute with the collapse of the inflation-led boom and with the dispute over the role of the welfare state that flared in the mid-twenties. After the world slump that began in 1929, the gulf between reduced state assistance and mass poverty became a yawning one.

7. The slump illustrated a more general dilemma of social policy. A notable expansion of social services could be financed only in a period of fairly steady economic growth. Conversely, as the Weimar economy went through phases of stagnation, disputes over resource allocation became more pronounced. Periods of acute crisis pointed up the near-absurdity of the social-policy cycle, whereby resources were least available at the times when they were most badly needed.

THE LIMITS OF SOCIAL ENGINEERING

The blithe unconcern with which the founding fathers of the Weimar constitution had written out their shopping-list of new welfare services and social benefits was a reflection of certain important prevailing assumptions in social thought. Since the 1890s, believers in the need for social reform had increasingly been tempted by the further, more ambitious conviction that all social problems could be rationally solved by state intervention and the application of science and social theory. This blind faith in the omnipotence of social engineering, which spread to all political parties, was founded, indeed, on some perfectly genuine social achievements.

The successes of social policy seemed to vindicate the view that the need for social regulation could, and should, be met by bureaucratic procedures and state intervention. At local as well as national level, the big infrastructure projects which were beginning to provide a remedy to the harmful effects of mass urbanization – the provision of water supplies and sewage systems, for example – encouraged the belief that a combination of action by the authorities, new technologies and scientific advances in public health could solve all the major problems that had been regarded as making up the 'social question'. Scientific understanding of serious diseases was advancing by leaps and bounds, and scourges such as smallpox, cholera and tuberculosis, in particular, seemed about to be conquered once and for all. In parallel, the professionalization of social work and the expansion of public services was leading to the enlistment of growing numbers of lawyers, doctors, teachers and engineers, who brought with them their specialist skills and their practice-oriented methods and attitudes. Altogether, a new instrumental and technical approach to diagnosing and solving problems was gaining ground: social questions were judged according to criteria of utility and the feasibility of social engineering.

At the same time, it should not be forgotten that such thinking was attacked by the classically educated critics of modernity who were active in the youth and educational-reform movements, while even the apparently sober, pragmatic, scientific belief in social planning had an admixture of middle-class unease and discontent, notably as far as contact with the lower social classes was concerned.

Solutions to specific types of social problem were seen as vitally conditional on the realization of grand utopian projects. The proposals of the new social engineers – whether concerned with youth welfare, public health or town planning – were imbued with the notion that the 'social question', as such, could finally be solved. As medical advances had put paid to bacteria, so an alliance of science and inter-ventionist social engineering could put paid to all outstanding causes of social unease. Architects would solve the housing question as well as all the other woes of urbanization; lawyers and educationists would together teach criminals to mend their ways; medical research and public-health programmes would abolish illness; psychologists and social workers would abolish 'asocial' behaviour; eugenists would 'eradicate' the genetic causes of abnormality.

It had been the utopian dream of the Enlightenment to secure the greatest good of the greatest number by harnessing reason in the public interest. This notion had descended from the philosophical heights and had become the prosaic guidepost of the new class of social engineers. The process, which had begun before the turn of the century, reached its culmination under the Weimar Republic. And yet it was now, too, that these ideas entered a state of crisis, as it became apparent in all areas of society that there were limits to what could be achieved by social intervention. We can illustrate this by reference to five different aspects of social policy.

The introduction of *unemployment insurance*[6] represented a fundamental, and fatal, extension of the centrepiece of social policy, the social-insurance system. War and demobilization had led to the issuing of provisional state regulations covering job procurement and unemployment relief. But it was not until 1927 that the constitutional commitment on unemployment was met and the Labour Exchanges and Unemployment Insurance Law was passed.

Labour exchanges now took over the functions of job procurement and vocational guidance which had previously been performed by local-government bodies, private agencies, trade unions and private individuals. Uncoordinated journeying or migration in search of work, which threw together vagrants and those genuinely looking for jobs, was replaced by an organized regional system of job placement. A public scheme of vocational guidance would supplement the state's role in apprenticeship training, while the dual system for apprenticeships, combining workplace and *Berufsschule* (vocational or technical school) was retained. Both employers and employees paid contributions into the unemployment-insurance scheme, with the state guaranteeing the viability of the scheme by adding a subsidy. The level and duration of insurance cover depended on the nature of the individual's previous employment. When a person's unemployment benefit ran out, emergency relief at a lower level was available for a set period of time. Thereafter, however, the individual had to fall back on local welfare services. In severe cases, in fact, the benefits provided by the insurance scheme were so low that local assistance was necessary in any case.

Although the general scheme was a radical, progressive one, the actual levels of projected benefits were far from lavish. And the effect of the world economic crisis was that they were cut back further. The skeleton of the unemployment-insurance system could be preserved only if its flesh, in the form of actual benefits, was pared down. But this meant that most of the unemployed had to have recourse to the degrading procedures and meagre handouts of the local welfare and relief institutions, despite the fact that local government was virtually bankrupt anyway. Nowhere, then, was the gulf between progressive ideals and shabby reality more pronounced than in this very showpiece of social policy.

Weimar legislation sought to free *public welfare provision*[7] of the odium of 'poor relief' and charity that had previously surrounded it (anyone receiving welfare assistance had lost the right to vote, for example). The First World War created a new clientele of 'superior' welfare recipients: servicemen's relatives, widows, orphans and disabled soldiers. They were granted benefits based on their previous standard of living and not calculated simply with reference to basic subsistence. The Reich Relief Law and Serious Disability Laws of 1920 provided further support for war victims, with special emphasis on rehabilitation for at least partial re-employment; pensions were set at a fairly low level, and could be supplemented by 'superior' welfare payments only if the individual failed to find work. In 1924 an emergency decree on welfare provision and a declaration of 'Reich Principles' on public welfare set out the legal entitlements of those in poverty, procedures for assessing need and providing assistance, and levels of benefit.

The new legislation, though, did not do away with the problem of the old welfare system, namely that the nature and extent of the benefits were so limited that those who were eligible availed themselves of them only when all other options had failed. For many, the level of benefits was sufficient only to cover basic subsistence. Once again, there was a gap between the generosity the Weimar Republic's modern welfare apparatus offered in theory and the meagreness with which it operated in practice, a gap made even wider by the degrading procedures imposed by the system's bureaucracy and by the substantial drop in benefits that took place during the world recession.

Financial policy[8] also had an increasingly important bearing on social policy. The rationale for the financial reforms brought in by the Reich

Finance Minister Matthias Erzberger, which assigned the responsibility for fiscal policy to the national government, was partly the unitary structure of the new state and partly the state's enhanced role in social policy. The financial reform of 1919 certainly led to a weakening of local government, and also to a dramatic increase in state spending as a proportion of national income: the proportion rose from 14.5 per cent in the immediate pre-war period to 43 per cent in 1919, and settled, once the inflation was over, at an average level of 25.8 per cent during the years of stability 1925–9. Alongside this, higher incomes were taxed progressively for the first time in Germany, while the need to finance the welfare state also led to considerable rises in contributions on top of direct taxes. The tax burden as a proportion of the national income, which had stood at 9 per cent in 1913, rose to 17 per cent in 1925.

Nevertheless, Reich tax revenues during the stabilization period were scarcely sufficient to cover increased administrative costs and state welfare expenditure, part of which had to be met through borrowing, particularly from the United States. Local authorities, the losers from the financial reforms, were especially badly affected. The world recession virtually drove them into bankruptcy as foreign credits were cancelled, while the Reich government used its deflationary policy to cut back further on its own benefit provisions, so driving the poor on to local welfare and charity. The progressive financial reforms, in other words, which on the face of it should have expanded the scope and impact of social policy, in fact had the opposite effect.

Conventional social policies were complemented by new developments in *public health*.[9] The extension of health insurance meant that the lower social classes were now able to benefit from medical care, and public health services expanded noticeably. Whereas in 1909 there had been only 4.8 doctors for every 10,000 people, the figure for 1930 rose to 7.4; similarly, the number of hospital beds rose from 63.1 per 10,000 people in 1910 to 90.9 in 1930, and the use of hospitals also increased in proportion, from 374.7 in-patients per 10,000 people in 1910 to 656.6 in 1930. During the same period there was a marked fall in the numbers of deaths from serious endemic diseases. Deaths from tuberculosis, which had stood at 143 per 10,000 people in 1913, fell to 87 per 10,000 in 1928; deaths from pneumonia fell from 119 to 93 per

10,000 people. On the other hand, cancer and cardio-vascular disease became more common as causes of death, and the maternal mortality rate remained high.

Public housing programmes were relevant to public health as well as being a part of social policy generally. Housing reformers were interested not only in town planning and the provision of adequate living-space, but in the physical and moral improvements that would come from better housing and living conditions. Weimar housing policies built up further the legislative apparatus for funding public housing that had been devised during the First World War. Taking 100 as the index for 1913, public spending on housing rose to 2,525 in 1925 and to 3,300 in 1929. Between 1927 and 1930 over 300,000 new or renovated homes were added to the housing stock.

It must be said, however, that improvements in public health – which also included advances in infant care, convalescence services, preventive medicine, sex education and nutritional reform – went together with questionable eugenist ideas and practices. It was not just the advance messengers of National Socialism but also humanistic, liberal and socialist writers on public health who looked ahead to radical new ways of improving the national 'genetic stock' through measures of prevention and 'eradication'. The proposed methods ranged from voluntary preventive counselling about hereditary conditions to mass sterilization of those with supposed hereditary diseases. Many conditions – from schizophrenia to mental deficiency, alcoholism to short-sightedness – were rather glibly pronounced to be inherited, and medical scientists and psychologists tended to explain forms of social behaviour in 'biological' terms, again encouraging the call for eugenic intervention. *Bevölkerungspolitik* accordingly became a meeting-ground for eugenic ideas arising from concerns about public health and the more radical versions of eugenics that sprang from racial biology, in which ominous comparisons were drawn between social or ethnic groups of 'lower value' producing large numbers of children, and groups of 'higher value' producing smaller numbers of children. It was not, however, until the grand designs of the social engineers were dispelled by the pessimistic mood that accompanied the onset of the world economic crisis, and the aims of *Bevölkerungspolitik* seemed to be threatened by a growing army of the sick, the weak, the poor and the 'asocial', that a doctrine of 'selection' (*Auslese*) began to be enunciated during the years 1930–33 – to be followed, after 1933, by the actual practice of 'eradication' (*Ausmerze*).

Finally, *special education*[10] became increasingly significant during the Weimar Republic. The Reich Youth Welfare Law of 1922 created a legal framework and an institutional structure which completed the reforms that had begun under the monarchy. The law, which proclaimed the child's 'right to [a good] upbringing', cleared the way for considerably more intervention by the state into the privacy of the family than had been possible under the restrictive terms of the Civil Code of 1900. The new powers included compulsory public guardianship for all illegitimate children, the widespread introduction of professional guardians, an extension of reform-school education and the institutionalization of youth services in a youth welfare office. This growth in the state's role, however, also made the system more susceptible to crises. By the mid-twenties the gulf between goals and achievements in special education had already become a yawning one. There were revolts and scandals in approved schools, which became the subject of much public discussion.

The arguments echoed a wider debate among educationists on the 'limits to educability'. Spokesmen for *Reformpädagogik* accused educators (themselves included) of hubris and attempted to establish a distinction between what special education could, and could not, achieve. But the controversy was also exploited by those who sought to pin the responsibility for 'ineducability' on the reform-school pupils. A protracted debate on whether the law should provide 'protection' (*Bewahrung*) or 'detention' (*Verwahrung*) for the 'ineducable', together with cuts in special-education provision during the economic crisis, paved the way, here too, for the emergence of a paradigm of selection and segregation before 1933, and the National Socialists then took the final step into 'eradication' after their assumption of power in 1933.

To sum up: it was the very expansion of the welfare state during the Weimar years that brought social policy up against the limits, both internal and external, to its effectiveness. This dilemma had gradually become clear in all areas of social policy even before the world depression; once the depression had set in, all talk was of the crisis of the welfare state and the need to curb its 'excesses'.

THE *KULTURSTAAT* AND ITS CONTRADICTIONS

The founding fathers of Weimar believed that the legitimacy of the new republic would rest on the fact not only that it was a welfare state, but that it would be a *Kulturstaat*: a 'culture state' or 'civilized society'. The discrimination against Social Democratic, Catholic and left-liberal cultural values that had been practised during the monarchy would be ended; the new constitution aspired to a genuine cultural pluralism. But in the event, these pluralist goals were diluted by empty formulas and short-term compromises; fundamental reforms were postponed indefinitely, for lack of votes in Parliament; and the attempt to translate the ideal of a *Kulturstaat* into reality led to bitter and unappeasable controversy.[11]

The Weimar Coalition was, in fact, extremely ill-equipped for developing a concerted approach to educational policy, since the secular educational aims of the Social Democrats and liberals were diametrically opposed to the religious goals of the Catholic Centre. On the other hand, as far as the central issue in education was concerned, namely schools,[12] the Social Democrats' policy of secular, comprehensive education, with its aim of giving all children equal educational opportunities, was very far from being acceptable to the educated middle classes, who, whatever their political colour, were strongly committed to the *Gymnasium* system. On this point, accordingly, the liberals were allied with the Centre. In turn, the Centre's insistence on denominational schooling, while provoking the opposition of its coalition partners, the SPD and DDP, was supported by the Protestant conservatives of the DNVP.

A way out of this tangled situation was provided, at least for a while, by a characteristic Weimar compromise, embodied in Articles 135–50 of the constitution, in the Reich Elementary School Law of 1920 and in the negotiations at the Reich School Conference of the same year. An accommodation was reached by simply excluding from consideration all issues on which consensus was not possible. The basic form of school would be the 'Christian non-denominational school' (*christliche Simultanschule*), in which the different denominations would conduct religious education separately. At the same time, denominational (or indeed secular) schools could be set up on parental request.

After the Weimar Coalition lost electoral ground in 1920, however, the Reich School Law which would have incorporated these changes fell by the wayside and the status of the existing denominational schools was left essentially unaltered, although civics had become a school subject in conjunction with religious education. The constitution had circumvented the thorny question of whether comprehensive schools should replace the divided school system, using an empty formula about continuing 'organic development' in education, which could be seen by one camp as a safeguarding of the traditional division and by others as a call for comprehensivization. Nevertheless, a common system of elementary education for all children was established. Schooling was made compulsory until the age of eighteen, and was to consist of eight years of *Volksschule* (elementary education) followed either by technical school or by *Realschule* or *Gymnasium*. A unified system of teacher training was also to be introduced, but this scheme fell through because of fears about the financial costs of implementing higher training standards and meeting higher salary demands.

The achievement of compromise in so controversial a field as that of school education should not be underestimated. All the same, the stalemate between the warring sectional interests, so typical of Weimar policy-making generally, began to have a damaging effect as early as 1920. Further progress was made, mainly at *Land* level, on a modest scale and as a result of trade-offs among the various interested parties, but problems at the centre remained unresolved. Ideological pluralism was not embraced for its own sake, as an opportunity for the Republic to strengthen its political identity, but was accepted, reluctantly and with much gnashing of teeth, as a consequence of purely semantic compromises. Despite many attempts to create greater equality of opportunity, the tripartite school system perpetuated traditional social divisions and, although the educational system was expanded in an institutional sense, the philosophies underlying it remained at loggerheads.

And yet the Weimar era is rightly seen as a 'great age' of educational reform.[13] Reformist ideas had gathered strength around the turn of the century, as *Kulturkritiker* questioned the utilitarianism and authoritarianism that had hitherto dominated the schools and higher education. Appealing to humanistic values, the educational reformers sought to give primacy to the actual educational situation as experienced by the child and looked to the youth movement and progressive rural boarding schools for models of new, comradely relationships between teachers and pupils. Under the Weimar Republic academic chairs in education were established, new institutions were founded and there was a flowering of debate on educational issues; the educational reformers became, in a sense, the spokesmen of the Republic's system of education. Admittedly, as far as teaching itself was concerned, both in schools and elsewhere, the reformers remained a small minority and circumstances often conspired against their experiments. Reformist ideas also had their own in-built limitations, being idealized extrapolations from the pattern of education and child psychological development characteristic of the cultivated middle classes. Even so, right up till 1933 the most thoughtful of the educational reformers remained committed to the goal of 'understanding' the everyday experience of the mass of the population and the pattern of socialization of working-class children, and of building a broader concept of education on this basis. Their work shows that there was certainly an articulate and imaginative alternative to the retreat from educational reform that occurred with the final crisis of the Republic. Equally, this fact did not prevent many educators from seeking a *modus vivendi* with the National Socialists when they came to power.

Possibly more significant than the debates over substantive matters of educational reform and philosophy were the institutional changes that were coming about as a result of growing professionalization in the educational system and in social and youth work.[14] Although an integrated system of teacher training was not established, the number of trainee teachers increased; on the other hand, career prospects in teaching, after a growth in the number of posts brought about by the immediate post-war reforms, rapidly deteriorated. The long-term pattern of expansion and contraction in the educational system meant that there was little room for recruitment into the profession during the years of the Republic itself. As a result, although there were considerable reserves of support for democratic ideas within the teachers' associations, there was a swing to the right among students and aspiring and practising teachers, and this swing became more pronounced in the final Weimar years.

Within social and youth work, too, a brief expansion of posts, caused by the formal establishment and development of training courses in social work and special education, was followed by a longer period in which there was a surplus of qualified applicants. Here again, those affected found themselves victims both of the wider crisis of the Republic and of a 'trade cycle' of institutionalization and professionalization within the educational system, whereby a short phase of rapid growth and rising demand for qualified personnel was followed by a much longer and more dismal phase in which the newly expanded supply of people with qualifications was chasing a drastically reduced number of new posts.

On the whole, then, the story of the *Kulturstaat* in the Weimar years was a sorry one, especially since even the founding fathers of the Weimar Coalition rapidly lost the will to compromise, let alone to achieve consensus. A telling sympton was the debate about a 'Law to Protect Young People from Harmful and Obscene Publications', introduced by the *Bürgerblock* government in 1926, which sought to ban pornographic and sensationalist publications.[15] Despite the effort of Theodor Heuss to make the legislation palatable to the left by claiming that 'there is not only a social policy of wage agreements – there is also a social policy of the soul', there was no meeting of minds. The right, together with the Centre, regarded modern civilization in general, and the Weimar public media in particular, as a latter-day Sodom and Gomorrah which could be countered only by a wholesale return to traditional values; the left, not without justice, viewed the use of youth-protection legislation as a pretext for the introduction of more general political and moral censorship. The law was finally passed in a diluted form, leaving each side equally dissatisfied and embittered, and even more anxious to prolong the dispute.

The *Kulturstaat* envisaged in the constitution did not come into being; in its place was a battleground of irreconcilable ideologies and sectional interests.

FROM RETRENCHMENT TO SELECTION

Even during the period of relative stability, the internal contradictions within Weimar social policy had become more pronounced. The provision of wider ranges of social services and benefits to larger numbers of people stretched social policy to the limits of what was financially attainable, and provoked demands for expenditure and services to be cut back. The disparity between generous promises and entitlements on the one hand and limited provision and humiliating administrative procedures on the other became patently obvious in daily life. Given the general dearth of resources, the bureaucratic way in which the system was run was bound to cause especial resentment. And in cases where tangible advances were actually achieved – in housing and health, for example – the state quickly came up against limits to its effectiveness. With the arrival of the world recession, the policy of piecemeal restrictions became a strategy of deliberate retreat: a policy to dismantle the welfare state altogether.

Certainly, the Reich government's policy of austerity and the insolvency of the *Länder* and local authorities were of crucial importance in leading to the dismantling of social services and benefits. But behind the policy of austerity lay a fundamental break with the principle of the welfare state as it had so far been envisaged. This was made clear beyond misconstruction by the Reich government of Franz von Papen on 4 June 1932:

Post-war governments believed that by means of ever greater state socialism they could relieve employees and employers of most of their material anxieties. They tried to turn the state into a form of public-welfare state, and thereby weakened the moral strength of the nation.[16]

Thinking of this sort became the new paradigm in social policy with the onset of the world economic crisis.[17] The expansion of welfare provision and the use of education as a means of social integration and discipline had reached the limits of its efficacy.

Even before the crisis, a critical re-examination of the relationship between social ends and means had got under way. A new basic distinction had begun to emerge, between the overall (and over-large) category of those in need and a new, smaller category for whom provision was said to be 'suitable' and 'likely to be beneficial'. Criteria for determining levels of benefits were canvassed, in order to stem the widely deplored flood of claims on the system.

The economic crisis ushered in a 'red pencil regime'. The government sought to legitimize the cuts by using the theoretical debate about the ends and means of social policy as the basis for a concrete system of classification. Possible recipients of benefits were categorized according to whether or not they were 'worth' helping, and whether or not the welfare support to which they would previously have been entitled would be 'useful'. It followed logically that those not explicitly selected for provision were implicitly labelled 'useless' and 'unworthy' of help.

To give an example: the Reich Youth Welfare Law of 1922, which had guaranteed 'every German child' the 'right to [a good] upbringing', was altered in November 1932 by an emergency decree that lowered the general age of discharge from reform schools below the age of majority. At the same time, provision was made for the 'ineducable' to be refused admission to, or be discharged from, reform school. In the space of a decade the aspirations of the educational reformers had been swept aside and replaced by the stigmatization of the 'ineducable'.

Although the welfare state had been put into reverse and new paradigms of selection and segregation had taken charge, the final outcome was still not settled. It was only when the National Socialists came to power that the policy of 'selection' was given 'scientific' respectability by means of racial biology, which had previously been of marginal influence. The elimination of left-wing and liberal critics gave the advocates of 'selection' a free hand, and the Nazis' lack of moral inhibitions made possible the ultimate step from 'selection' to 'eradication'. But although even the harshest foes of the Weimar welfare state had not sought a 'final solution' of concentration camps and gas chambers, by starting the process of dismantling the welfare state in the early thirties they had undoubtedly helped to pave the way for it.

7. SOCIAL MILIEUX AND POLITICAL FORMATIONS

In the last thirty years of the nineteenth century, in conjunction with the process of industrialization and the consolidation of a unified national state, a pattern of political culture evolved in Germany in which particular regional, religious and social groupings became associated with distinctive ideologies and beliefs and with different party-political allegiances. Each of the major political parties became linked with its own socio-denominational milieu, and this pattern retained its cohesive force into the 1920s, after the collapse of the monarchy.[1]

Broadly speaking, there were four major political camps at the end of the nineteenth century, each with its corresponding social milieu.[2] The Conservative camp had its roots in East Elbian agrarian society, which was Protestant and dominated by big landowners. The National Liberals derived much of their support from Protestant urban areas, where leading middle-class citizens played an influential role. The Centre Party represented a majority of Catholics of all social classes, as it had done since the *Kulturkampf* of the 1870s. The social ambit of the Catholic church, in fact, was wide, taking in rural and small-town areas that were still virtually pre-modern and the new industrial districts in the Ruhr and Rhineland, where the Catholic workers' movement provided an ideological and organizational base for the new 'fourth estate'. The Social Democrats, finally, were rooted originally in the older industrial districts and towns, spreading only later to the new industrial regions such as the Ruhr. Particularly during the period of the monarchy when they had been persecuted under the *Sozialisten-gesetz* (Socialist Law), the Social Democrats built up an entire social milieu of their own, providing an alternative to the society in which they were debarred from full participation. This counter-society was the setting for the lives of the working class, if not from cradle to grave, then from *Jugendweihe* (consecration of youth) to cremation, and it offered a great range of social and political activities, from theatre visits to trade union work.

The Bismarckian constitution, under which governments were not formed from majorities in Parliament, and the exclusion of so-called 'enemies of the Reich' from political life further reinforced the tendency for the political parties to become separate socially based camps. Before the First World War a first loosening of these divisions had begun to become apparent, both politically and in daily life, and the process was highlighted in dramatic, but short-lived, fashion in the 'Volksgemeinschaft' euphoria of August 1914. During the war, however, the political camps remained as tightly integrated class parties, even though there was a certain softening of social differences as a result of military service. The election results of 1919 represented a continuation of the trends of 1912 and demonstrated that the cohesion of the separate political camps was still strong.[3]

SOCIAL MILIEUX IN THE 1920s: LEVELLING AND NEW SEGMENTATION

During the 1920s the main political groupings, and the social and denominational ideologies associated with them, were subjected to two conflicting sets of pressures. On the one hand, as industrial society became more mobile, the social patterns that had become solidly fixed during the Wilhelmine era began to shift and there were clear signs of levelling. In tandem with these changes, the political parties made various efforts to extend and reorganize their support by offering broader-based forms of integration. On the other hand, the post-war crisis in politics and society began to open up new social divisions, which in turn caused new socio-political groupings to split off from the old. These new forms of segmentation did not run in one single direction: tensions arose between, for example, gainers and losers from inflation; between different groups vying more fiercely than before for a greater share in the stagnating national income; between the younger and older generations; between men and women competing

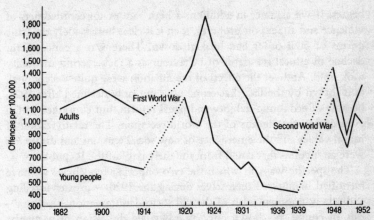

Figure 7 Youth and adult crime in Germany, 1882–1952 (numbers of criminal offences per 100,000 people of responsible age)

Source: C. Kennert, *Entwicklung der Jugendkriminalität in Deutschland 1882–1952*, dissertation, Berlin, 1957, p. 38

for jobs; between white- and blue-collar workers; between the skilled and the unskilled; between those whose qualifications enabled them to profit from modernization and those whom modernization left de-skilled; and between the employed and the unemployed.

This incomplete list gives an idea of the new fissures that were spreading across the old terrain of social attitudes and allegiances. In addition, there was a general weakening of traditional social and moral ties as a result of war, revolution and inflation. This instability, much discussed and deplored at the time, is strikingly reflected in statistics of crime (see figure 7).[4] Youth crime had already increased dramatically during the war, signalling a collapse of established authority. There were complaints about insubordinate behaviour, criminal rowdyism, larceny, offences against public order and provocation of public authorities, involving not only young people but also, in growing numbers, women faced with financial hardship on the 'home front'. Although recorded adult crime rose from 1919 to 1921, it nevertheless remained on a level comparable with the immediate pre-war period. But with the inflation of 1922–3 it too exploded: mass crime on this scale had never been seen in Germany since the compilation of statistics had begun. If we assume, in addition, a high rate of unrecorded acts of violence and attacks on property, then it is clear how widely the basic norms of civil order had broken down. There was a concomitant decline in ethical standards of behaviour as a racketeering mentality took hold. And yet the effects of the inflation were quite exceptional, as is shown by the fact that crime rates not only declined after 1924, because of economic stability and penal reform, but continued to fall even during the rigours of the world recession. The relativization of moral values and the emergence of new social tensions and disparities were an incubus that dated from the early days of the Republic.

The specific ways in which the two opposing tendencies we have identified manifested themselves during the 1920s – greater levelling and a new fragmentation of the old socio-denominational milieux – can, of course, be shown only by a detailed discussion of particular cases.[5] In what follows we shall take socialist working-class society as our principal illustration, also referring more briefly to the position of German Catholics. In addition, we shall consider two marginal phenomena which do not entirely fit into the explanatory framework of socio-political camps: namely the relationship between the new breed of white-collar workers and the old middle class, and the position of the German Jewish community, as it found itself caught between full emancipation and mounting discrimination.

SOCIALIST WORKING-CLASS SOCIETY

Before 1914 the Social Democratic movement was, along with the Catholic Centre, the classic instance of the political camp centred on a social milieu. Social Democracy was rightly seen as akin to a full-dress alternative society, headed by its 'alternative Kaiser', Bebel: a quintessential part of the Wilhelmine world, so to speak, precisely by virtue of its being excluded from it.[6] War and revolution brought an end to this state of 'negative integration', but the Republic did not usher in a corresponding form of positive integration on the same scale. Instead, during the years 1919–20 the unity of socialist working-class society was irreparably destroyed.[7] From late 1920 onwards various conflicts among specific social groups, which had always existed but which had now become more polarized – conflicts, for example, between skilled and unskilled workers, young and old, those in large firms and those in small ones – were joined by the new splits that had been provoked by the collisions of civil war to create an irreconcilable gulf between the Communist and Social Democratic camps.[8]

In the Reichstag elections held from 1924 to 1932 the KPD polled between 9 and 16.9 per cent of the votes, while the SPD's vote ranged from 20.4 to 29.8 per cent. In 1928 the two working-class parties together attracted 40 per cent of the votes. This was less than the SPD and USPD had achieved in 1919, but it demonstrated the continuity in support for the left since the collapse of the monarchy. The left's combined statistical strength, however, was of little account, since all co-operation between the KPD and the SPD was ruled out by their deadly political enmity, which had been exacerbated by the civil war.

Behind the political animosity, furthermore, lay sharp differences in the memberships of the two parties.[9] Generalizing very broadly, we may say that the members of the KPD were much younger than those of the SPD, and the same was true of the two leaderships. The Communist Party also contained a higher proportion of unskilled workers. Whereas the typical member of the SPD was the skilled worker ambitious to use his training in order to gain promotion and, especially, to improve the social and educational opportunities of his children, young Communists were drawn towards the radicalized political counter-culture of the Weimar left by a sense of disillusion: a belief that education and skills would do nothing to improve their future prospects. The KPD, in particular, became the party of the unemployed: even before the world recession a majority of its members had been unemployed, and with its onset almost all of them became so.

The political outlooks of the two parties accordingly reflected these different sets of social and personal experiences and attitudes. Social Democrats were receptive to proposals for developing orthodox Marxism into 'popular socialism' (*Volkssozialismus*) and 'cultural socialism' (*Kultursozialismus*) within the context of a democratic state, whereas the Communist Party clearly echoed the bleaker experiences of its supporters when it proclaimed the sterility of the capitalist system, the illusory nature of reformist measures and the need for radical and violent change.

The political and social split within the working class was not so profound as to sever all contact between the two estranged brother parties. For one thing, the account we have given is an ideal-type dichotomy, whereas in reality the distinctions were much less clear-cut and predictable. Furthermore, daily life within the family and in the workers' housing estates, leisure time spent in clubs and *Gasthäuser* and working conditions in the factories were very similar for all workers, whatever their political persuasions. Nevertheless, the amount of common experience diminished rather than increased over the course of time. During the depression, particularly, social seg-mentation became more pronounced and the political gulf grew wider. After 1928, following a period of experimental joint action, the KPD line switched to one of fierce competition with the Social Democrats. The trade unions were split, and divisions within the rich life of the workers' clubs and associations also became more marked.

The political labour movement had already propagated a highly ramified set of organizations under the monarchy, its institutions and activities ranging from the trade unions[10] to workers' sports clubs and free-thinkers' societies. These activities, however, developed yet further in the Weimar period, both in scope and number. New organizations such as the Workers' Radio Association sought to exert an influence on the emergent mass culture and its communications media. Other bodies, such as the Workers' Youth Movement, were now able to throw off the shackles that Wilhelmine authoritarianism had imposed on them. There were efforts to extend democracy in civic institutions and to bring social considerations to bear in education and culture. Workers' educational and social clubs and associations proliferated as never before,[11] though at the same time mounting competition from the new, non-political mass media and from new forms of leisure already indicated that the influence of the workers' bodies would be limited.

The split between the 'mass organizations' of the labour movement also damaged the movement's political effectiveness. In the short run, it is true, political radicalization led to a new upsurge of activity. Intellectuals committed or sympathetic to the Communist Party were particularly active in trying out new forms of communication and propaganda and path-breaking approaches and experiments in the arts. There was a boom in workers' songs and street theatre, for example, and John Heartfield's technique of photomontage and the theatre of Bertolt Brecht emerged as revolutionary new modes of artistic expression.[12] Yet the political radicalization that was part and parcel of these innovations also mirrored and reinforced the political impotence of the left as it faced the general rightward movement in the country and the rise of National Socialism in particular.

The split in the labour movement not only diminished the political strength of the two parties but diverted a large portion of their organizational energies into their own internecine struggles. The SPD was caught in a dilemma: despite trying to make itself a broader-based party, in order to retain and extend its role in the political centre ground, it was constantly forced to steer back towards the left for fear that its supporters would desert to the Communists. It is questionable, in fact, whether the SPD's attempt to broaden its base was ever a realistic option, given the swing to the right among liberal voters and the presence of the socio-cultural and economic factors that had led to the split on the left. The KPD, for its part, could preserve its identity within a non-revolutionary situation only by alternately offering cooperation and insisting on separateness. Accordingly, the party line on the question of a united front with the Social Democrats kept changing. After 1928, in keeping with the switch of policy by the Soviet Communist Party and the Comintern, the party leadership was committed to a fierce and politically senseless struggle against the SPD 'social fascists'. The new line was later deemed to have been vindicated when the world economic crisis descended in 1929 and political capital could be made out of the mounting radicalism of the party's rank-and-file supporters.

Thereafter the two working-class parties remained fixed in a posture of irreconcilable confrontation, despite the growing danger from the National Socialists. Each tried to overcome its isolation and to put an end to the rivalry by experimenting with new forms of organization. The KPD, by putting its members, especially the young and militant, into paramilitary units, played a considerable part in giving an increasingly violent turn to the political quarrel at the end of the 1920s,[13] while the SPD, with its *Reichsbanner* and *Eiserne Front*, went along with the upsurge in paramilitarism in an attempt to defend democratic values.[14]

Despite all this visible political activity, the two parties of the left had become increasingly bogged down by the early thirties. The Social Democratic leadership was growing old, the party was losing votes and after 1930 it was excluded from the role in democratic government to which it had become accustomed. The immobilism of the Communist Party, on the other hand, was due to the fact that its radicalism, while swelling its numbers, also debarred it from all co-operation with the SPD. The KPD was trapped in a ghetto of its own making.

The crisis in socialist working-class society in the early 1930s thus involved far more than the purely political split between the parties. Growing social segmentation and deep divergences in the experience of different sections within the working class had stemmed the advance of the labour movement as a collective force, despite the wide range of institutions and new initiatives the movement had created, and had robbed it of its capacity for decisive political action.

CATHOLIC SOCIETY

The same grim verdict applies to the German Catholic milieu in the closing years of the Weimar Republic, and to the two political parties which represented it, the Centre and the Bavarian People's Party (BVP), despite the fact that since 1918 the Catholic parties had been operating under the most favourable conditions for which they could have hoped.[15] Bismarck's *Kulturkampf* had led to the forging of the alliance between the Centre and grass-roots Catholic society, and the Catholic political movement retained this basic identification as it progressed towards government, at first advancing slowly under Wilhelm II and then becoming a full coalition member under the Republic. Although a social minority, it had moved into the political centre,[16] albeit at the cost of becoming an increasingly rigid traditionalist organization.

The active heart of the Catholic social milieu was Catholic parish community life and the system of Catholic clubs and associations.[17]

In traditionalist rural and small-town communities and in the new industrial districts of the Rhineland and the Ruhr, the authority of the priests remained strong; life still revolved around the faith, ritual and moral teachings of the Catholic church, despite the fact that by the 1920s secularizing tendencies had begun to weaken social ties. The parish was the centre around which people from highly disparate social backgrounds came together: Catholic landowners, prominent middle-class citizens and working people. Catholic clubs and associations, by contrast, were clearly differentiated in terms of class and status. The Catholic workers' movement, with its strictly denominational workers' associations and its (theoretically) non-denominational Christian trade unions,[18] provided a mass base for Catholic politics, but remained too weak to claim the leadership of the Centre Party.

As the *raison d'être* of the Centre came under challenge, with the ending of official discrimination, the rise of secular attitudes and the emergence of internal social and ideological conflicts, the party resorted to the tactic of offering those who voted for it (it was not a party with strong grass-roots membership) unifying compromise formulas on contentious political issues. The election of Prelate Kaas as party leader in 1928 was a similarly characteristic move, in that an ostensibly neutral priest was put in charge at a time of political in-fighting. The continuous presence of the Centre in government was also important for its continued survival, providing its members with jobs in the public service, especially in Prussia, on a far greater scale than had been possible under the monarchy.

On the other hand, the Centre, despite its permanent role in government, was unable to push through central features of its policies beyond the limits set by the Weimar constitutional compromise, though it could claim a fair number of victories on matters of social and educational policy (including the Harmful and Obscene Publications Law and unemployment insurance). Despite – or perhaps rather because of – its constant presence in government, then, the standing of the Centre was gradually undermined. It suffered a steady, if slow, loss of electoral support, falling from 13.6 per cent in 1920 to 11.2 per cent in 1933. Leaving aside Bavaria, barely two-fifths of all Catholics (60 per cent of them women) remained Centre Party voters.[19]

It is, of course, impossible to speculate how Catholic society and the Centre might have fared if the National Socialists had not come to power in 1933. As far as the Weimar period is concerned, however, it is important to note that the Catholic political movement was highly resistant to the electoral blandishments of the NSDAP. On the other hand, the collapse of the Centre in 1933 would scarcely have happened but for the weaknesses that had accumulated in the preceding years.

In this sense, the signs of political immobilism in the socialist and Catholic milieux were comparable phenomena.

WHITE-COLLAR WORKERS AND THE OLD *MITTELSTAND*

The middle classes, for all their grievances, had properly regarded themselves as the bulwark of the monarchy before 1918. The upheavals of 1914 to 1924 and the new social and political order established by Weimar hit them hard. This explains the great surge of resentment and hostility to the Republic which built up among different sections and representative bodies of the so-called old *Mittelstand* (middle class) of craftsmen and shopkeepers, and also their reactionary, romanticized glorification of anti-modern notions of *Stand* (estate).[20]

Some craftsmen and tradesmen suffered badly from the effects of interventionist economic policy during the war, and then from the inflation.[21] As well as sustaining losses of income, they were robbed of their relatively privileged social position and of the trappings of monarchy and empire which had been a particular focus of identity for them. The style of the new republic was not glamorous, and it went hand in hand with the oppressive, polarized big-business and trade union corporatism that dominated economic and social policy once the phase of co-operation came to an end in 1924. Appeals to a revival of the old 'estates' and of a state based on them should therefore be seen, in part, as an attempt to mobilize resistance against the domination of society and the economy by organized big business and mass-membership trade unions.

This analysis is borne out by a close study of the most significant psephological event in the history of the Weimar Republic, namely the gradual erosion of the liberal middle-class vote from the mid-1920s onwards. Whereas the DDP and DVP had together polled over 20 per cent of the votes in the 1920 elections, continuing the liberal tradition of the pre-war period, thereafter the two parties steadily declined, achieving only 4.9 and 8.7 per cent respectively by 1928. German liberalism was on the wane even before the years which saw the rise of the NSDAP, which was to mop up many of these defecting middle-class voters (though not only these). In a transitional phase, however, former liberal voters first sought political expression in a variety of special-interest parties.[22] The liberal political network had been made up of groups of local community leaders; already less tightly held together than it had been, this network began to fall apart as the 'panic in the *Mittelstand*' took hold and was replaced by a host of splinter organizations, which then, in turn, succumbed to the success of the National Socialist movement.

Generalized assertions about the political behaviour of the middle classes are bound to be questionable, because the middle classes were not a single, homogeneous group. This had already been true of the old *Mittelstand*, but it was virtually a defining fact about the so-called new *Mittelstand* of white-collar workers (*Angestellten*).[23] White-collar workers were employed rather than self-employed, and in this sense were like blue-collar workers; but they regarded themselves as distinct from the working class by virtue of having a more privileged status and, to an extent, higher salaries. This half-and-half position led to a fairly rapid turnover of conflicting social and political attitudes. Broadly speaking, in 1918 white-collar workers were reasonably well disposed towards the Republic and towards the principle of trade union representation, but this stance was soon followed by a retreat into non-political disenchantment, while some became radicalized and threw in their lot with the far right.

In social and cultural terms, white-collar workers, for all their apparent traditionalism, were largely a *tabula rasa* on which the effects of the process of modernization were being particularly vividly imprinted. In his mordant but sensitive study *Die Angestellten* (published in 1929), Siegfried Kracauer portrayed the white-collar class, by virtue of its very self-contradictions, as an ominous symbol of the rationalistic, empty, consumption-dominated world of industrial modernity.[24] According to Kracauer, despite the obvious differences in qualifications and types of job that separated secretaries and salesgirls from engineers and managers, there were certain central defining features of the white-collar phenomenon in the twenties: mechanization, the disappearance of traditional attitudes towards work, anonymity, the interchangeability of jobs and a labour market in which preference was given to young, highly productive workers. The new white-collar species was a creature of the urban and big-city world of leisure, a world dominated by the mass media and sated by consumerism: 'The exact counterpoise to the machine world of the office ... is the world of bright lights. Not the world as it actually is, but the world as it is portrayed in hit songs. A world which has been gone over by a vacuum cleaner, so that not a single speck of the dust of everyday life remains.'[25] Kracauer was writing about Haus Vaterland, a Berlin place of entertainment popular with the white-collar class, an omnium gatherum of the clichés of international tourism: 'At the very moment when firms are being rationalized, so these places are rationalizing the pleasures of the white-collar multitudes.'

Modernity, a fictive status of non-proletarian superiority, aspirations to upward mobility and fears of its opposite – this combination of factors underlying white-collar attitudes made for a volatile mixture. Once the hopes engendered by rationalization in the 'golden twenties' had been dashed by the world economic crisis, a noticeably high proportion of members of the white-collar class found their way into the ranks of the NSDAP.[26]

THE JEWS: EMANCIPATION, ASSIMILATION AND DISCRIMINATION

The social groups whose history under the Weimar Republic we have discussed so far were characterized by growing insecurity and paralysis and, at the close, were subjected to increasingly strong pressure from the right. The same applied, in even greater measure, to the Jews as a social group.[27]

The establishment of the Weimar Republic completed the process of Jewish emancipation in Germany. The formal and informal barriers which had effectively excluded Jews from higher positions in the public service and the academic world under the monarchy were removed. Jews now assumed an important part in post-war public life, in the liberal parties and the parties of the left, in universities and the mass media, and in certain branches of business, especially commerce. Educated middle-class Jews in Germany had become highly assimilated during the nineteenth century, blending into German culture both as producers and consumers. This process became even more pronounced in the 1920s, when, despite the conservatism of the majority of middle-class Jews, many Jewish intellectuals embraced modernism and the art of the avant-garde. There were first glimpses of the possible emergence of a new international, secularized culture which would sweep aside the traditional and nationalistic barriers on which anti-Jewish discrimination had rested.

The new mobility and cultural influence which Jews enjoyed under the Weimar Republic, however, cloaked the fact that German Jewry also had its own internal problems and was facing an alarming rise in anti-Semitic discrimination. The German Jewish community was fearful for its identity and its survival, since it was undergoing a steady decline both in absolute terms and as a proportion of the population of the Reich. The reasons were partly a low birth rate and partly the pull of secularization. Jews were not so much becoming converted to Christianity as unobtrusively losing their faith, abandoning religious observance, contracting mixed marriages and bringing up their children either under Christian auspices or without any religious education at all. From their different points of view, both Orthodox Judaism and the Zionist movement tried to stem this loss of Jewish identity.

A further challenge to the German Jews' self-image came from the immigration of *Ostjuden*, or Jews from eastern Europe. The new migrants differed from the existing German Jewish community socially, culturally and in their forms of worship, and their presence became a cause of intra-community conflict. In addition, with their strange accents and unfamiliar forms of behaviour they became a particular focus for anti-Semitic prejudice. In the crisis-torn atmosphere of the Republic, foreign migrant workers were unwelcome generally, and *Ostjuden* were regularly deported by the German authorities (here taking a leaf, admittedly, out of the monarchy's book).

A mass expulsion ordered by the Bavarian government in 1923 marked a new level of hostility.

The same year saw a shocking anti-Jewish riot in the Scheunenviertel in Berlin, a district heavily populated by *Ostjuden*. The *Vossische Zeitung* reported on 6 November 1923:

Howling mobs in all the side streets. Looting is going on under cover of darkness. A shoe shop on the corner of Dragonerstraße has been ransacked, and the smashed fragments of glass from the shop windows are littered on the street. Suddenly there is a whistle. The police advance in a long cordon, stretching right across the road. 'Clear the street!' an officer calls. 'Everyone indoors!' The crowd moves on slowly. On all sides, the same cry: 'Kill the Jews!' The starving have been worked on by agitators, and they are now in a state to set upon the wretched folk who pursue a miserable livelihood in the Dragonerstraße cellars ... It is inflamed racial hatred, not hunger, that has driven them to looting. If anyone with a Jewish appearance walks past, he is followed by a group of youngsters who pick their moment and then fall on him.[28]

The Scheunenviertel riot can be seen as a portent of the anti-Jewish boycott of 1 April 1933 and the 'Reichskristallnacht' of 9–10 November 1938. But there were also differences: in 1923 the police still cleared the anti-Semitic mobs from the streets; and the Nazis' invocation of an abstract demonized image of 'the Jew' played a far more important part in the later episodes than Germans' actual encounters with the unfamiliar *Ostjuden* did in the 1920s. In these respects, the Scheunenviertel episode was more akin to a traditional outbreak of anti-Semitic hostility or a pogrom prompted by mob rioting.

The history of the Jews during the Weimar Republic, therefore, cannot be viewed solely in the light of their terrible fate during the Third Reich. Anti-Semitic discrimination certainly existed, but the situation was a complex one, involving conflicting tendencies within the Jewish community and wider factors in society as a whole. Many Jews were becoming increasingly assimilated, while others were finding themselves more sharply isolated. What is clear is that the rise of anti-Semitic discrimination and the role of anti-Jewish racial hatred within National Socialist ideology were not the outcome of events within the history of the Jews in Germany, but are to be accounted for as part of the evolution of the German radical right.

THE TRANSFORMATION OF THE PUBLIC DOMAIN

The 1920s saw fundamental changes in the nature of the public domain: changes that were the result of a combination of many different political, socio-cultural and technological factors.[29] The dominant common image symbolizing these changes was that of the regimented mass. It was a period of mass marching columns, huge rallies, great sporting events and mass spectacles in the theatre, as well as of mass production in industry and mass construction in the new architecture. The organizing principle underlying this generally more regimented public sphere was the standardization of the individual unit: uniform behaviour on the part of the people involved, and the reduction of the basic component elements to highly simplified, often cubist, forms. In turn, the large-scale assemblage of replicated basic units served to produce new massive geometrical structures. The purpose of such large formations might be functional, or it might be to create a species of overwhelming, unprecedentedly monumental mass ornamentation. Often, indeed, the very function of the mass structure was to generate a huge, choreographed totalitarian spectacle.

Among the political movements, the totalitarian parties made the ornamentalized regimentation of the masses their special trademark. The unquestionable fascination which these displays exerted over their followers persuaded the other political organizations that they too had to fall in with the new ways of operating within the public domain: the Social Democrats, for example, came up with the symbolism of the *Eiserne Front* (the alliance of party, unions and paramilitary *Reichsbanner*) as a response to the propaganda gains that had been made by the NSDAP and the KPD. But powerful and wider social and cultural trends and new patterns of mass organization were also pushing in the same direction, as the widespread fascination with mass spectacle in the twenties demonstrates.

Before the First World War both political and non-political forms of association in the public sphere were bound up with the world of local clubs and societies, in which relatively small numbers of individuals, already associated in their daily lives, came together voluntarily in pursuit of a common goal. The only way in which larger-scale public activities could be generated was through the traditional print media or in meetings whose size was more or less circumscribed by the range of the spoken voice. Even mass rallies consisted of groups gathered round a number of different speakers' platforms, and there was a limit to the excitement that could be stirred up by music, posters and the chanting of slogans.

In the twenties not only did people become more receptive to the idea of mass mobilization, so that there was a greater demand for larger-scale forms of public expression, but the technological means of staging public events also advanced. A mass body of supporters could be 'bused in' by mechanized transport, large runs of posters and leaflets could be printed, organizers were able to communicate widely, rapidly and efficiently by means of the telephone system, and improvements in methods of sound amplification meant that vastly greater numbers of people could now be brought within earshot of a single speaker, unifying his audience through his control of the microphone.

Technological innovations in the field of leisure also provided new means of mass mobilization and created centralized forms of dominance. Big new cinemas were built, especially after the introduction of the talking film in 1929. Radio had gone beyond the do-it-yourself crystal-set stage, so that broadcasting stations could reach much larger audiences, but the *Volksempfänger* (popular radio set), which allowed most people to listen in privacy in their living-rooms, was not to come in until the thirties, and so for the time being listeners often gathered around the new radio receivers in larger groups. In transport, similarly, the dominant technology was that of mass transit, while privately owned cars were still relatively few in number. On top of all this, mass production and mass consumption helped give these large-scale forms of public activity an image of attractiveness and modernity.

The crisis of the old liberal and the old authoritarian political models, together with the mobilization of the masses that had taken place during the First World War, had generated a demand for new mass forms of political expression, and this demand could be met by the new opportunities created by changes in society, culture and technology. The political camp became a way of life; the marching column became a symbol of the political 'movement'. Uniform, militarized behaviour spread from the radical fringes of politics to what had previously been the middle ground, and by the start of the 1930s had established itself as the dominant style of a political culture fractured along political lines. The outward style became universal, even when the political programmes that went with it were profoundly at odds with one another. This central feature of German – and, in a sense, of all European – politics between the wars did not disappear until the end of the Second World War. After the war, of course, serried ranks lost their appeal and gave way to a world of material goods and mass media, standardized yet tailored to the individual consumer: a world of cars and television sets owned by individuals and families. But in the twenties and early thirties no one could foresee that totalitarian structures would prove to be only a transitional phase in the process of the modernization of the public domain. Rather as Eduard Bernstein had said that the socialist movement meant everything to him, but its ultimate goal nothing, so the form of the mass movements of the inter-war years had become their *raison d'être*. Mass structures had become a species of ornamentation.

8. MASS CULTURE AND THE *NEUE SACHLICHKEIT*

The mystique of the 'golden twenties' remains potent today. Culturally speaking, 'Weimar' is still synonymous with 'modernity'. And Weimar avant-garde culture reached the height of its influence only to fall victim, in 1933, to the most rigorous rejection of cultural modernity that this century has witnessed. With the passing of National Socialism, the culture of Weimar has enjoyed a number of new leases of life. New aspects of this complex phenomenon – which lasted, after all, little more than a dozen years between the First World War and the Nazi seizure of power – have repeatedly been rediscovered as revisionist attacks have been mounted on prevalent historical interpretations.[1] The very intricacy and variety of Weimar culture, and the tensions it contained, have made it the archetypal emblem of what we understand by modernity.

Weimar's modernity was far from homogeneous. It did not consist merely of the formalist avant-garde, as writers in the 1950s argued, nor of the agitprop culture of the left, as was sometimes claimed in the 1960s. Furthermore, like other areas of society, the features that are commonly singled out as typical of Weimar had already begun to take shape around the turn of the century or in the years immediately before the First World War. In the cultural sphere as elsewhere, therefore, it is advisable to regard the era of 'classical modernity' as consisting of the entire period from the 1890s to the 1930s, and then, within this period, to distinguish the formative phase before the war from the subsequent phase of development and crisis.

To give even a schematic summary of the wealth and scope of Weimar culture would be to exceed the parameters of this study. We shall therefore confine ourselves to a discussion of two basic questions, in which problems of cultural modernity, and problems of social modernization in general, intersect. These issues are, first, the relationship of writers and other artists to the new mass culture of the world of consumer goods and the media; and, second, the controversy, manifested in *Kulturkritik* and the debate about 'Americanism', concerning the attitude that should be adopted towards modern life.

LATE-WILHELMINE AVANT-GARDE AND REPUBLICAN PLURALISM

After the turn of the century, the field in which the avant-garde's break with the post-Renaissance European tradition of art was most clearly evident was that of painting. The Expressionists and Cubists decisively liberated colour and form respectively from their representational function. Even the final logical step in this process of detachment, namely abstractionism, had been taken shortly before the First World War. Analogous developments marked the rise of Expressionism in literature.

World war and revolution gave the Expressionists, with their utopianism and their use of highly charged emotion, a new and wider audience. Through their revolutionary rhetoric, and indeed commitment, Expressionist artists tried to forge a liberating alliance with 'the masses'. But grand gestures were soon followed by a cooler counter-reaction. Dadaism, originating in Zurich in 1916, set itself against intensity of expression and idealized visions of a mass age of revolution, and made play instead with irony and self-mockery. And yet Dada actually constituted an even more radical break with tradition, because it abolished the barrier shielding the realm of art from that of everyday life. Equally, by turning banal utilitarian objects and texts to artistic account in its collages and provocative performance art, it opened the way for artists to operate in the field of mass artistic reproduction. John Heartfield's photomontage technique was one such result.

Expressionists, abstractionists and Dadaists continued to be influential on the Weimar cultural scene after the initial phase of revolutionary political upheaval, but by about 1923 a new and original cultural trend had begun to emerge, spreading outwards from painting and literature to become the dominant style of the twenties: the *neue Sachlichkeit*, the new objectivity or matter-of-factness. Many of the leading figures of the *neue Sachlichkeit* were keen to take up the challenge offered by mass culture and the mass media and to develop forms of expression appropriate to them, and we shall discuss their work in more detail presently. It should also be remembered, however, that with the crisis of the early thirties the optimism of the *neue Sachlichkeit* began to falter, giving way to *Kulturpessimismus* and political polarization.

The major artistic styles which made up classical modernism not only arrived on the scene in breakneck succession, but were actively in competition with one another. No single style was powerful enough, or lasted long enough, to impose its image on the Weimar era as a whole. Besides the avant-garde movements, traditional styles remained current in all branches of the arts and retained their pre-eminence among a wider public: avant-garde art, of whatever stripe, was a minority taste even during its own classical phase. At the representative Allgemeine Kunstausstellung in Munich in 1930, for example, modernist artists accounted for only 2 per cent of nearly 1,000 artists showing their work, and modernist works for only 5 per cent of the 2,700 exhibits.[2]

These considerations suggest, in fact, that the central and characteristic feature of the culture of the period was its very diversity. It was an era in which conflicting styles existed alongside one another or surfaced in rapid sequence, in which the practitioners of rival styles had no common language, and in which there was a matching proliferation of outlets for artistic production. As the art market opened up, and the symbiotic relationship between the creative artist and the cultivated artistic consumer that had characterized the era of the educated bourgeoisie began to dissolve, so there was a shift away from the norms of naturalism and representationalism, and, to use Walter Benjamin's terms, the work of art began to shed its 'aura'. In an 'age of mechanical reproduction', there had to be a new definition of art.

These profound changes in artistic production and in aesthetic theory were reinforced in a very direct way by the 'hardship of the intellectual workers' that set in during the decade of inflation.[3] Previously, a section of the middle-class intelligentsia had been able to live reasonably securely off modest (or more than modest) returns on invested capital. Intellectuals and artists might take employment or be paid freelance fees, but the sense of security, independence and leisure created by the possession of private means played a far more important part in shaping the conditions under which they produced their work. Inflation expropriated the entire *rentier* class, and made intellectuals totally dependent for their livelihood on selling their work or taking employment. The Bohemian who had been the stock caricature figure of the pre-war *rentier* intelligentsia was now replaced by the journalist who was beholden to the market or the goodwill of his boss.[4]

Among the members of the independent professional classes – doctors, authors, journalists, actors – having two jobs is now virtually the rule; people are running round in all directions looking for ways of earning money; the leisure which used to nourish intellectual activity and permit the cultivation of ideas is no more; the sense of security in old age, that cushion for those who live on their wits and nerves, has vanished; and the landscape is dotted with poor, hunted creatures, roaming in fear of the spectre of poverty, no longer able to offer disinterested service to the life of the mind.[5]

This woeful outburst dates from 1923, the year of hyperinflation: the year when the Expressionist writer George Kaiser was sentenced to twelve months' imprisonment for theft because he had not been prepared to see his family starve.[6] Clearly, over and beyond their immediate material plight, intellectuals were in a fundamentally new situation now that they were having to work within a market society and a mass culture.

TOWARDS A MASS CULTURE

Weimar intellectuals, made sensitive by their own experience of social change, were vividly aware of the contrast between the old 'life of the mind' lived by the bourgeois artist or writer and the new world of the cultural producer, operating as a creator of artistic use and exchange value on the mass-cultural market. The transition to a mass culture was a final stage in the process of the mechanization of the world, a process from which artists had hitherto been able to hold themselves aloof through criticism or escapism, but into which they had now, however reluctantly, been dragged. A new concept of art itself was called for:

But what if [artistic] form – that is, all known and familiar forms – has become a lie, because the present age, as a cultural epoch, has no form – creates no forms other than steel structures, machines and other technical marvels? What if the present age, both in its material externals and in spiritual, cultural and artistic terms, is itself a formless, disintegrated mishmash – if it is as God-forsaken and futile as any age has ever been? ... Who can doubt that a casualty of this age will want to vent his cries of despair? Anyone who does not want to do so can always go away and read Mörike. But in this age of cinema, radio and Stinnes, he will have to hoodwink himself if he is going to find Mörike the perfect answer. He will have to pretend that the express-train tempo of modern life is a post-chaise canter, that the stink of petrol is like rose petals, and that a stock-exchange wizard has a fairy-tale heart of gold.[7]

The historical achievement of the *neue Sachlichkeit*[8] was to come to terms with the new reality of the express train, the stink of petrol and the stock-exchange wizard, and to draw up a new aesthetic that did not consist merely of cries of despair or escapist evocations of rose petals. Painting became representational once again, but it now incorporated the effects of the earlier formalist break with the nineteenth century and was quite remote from contemporary traditionalism in technique as well as in its modern social subject-matter. Whether in the social criticism of Dix and Grosz or the cool portraiture of Felix-müller and Schad, a new constructivist element was now present: a self-reflexive gap between the art-object and its subject-matter.

As far as writing was concerned, the Weimar years saw a burgeoning of reportage, a literary form whose aim was similarly to achieve the utmost authenticity, but to communicate information without sacrificing considerations of formal design. Practitioners of this genre ranged from the openly party-political 'hotfoot reporter' Egon Erwin Kisch to the more sceptical, detached Erik Reger and the essayist Siegfried Kracauer, who was highly critical of the shallow and specious investigative work of mediocre *neusachlich* writers:

But life cannot be captured by being relived, once if you are lucky, in a documentary report. Reportage has been a legitimate riposte to idealism; but no more than that ... A hundred reports from a factory do not add up to the reality of that factory ... Reality is a construction.[9]

Kracauer was distinguishing two possible ways in which the new factuality could deal with the modern world of technology and mass culture. One option was a bland, trite surrender to the world of the assembly line and the market, a degeneration into machine-worship and affirmation of the new mass man. The alternative was to work towards a critical reconstruction of reality.

In the hectic atmosphere of the 1920s, these two approaches were by no means always clearly separated. The new communications media might be hailed as 'democratic', on the grounds that they were mass media, while at the same time the 'new man', new production techniques and the new society would be lumped together in a utopian celebration of functionalism and 'rationalization'. At the same time, of course, exuberance was far from universal. There was a considerable gap between the old educated middle class and the younger intellectuals who were seeking to conquer the new media.

One writer who made extensive, but not untypical, use of the new possibilities was Alfred Döblin, whose *Berlin Alexanderplatz*, published in 1929, burst the bounds of the classical novel by incorporating collage, montage and techniques borrowed from the cinema. Consistently enough, the book itself appeared in other media too: in a radio-play version in 1930 and as a film in 1931. Similarly, Bertolt Brecht recycled his *Dreigroschenoper* as a novel and a film, and, when the film provoked a lawsuit, also produced a long theoretical essay on the very conflict of media involved. Brecht, indeed, was one of the most influential writers, though by no means the only one, to think theoretically about the new conditions of artistic production, seeking not only to make use of them but to alter them.

In music, too, while the twelve-note composer Arnold Schoenberg and his followers introduced techniques that were highly innovative but not widely influential, there were interesting attempts by composers such as Paul Hindemith, Kurt Weill and Hanns Eisler to forge links between the new music and the wider, more actively involved audiences that had been created by radio and the gramophone.

In writing and the theatre there was a search for new forms appropriate to a mass audience. Small-scale cabaret forms were one result; another was the multi-media political theatre of Erwin Piscator. Agitprop theatre groups campaigned on the streets, while for less political, more consumption-minded theatre-goers there were musicals and revues. The theory of 'epic theatre' was an attempt to fuse these different stylistic elements into a concerted whole. In journalism, it was hoped that the use of 'worker correspondents' would help to challenge the monopoly control exerted by newspaper proprietors, while 'Rote-Eine-Marks-Romane' were intended to circumvent the power of the big publishers.

Undoubtedly, however, the pioneering mass media were the cinema and broadcasting. Some of the hopes that were invested in these new forms were clearly unrealistic from the outset:

> For us, then, the most important thing is that film has been democratic since its inception ... Film began as an art of the masses: as theatre for the common herd. And a film which goes against the masses is quite out of the question.

> There are 3 million families listening to about 3 million radio sets: in other words, there is a radio audience of about 9 million people. Art is publicly available on an unprecedented scale. Art has been taken into public ownership.[10]

The new forms of communication certainly reached sections of the population to which the traditional media and the cultural products of the educated had not previously had access. A good number of intellectuals contributed to radio programmes and wrote film treatments and screenplays. But opportunities for direct public influence remained limited. The ostensibly democratic new media were capital-intensive and were run on highly commercial lines. The introduction of talkies and the need to compete with Hollywood, in particular, drove up film production costs and made producers less willing to take artistic risks. In addition, the newly emergent media organizations were dominated by strongly conservative forces, the most notable case being UFA, which was controlled by the nationalist press baron Alfred Hugenberg. At the same time, state film censorship and public controls over broadcasting stifled any projects whose subject-matter, presentation or political thrust were regarded as controversial.

Nevertheless, the cinema exerted its fascination over intelligentsia and general public alike. Pre-war films had never quite risen above a penny-dreadful sort of unsavouriness, but during the war, as their potential propaganda value became apparent, they acquired a new respectability. The Weimar years saw the building of huge picture-palaces, splendid and glamorous buildings for the masses which assumed the function that opera houses had had for the bourgeoisie in the nineteenth century.

In aesthetic terms, too, cinema reached maturity after the war.[11] Art films influenced by Expressionism were made, which are now seen as icons of the twentieth century: *Metropolis, Das Kabinett des Dr Caligari* and *Dr Mabuse*. The American cinema also had considerable impact on public taste, thanks in part to Charlie Chaplin's powerful blend of comedy and deep humanity, but also to the shallow sentimentality and sensationalism of Hollywood's mass output. The American cinema strengthened its commercial lead when talkies were introduced in 1928–9, the new genre of the musical film proving especially popular.

There was no regular radio broadcasting service in Germany until 1923.[12] By 1926 a million listeners had already been officially registered, and the figure rose to 2 million in 1928, 3 million by the end of 1929 and 4 million at the start of 1932. By this last date there were 24 radio sets for every 100 households, and in large cities the proportion was almost 1 in 2. The broadcasting service was the creation of privately financed companies, but it was subject to strict state control and in 1932 became a *de facto* state system. The degree of informality in the early days of broadcasting, however, should not be underestimated, and many intellectuals, including left-wingers, took part in programmes. Broadcasting also gave rise to new forms, such as the radio play. The labour movement experimented with ways of using radio both to reach its supporters and to encourage a critical attitude towards the new medium.

But the paramount feature of the old as well as the new mass media was concentration. Big press combines like that of Alfred Hugenberg not only controlled their own newspapers but exerted further influence on public opinion through their news agencies and by supplying syndicated copy to the nominally independent provincial press.[13] On the left, Willi Münzenberg, an energetic and enterprising Communist, tried to build up a competing communications apparatus centred on the International Workers' Relief organization of which he was the director. Münzenberg's operation included publishing houses, newspaper titles such as the *Arbeiter-Illustrierte-Zeitung*, a network of worker photographers and correspondents, a distribution system closely tied in with the Communist Party and a film distribution service. Left-wing intellectuals and artists such as Brecht and Heartfield also contributed.

The old workers' educational movement was still very much alive – was attracting, indeed, larger numbers than ever – and the mass media enabled it to take on a more prominent public role. A greater amount of energy and hope was invested in the attempt to mobilize support and encourage participation through the new means of communication than at any other period of German history, before or since. Many of these efforts failed to come to fruition or were thwarted by the sectarianism of the hard-left Communist Party intelligentsia. But what was achieved, during this brief period, was impressive.

RADICALIZATION AND POLARIZATION

Writing in 1928, Erwin Piscator combined his call for a political mass theatre with a polemical attack on the conventional individualistic view of art: 'In a world in which the real upheavals are caused by the discovery of a new goldfield, by oil production and by the wheat market, why should we worry about the problems of people who are halfway out of their minds?'[14]

Of course, neither the *neusachlich* groundswell of enthusiasm for technology nor the rising chorus of anti-capitalist agitation deterred individual artists from going their own way in defiance of prevailing trends and struggling to give expression to basic concerns of human existence. But in 1928, when Max Hermann-Neiße, in the *Neue Bücherschau* – a journal which had always opened its pages to a broad spectrum of left-wing opinion – combined a favourable review of poems by Gottfried Benn with an attack on Communist Party writers of the Johannes R. Becher stamp, the controversy was sufficient to lead the enraged KPD to break with the magazine.[15] With the founding of the League of Proletarian Revolutionary Writers, together with its own journal *Linkskurve*, the split became complete, and left-wing writers proceeded to belabour one another even more vigorously in print.

The world economic crisis finally knocked the bottom out of the *neue Sachlichkeit*. The cultural scene became increasingly polarized. But the collapse of concerted action by left-wing supporters of the Republic and Communists committed to purely party agitation was by no means the only consequence. A more ominous phenomenon was the rise of support for the far right. Even during the Republic's palmiest days, right-wing critics had not remained silent, and traditionalists in literature and the arts knew that they had the ear of a mass audience. For many, the arrival of the final crisis gave the lie to the claims for modernity made by the *neue Sachlichkeit* and the avant-garde. Defenders of democratic parliamentary procedures likewise came under suspicion. The new mood had already begun to become apparent in the public response to Erich Maria Remarque's pacifist novel *Im Westen nichts Neues* (All Quiet on the Western Front).[16] Within four months of its publication in January 1929 the novel had sold half a million copies. But although the book was generally well received, a few malicious voices from the far right could also be heard, saying that it sullied the honour of the soldiers who had fought in the trenches. Showings of the film of the book, which was released in December 1930, were systematically interrupted from the outset by the Nazis, and in some cases the riots caused performances to be banned. From then on, attacks on Remarque by the hard right were unceasing. At the same time, an extensive repertoire of nationalist war literature had been accumulating, with films of its own to match. The closing years of the Republic were marked by a new glorification of war, which publicized fascist ideas and paved the way for the dissemination of fascist propaganda on a mass scale.

It was already clear by the beginning of the thirties that many intellectuals, in response to the polarization and radicalization of the cultural scene, had begun to retreat from the discussion of public issues and were turning again to *Innerlichkeit*: 'The subject for today is: the masses, clamour in the streets. The aim: documentation. The subject for tomorrow will be: the inner life, the self, silence. The aim: creation.'[17]

MASS CONSUMPTION

The challenge of mass culture which faced intellectuals in the 1920s was the result not only of technological innovation and the new openness of the political system, but of changes in economic conditions and living standards. Industrialization had created the possibility of mass production and mass consumption. Urbanization had led to a fall in the proportion of households functioning as privately owned businesses, while the rise in real wages in the decades before the First World War had generated a certain degree of mass purchasing power (though pre-war levels were only regained with difficulty in the post-war period).

Henry Ford's methods of using streamlined production techniques to raise productivity, thereby simultaneously lowering prices and increasing wages, and hence kindling mass consumption, were watched with great interest in Germany, but the model was hard to copy in view of the state of the German post-war economy. Nevertheless, the supply of mass-consumption goods based on new technology eventually reached a respectable middle-of-the-order European level.[18] By 1932 there were 66 radio listeners, 52 telephone subscriptions and 8 private cars for every 1,000 people in Germany, compared with European average figures of 35, 20 and 7 respectively. In the USA, on the other hand, there were 131 radio listeners, 165 telephone subscriptions and 183 private cars per 1,000 inhabitants – a graphic illustration of the size of America's lead in the field of mass consumption.

At least during the brief 'golden' years of the twenties, from 1924 to 1929, the German public viewed the gap between American and German consumption levels as a promise of better things to come in the future. Radio and the press ran eager reports on new forms of transport such as the motor car and the aeroplane, even though the great mass of the population had no chance of using them. Aviators like Charles Lindbergh (who crossed the Atlantic) and racing-car drivers became the new heroes of the twentieth century.

The apparently limitless potential of modern technology was a theme explored by many writers;[19] futuristic utopias became a new genre. Visual artists similarly took the world of cities and machines as their subject,[20] but they did more than merely portray the changes in the human environment. Even before the war, the Deutsche Werkbund movement had tried to develop a new stylistic language appropriate to modern technology, from architecture to industrial design.[21] With the coming of the Republic, the Bauhaus was established, first in Weimar and then in Dessau, with the aim of uniting under one roof art and crafts training, the design of utilitarian industrial products and the search for new forms of artistic expression.[22]

Even though there remained a gulf between, on the one hand, the lofty ideals and achievements of the Bauhaus and, on the other, the common run of mass-produced objects with highly variable standards of design, an important result of mass production was that modern styles made far greater headway in advertising and industrial design than they did in the realms of high culture. The design language of everyday objects remained modern even after 1933, while the National Socialists imposed strict rules of expression on painters and sculptors.

Although the weakness of purchasing power in Germany meant that the ownership of consumer durables lagged behind the levels made possible by American-style production methods, nevertheless modern ways of living, often imported from America, were making irreversible advances in the field of leisure. By introducing the forty-hour week and the first negotiated agreements covering holidays, the Weimar Republic actually established a framework of leisure for wage-earners for the first time. Pleasures that had previously been reserved for the middle classes were now, potentially at least, available for all. Modern leisure, indeed, dates from the twenties.[23] Clubs and associations prospered, the *Schrebergarten* movement spread, bringing gardens and allotments to the outskirts of cities, and fun-fairs, variety shows, dance-halls, cinemas, boxing arenas and cycle races came to compete with more serious institutions such as the theatre, public libraries and adult education. More popular than all other forms of leisure activity was sport. Sports clubs increased their membership, modern competitive sporting tournaments expanded and the sporting event *qua* mass spectacle came into being. By the late 1920s radio commentary had created a further revolution in mass sport. National sporting events could now be followed by audiences in the millions; indeed, it was only now that they became major 'events' in their own right.

Young people adapted most speedily to this new world of sport and commercialized leisure. They were also the pioneers of modern tourism. Weekend rambling in the countryside surrounding the big cities had begun to become popular around the turn of the century, and by the twenties it was a very widespread pastime. Longer hikes and journeys were made possible by an increase in the numbers of campsites and youth hostels, but long-distance travel to hotels and boarding-houses in spas and seaside resorts remained a middle-class preserve.

Mass consumption and the new culture of leisure gave large sections of the population a greater opportunity to shape their own lives and led to a certain amount of cultural assimilation. By the end of the twenties people at the lower and higher ends of the social scale danced to the same rhythms and listened to the same hit songs and radio programmes. On the other hand, as far as the traditional branches of culture were concerned, especially those in which purchasing power was a critical factor, class differences remained intact.

Mass consumption was also far from meeting with universal approval. In particular, department stores – latter-day temples of consumerism – attracted as many fierce critics as they did fascinated customers.[24] Small shopkeepers, who had been badly shaken by wartime controls, inflation and stagnant consumer demand, saw the powerful competition emanating from the department stores as a threat to their existence. The big stores were a symbolic amalgam of all their *bêtes noires*: international high finance, the Jewish shopkeeper, under-cutting, poor and uncraftsmanlike quality of goods, modern design, modern social habits, anonymity and rootlessness. These ideological stereotypes, which soon became the stock-in-trade of National Socialist demagogues, show that mass culture and mass consumption had become the special target of the resentment of those social groups which were the losers from social change. But they also suggest that the new, modern world inspired a very mixed reaction in general and was, for this reason, perceived as a source of anxiety and insecurity. In the next chapter, accordingly, we shall explore the ideological forms that this unease with modernity took and the new aspects of life that had given rise to it.

9. 'AMERICANISM' VERSUS
KULTURKRITIK

Writing in 1929 about 'proletarian youth' in the big cities, the educator and Protestant cleric Günter Dehn observed:

If we were to ask them about the meaning and purpose of life, the only answer they could give would be: 'We don't know what the purpose of life is, and we're not interested in finding out. But since we are alive, we want to get as much out of life as we possibly can.' Earning money and enjoying themselves are the twin poles of their existence, their enjoyments taking in both the high-minded and the squalid – primitive sexuality and jazz on the one hand, and the modern working-class concern, artistically unexceptionable, for home decoration and sensible personal hygiene on the other. One thing, however, is certain: these young people are utterly resolved to 'stand with firm, strong bones upon the well-founded, enduring earth'. They wish to get from this world, and from this world alone, whatever can be got from it. The nation's thinking has indeed become Americanized, through and through, consciously so – and yet, of course, superficially. Coming into contact with the people, one is constantly made aware that it is not socialism but Americanism that will be the end of everything as we have known it. Scarcely any proletarian girls now have their hair dressed in the old way: they wear it bobbed, of course – a style truly bereft of metaphysics. Here is a meaningful symptom of the entire attitude to life we have described.[1]

In the twenties 'Americanism' became a catchword for untrammelled modernity. The public debate about 'America' was really a debate about German society itself and the challenge that modernity posed to it. What was at issue was the value to be placed on a 'rationalized' form of life emptied of all the ballast of tradition. The debate was a tug-of-war between two extremes: passionate enthusiasm for rationality and efficiency on one side, and hostility to modern civilization on the other.[2] In this chapter we shall first ask – taking modern architecture and urban life as a specific illustration – what 'Americanism' meant, both as a ideology and as a phenomenon of daily life, and shall then go on to trace the origins and varieties of Weimar *Kulturkritik*: the diverse forms of criticism that were made of German, and modern, society and culture.

'AMERICA', FOR AND AGAINST

For all their apparent archaism, the romantic national folk-mythology and imperial bombast that had accompanied the process of social, technological and economic change in the Wilhelmine era had represented an affirmation, not a rejection, of modernity. The abandonment of traditional attitudes and practices had been seen as a gain, not a loss, as Germany strode towards her 'place in the sun'.[3]

After Germany's defeat in the war, and more especially after the achievement of economic and political stability under the aegis of the United States in 1924, a mythicized version of 'America' that had already been gaining currency in the earlier years of the century now emerged as the symbol of modernity *tout court*.[4] The American mystique was fed by many different tributaries: the image of the dazzling conqueror from overseas; the myth of the land of limitless opportunity; America's economic and financial strength; her lead in mass production and consumption; notions of unimpeded efficiency and unhidebound innovation; pioneering innovations in the new mass culture; and the growth of new forms of communication and everyday life-styles.

American dance music, which seemed to constitute a radical breach with the European musical tradition, and was hailed, or decried, as 'negro music'; spectator sports such as boxing, which were a display of physical skills and competitiveness before a mass audience; Henry Ford's autobiography, published in German translation, which claimed that a society could escape the messy free-for-all of the class struggle by means of modernization, higher living standards and productive efficiency; Hollywood films, which promoted a new, instant and truly international style in dress and ways of living – these and countless

other products of the American way of life had made 'America'
synonymous with 'progress'. 'America' stood for the unencumbered,
common future of industrial society.

The American mystique offered people a way of recovering from
the four traumatic years of trench warfare that had divided the old
European nations, and also of coming to terms with the problems that
preoccupied the educated European middle classes. Rudolf Kayser
wrote in 1925: 'Americanism is a new European method ... a method
which uses concrete terms, and energy, and is entirely adapted to
intellectual and material reality.'[5] Even the depersonalized, purely
ornamental effect created by a line of American chorus girls was seen
as a symptom of the modern 'American way of life':

The Tiller Girls ... were a brand of dancers ... dancing bodies drilled and
trained in certain simple techniques, mobile machines: they made a very
striking impression, but they also gave considerable pause for thought. They
were the product of an American mentality.[6]

Alfred Polgar was more critical:

There is more than just erotic magic in the appearance and behaviour of the
girls: there is the magic of militarism. The trained precision, the straight
lines, the regular rhythmic beat ... the obedience to invisible but ineluctable
orders, the marvellous 'drill', the submersion of the individual into the group,
the concentration of bodies into a single collective 'body'.[7]

'Americanism', then, perceived as the supersession of the old world
by the New World, the displacement of the self of the traditional
culture by the unconditioned mass personality of modern rationalism,
had its opponents as well as its enthusiasts. Herbert Ihering's obser-
vations on the millions who were flocking to see Hollywood films by
1926 cannot be dismissed as the mere know-nothingism of a member
of the tradition-bound educated middle class.

They are all being subjugated to American taste; they are being standardized,
made uniform ... The American cinema is the new international militarism.
It is advancing. It is more dangerous than Prussianism. It is swallowing up
not just individuals but the personalities of whole peoples.[8]

The dispute between the advocates and opponents of 'Americanism' in the twenties, in other words, was by no means simply a confrontation between progress and reaction, between liberating modernity and stultifying tradition. This confrontation was certainly real enough, and the international economic crisis made it all the more sharp. But the debate about 'Americanism' was also a focus for the concerns of those who feared for the future of humane values within an unregulated industrial society yet did not want to urge a retreat into a pre-industrial golden age. For such people, freedom and human dignity would certainly not be served by exchanging the old chains of European traditionalism for the new conformity of a rationalized, modular-built American future.

The most instructive example we can use to illustrate the controversy about the new 'Americanism' is that of housing and urban life.

'MODERN LIVING' AND THE MODERN CITY

The city was the quintessential modern habitat: on this point, at any rate, both supporters and detractors of urban life were in accord.[9] By the turn of the century the process of urbanization was, in a sense, beginning to come to a close. From this time onwards, big cities continued to grow merely at the pace of population growth in general, or as a result of the incorporation of outer suburbs, which altered administrative boundaries but did not, as such, affect the character of urban or suburban life.[10]

A symbolic moment occurred in 1920, when, with the creation of metropolitan 'Greater Berlin' as an administrative entity, the city's population became 4.3 million, making it the third largest in the world after New York and London.[11] By the mid-1920s the German population was divided roughly equally between the big cities, the countryside and the smaller towns. But it was urbanism that embodied the spirit of the times, and the provinces inevitably suffered from the comparison. They were regarded as unable, by definition, to match what the metropolis had to provide, and the aspersion was a source of much provincial resentment of the 'asphalt jungle'. Conversely, the urban and metropolitan spirit was fuelled by the sense of liberation from convention and the reins of community which the city offered, with its anonymity, its multiplicity of activities and its great arrays of goods and entertainments, newspapers and magazines. At the same time, however, the city came under a different sort of attack from within itself, as a place of personal isolation and alienation, unfriendliness and merely mass identity. The debate about 'modern architecture' and 'modern living' offers a good example of the way in which the avant-garde was faced with a two-pronged attack, not only from traditionalists but also from within the modernizing camp.[12]

When urbanization was at its height, from the end of the nineteenth century onwards, new instruments of town-planning policy and infrastructural services had been created to cope with the expansion of urban areas. The First World War and the period of the Republic saw the granting of administrative powers to local authorities that enabled them to implement ambitious plans for public housing. The general principles of the 'new architecture' had also been taking shape since the turn of the century, and its proponents were now able to put their ideas into practice on a much larger scale, in Weimar Germany as in Social Democratic 'Red Vienna'. Avant-garde public buildings and luxurious villas continued to be built, of course, the Weißenhof estate in Stuttgart (1927) being a much quoted and controversial example, but most of the avant-garde's utopian town-planning schemes did not actually get beyond the drawing-board, at any rate until the period of reconstruction after the Second World War. Nevertheless, thousands of families embarked on a new way of life in blocks of flats on housing developments built by co-operatives or other non-profit-making associations or by local authorities.

The new public housing schemes varied greatly in detail, but their common feature was a combination of the new functionalist aesthetic and an attempt to create healthy living conditions while using economical design and construction methods. Sometimes these aims were successfully reconciled, but in other cases the result was an austere functionalism that paid little heed to people's individual needs. Flats were of standard design with small families in mind, despite the fact that the small family was still far from being the norm among the prospective working-class occupants. Small, functional kitchens designed according to ergonomic principles might be labour-saving, but they could also hamper the many activities that had taken place in the old *Wohnküche*, the kitchen that had also been a living-room. The new efficiency was meant to save time, but it also entailed more costly new standards of cleanliness and hygiene. Modernist canons decreed that household furniture and fittings should be streamlined and functional, but this style did not satisfy the aesthetic needs that had previously been met by curlicues and *Kitsch*.

The spokesmen of modern design were well aware of the gulf that existed between the conventional tastes and living conditions of the majority and the ideals of the new style. Indeed, they saw themselves as pioneers and teachers, who would use the new architecture to shape a new kind of human being. Hannes Meyer provided a portentous statement of the case in his article 'bauhaus und gesellschaft' in 1929:

> the new architectural theory
> is an epistemology of being.
> as a design theory
> it is a hymn to harmony.
> as a social theory
> it is a strategy for balancing
> the forces of co-operation and the forces of individuality.
> within the community of a people ...
> it is a taxonomy of the structure of living,
> and it resolves equally the claims of
> the physical, the psychological, the material, the economic.
> it explores, defines and orders the domains
> of the individual, the family and society.[13]

Such fantasies of omnipotence were by no means rare in the 1920s.

We should give functionalist architects the credit for being prepared to spell out ways in which the complex demands of life in an industrialized society might be met. Furthermore, the building projects of the twenties were exploratory in a way that was not true of the hackneyed mass housing and urban schemes that followed the Second World War. Yet it must also be said that contemporary critics of functionalist architecture were not always simply voicing conservative resistance to innovation, but were articulating needs which the new style, partly unwittingly and partly with deliberate proselytizing intention, had ignored – namely people's desire for the human scale, for space in which to develop without being cramped by utilitarian norms, for continuity with evolved forms and traditions and for superfluous but decorative detail.

Of course, functionalist architecture did not enjoy unqualified dominance in the 1920s in any case, either in quantitative terms or in the debate within the profession. Older, established styles were still generally favoured for public buildings: either the international rhetoric of neo-classicism or regional variants of *Heimatstil*, in other words vernacular approaches seeking (with varying degrees of success) to exploit traditional forms for modern uses. As competition and argument between the avant-garde and the neo-classical, traditionalist majority within the architectural profession became fiercer, so the ideological gulf between the two groups widened. A traditionalist German *Blut und Boden* style was posed as the answer to 'soulless' internationalism; schemes for mass rural private-housing settlements were keenly promoted as antidotes to the evils of the modern metropolis.[14] The National Socialists, when they came to power, effected a shotgun resolution of the ideological conflict, using the new functionalist technology but making it serve the ends of their own brand of mass housing programme.

All the same, the argument had been an important one. It had been a searching debate about different possible ways of living within an industrialized urban society and about the relationship between tradition and function in the modern built environment, and its influence remains.

THE TWO FACES OF *KULTURKRITIK*

The utilitarian 'Americanized' rationalism of modern life came under attack, as we have said, from writers and artists who were nevertheless profoundly fascinated by various aspects of modernity and were, as far as artistic technique was concerned, members of the modernist avant-garde. Bertolt Brecht and Gottfried Benn, for example, both exemplified this hostility, despite the fact that they belonged to very different political camps. In his poem '700 Intellectuals Worship an Oil Tank' Brecht mocked the cult of technology in the *neue Sachlichkeit*:

... God has come again
In the form of an oil tank.

Thou in Thy ugliness
Thou art most fair!
Violate us
O Object!

Extinguish our self!
Make us collective!
For, not as we will
But as Thou wilt ...

What is a patch of grass to Thee?
Thou sittest upon it.
Where there was once grass
There sittest Thou now, O Oil Tank!
And before Thine countenance an emotion is
Nothing.

Therefore hear our prayer
And deliver us from the evil of mind.
In the Name of Electrification,
Reason and Statistics![15]

At the same time Gottfried Benn was writing:

There is a group of poets who believe that they have written a poem if they
write the word 'manhattan' [...] All German literature since 1918 has been
trading on the slogans 'tempo', or 'jazz', or 'cinema', or 'overseas', or
'technical activity', while all problems of the mind and the emotions have
been pointedly dismissed [...] I, myself, am against Americanism. I am of
the opinion that the philosophy of pure utilitarianism, of optimism *à tout
prix*, of the permanent grin – 'keep smiling' – is not appropriate to western
man and his history.[16]

The two writers were arguing from different perspectives, of course:
Brecht was attacking the appeal to technology and 'objectivity' for its
cloaking of power relationships, while Benn was concerned with the
conflict between utilitarian optimism and the intellectual and spiritual
depth to which the *geistige Mensch* aspired. Both, however, deplored

the damage inflicted on nature, culture and human emotion by the onslaughts of a purely instrumentalist technology. And in attacking modernism from within the modernist fold, pointing to present short-comings and predicting future problems, they were representative of a major current in German intellectual history from the turn of the century.

In 1920 Max Weber repeated his gloomy prediction that western rationalism would evolve into a 'steel-hard shell' of serfdom regulated by bureaucracy:

Then, indeed, the 'last men' in this process of cultural evolution might truly be said to have become 'specialists without spirit, hedonists without heart'. And these nonentities imagine they have reached greater heights than human beings have ever previously scaled.[17]

In a quite different field, Sigmund Freud, who by developing an accepted language for speaking about the unconscious had provided a central element in the modern conception of human nature, reached a similarly sceptical view of 'civilization and its discontents', arguing that 'many cultures, or cultural epochs, possibly the human species as a whole, have become "neurotic" as a result of their aspirations to civilization'.[18]

The literature of the 1920s similarly reflected the ambivalent reactions which modernization had provoked. The alienated world of the novels of Franz Kafka is an obvious example. Ernst Jünger underwent a sequence of seismographic changes of attitude: first glorifying war and making a highly provocative but psychologically searching case for 'battle as an inward experience' (*Der Kampf als inneres Erlebnis*); then (in *Der Arbeiter*) celebrating the age of the masses and hailing the idealized 'worker' as the new mass man; and finally recording the retreat of wounded individuality in *Auf den Marmorklippen*.[19] The paradigm example of a sceptical response to modernity was Thomas Mann's ironic, distanced portrayal of the decline and fall of the bour-geois order in *Der Zauberberg*. Max Weber had already argued that the 'disenchantment of the world' – *die Entzauberung der Welt*, the freeing of the world from magic – was an unprecedented event and the main distinguishing feature of western rationalism. But the emergence of modern ideologies did not mean the end of conflict:

'The old gods, robbed of their magic, and therefore assuming the guise of impersonal forces, rise up from their graves, strive to exert power over our lives and once more resume their eternal internecine struggle.'[20]

These grim diagnoses cannot convincingly be accounted for as symptoms of the failure of the educated German middle class to make an accommodation with the forces of modernity and progress: as products, in other words, of Germany's pursuit of a 'Sonderweg', or 'special path of development', during the Bismarckian and Wilhelmine eras.[21] This sort of hostility to modernization did not spring from an antiquated clinging to tradition but from an informed awareness of current changes and trends. It was, however, characteristic that both optimistic progressives and pessimistic *Kulturkritiker* commonly thought fit to maintain that a comprehensive solution of all the problems facing humanity was possible. Nothing less than a 'New World' or a 'New Man' would usually do. This utopianism was itself a reflection of the dizzying pace that modernization had set, of its promise that anything and everything was possible, even while it also expressed the deep uncertainty, not to say shock, that people felt in the face of such profound transformations – transformations so radical, indeed, that it seemed they could be accommodated only by even more radical comprehensive solutions.

It was precisely because the process of modernization had been so blatant and rapid since the end of the nineteenth century, and because even the last surviving trappings of Wilhelmine tradition were then jettisoned after 1918, that opposition to modernization in Germany was so radical and so self-tormenting.

It should be recognized that the language used by those opponents of modernization who came from within the broad modernist fold contained many of the same metaphors that were used by the conservative, traditionalist critics of modernization. This overlapping of discourses led contemporaries, as it has often led later historians, to fail to distinguish analytically between the reactionary and post-modernist forms of *Kulturkritik*. In view, furthermore, of the National Socialists' demagogic technique of taking over many of the highly disparate currents of thought that were prevalent in Germany and fusing them into an all-purpose amalgam of ideological resentment, it is perhaps not surprising that many anti-fascist historians writing after 1945 have mistakenly concluded that the central thrust of German social thought was the 'destruction of reason': that a reactionary tradition of hostility to modernization led in a straight, descending line from Nietzsche to Hitler.[22] Yet in fact the 'politics of cultural despair'[23] cannot be properly understood unless the accuracy of many of its criticisms of modernization is also acknowledged.

The feverish intellectual climate of the Weimar Republic created almost laboratory-like conditions in which every conceivable solution to the problems of modernity could be put to the test, however sharply at variance or ill-sorted these proposed solutions might be. And one current of thinking that flourished and became ominously more popular with each successive crisis was, certainly, a resentful anti-modernism pure and simple, which made particular headway in the political movements that were hostile to the Republic, notably National Socialism. Yet the crucial point is surely that the barbarism which Nazism embodied was itself an extreme and infamous aspect of the very modernity against which Friedrich Nietzsche, Max Weber and Thomas Mann had inveighed.

The fact that perceptive *Kulturkritik* was so heavily swamped by hysterical *Kulturpessimismus* was also a result of the social changes that had affected the German educated middle class.[24] Grievances which had found release in jingoism during the Wilhelmine period and the First World War reasserted themselves under the impact of military defeat, the offence to nationalist pride caused by the Versailles settlement and its aftermath, and the collapse of middle-class living standards brought about by the inflation. Anti-modern sentiment became increasingly inseparable from anti-republicanism, even though the latter was not a logical consequence of the former.

We should acknowledge the positive face of *Kulturkritik*. Its attacks on the sterility of the educational system, on blinkered, mechanistic conceptions of culture, on utilitarianism in economics and on blind faith in the panacea of technological progress – all of these attacks an outgrowth of Nietzsche's mordant criticisms of German *Bürgertum* – helped pave the way for new thinking in the humanities (in Dilthey, for example), for a greater emphasis on artistic creativity and spontaneity, and for personality-centred reforms in education. The con-

frontation between neo-Kantianism and non-academic philosophy led
to the varieties of existentialism elaborated by Jaspers and Heidegger.
Taken together, these changes represented a great potential for cultural
renewal: a rejection of modern rationalistic functionalism, and an
ambitious affirmation of ways of coming to terms with the modern
world and exploiting the new opportunities it offered. The reformist
educational ideas proposed by Herman Nohl, Eduard Spranger and
Theodor Litt were a good example of a new spirit of self-criticism and
a desire to respond positively to the challenges arising out of everyday
life.

Kulturkritik undoubtedly had its negative face. There was no shortage of 'Inflationsheilige', pedlars of redemptive nostrums and chiliastic
visions who were happy to fish in the murky waters of conservative
mistrust of the iniquities of the big city. Trading on the stubborn
desire of the petty bourgeoisie to cling to its long-lost advantages of
status and on the growing uncertainties about values and goals that
had been created by the post-war crises, they confidently propounded
all manner of weird and wonderful utopias.[25] And as the brief interlude
of calm and relative stability in the mid-1920s was succeeded by the
world economic crisis and people's sense of security was shattered once
more, so the campaign against modern civilization was taken over by
National Socialist propagandists. Healthy *Blut und Boden* 'German-
ness' would declare war on the pernicious and corrupting influence of
modern, metropolitan life:

The German farmer in the countryside has begun to rebel against what is
going on in Berlin, and the educated German is going to resist the ideas
being promoted by the Berlin intellectuals. The spirit of the German people
is in revolt against the spirit of Berlin. The call is clear: the countryside must
rise up against Berlin.[26]

And yet, at the same time as these words were being written,
Sigmund Freud was setting down his sceptical thoughts on 'civilization
and its discontents'. Here was the true, discerning voice of *Kulturkritik*:

The fateful question that the human species faces, in my view, is whether
and to what extent it will succeed, through cultural evolution, in overcoming
the disturbance caused to its communal life by the instinct of aggression and
self-destruction. The present age is perhaps a particularly interesting one in

this respect. Human beings have made such great strides in controlling the forces of nature that they will have no trouble in harnessing these forces to exterminate one another, until there is no one left on earth. They know this: hence, in large measure, their present ferment, their unhappiness, their sense of anxiety. And so we can expect the other of the two great 'heavenly forces', eternal Eros, to strive to hold its ground and do battle with its equally immortal opponent. But who can forecast the victor, or the final outcome?[27]

IV. DECEPTIVE STABILITY, 1924–9

=====

More losses are sustained in the trenches of government than behind the lines in opposition.

Gustav Stresemann, 1924.

Our grandfathers may have seen their threadbare ideals transformed into reality. But that was a cheap garment: too much a ready-made product of 1848 to last. Young people take the view that the revolution has to be finished off properly.

Ernst Jünger, 1929

10. REVISIONIST ALTERNATIVES IN FOREIGN POLICY

In a sense the Weimar Republic underwent a *Stunde Null*, its equivalent of the 'zero hour' of 1945, in late 1923 and 1924. Conditions both at home and abroad had reached a nadir. After several years in which the Germans had refused to accept the consequences of wartime defeat, the catastrophe in the Ruhr finally made it clear that there could no longer be any illusions about the constraints on the country's freedom of action. Unpleasant facts had to be faced. The collapse of German foreign policy meant that in 1924 there could at last be a shedding of the ballast of unrealistic assumptions that had so far prevented the country from making a fresh start.

Stresemann's conduct of foreign policy between 1923 and 1929 brought about a rapid change in Germany's position on the international stage: a far more rapid change than anyone had at first imagined possible.[1] For a few years Germany seemed to be willing to adopt a new co-operative role in international relations. While recognizing Stresemann's achievement, we should not forget that a number of serious domestic and external factors which were capable of generating tensions in foreign policy continued to exist and that these factors, as conditions later deteriorated in the early 1930s, helped lead to a fateful change of policy direction.

Stresemann's foreign policy can be considered under five main general headings. While his aims on each of these counts were constructive, they were nevertheless hedged around with provisos or subject to countervailing pressures in the sense we have mentioned.

First, he accepted the prevailing balance of power and existing treaty obligations, combining the policy of fulfilment of the terms of the Versailles Treaty with the aim of piecemeal revision. In order not to lose sight of the long-term goal of revision and to reassure the inflamed sensibilities of the German public of his trustworthiness as a national leader, Stresemann also kept up the traditional nationalist rhetoric of earlier leaders. By so doing, however, he became a prisoner of the expectations he himself had aroused.[2]

Secondly, the consolidation of the German economy and of German foreign policy was largely due to the United States. As a beneficiary of American policy, Germany obtained a more realistic settlement of the reparations burden, more favourable credit conditions and a greater degree of access to world markets. At the same time, this made her more dependent on the American economy and more vulnerable to the instabilities of world markets.[3]

Thirdly, the German Foreign Office pursued a policy of rapprochement with the west, especially France, recognizing and seeking to accommodate the west's legitimate security interests. Rather than place her faith in an open-ended system of collective security, Germany hoped to remove on a step-by-step basis the restrictions on sovereignty which the Versailles Treaty had imposed on the Reich. But even though the policy of rapprochement yielded some successes, it did not resolve a central issue: namely whether Germany, having regained her freedom of action in international affairs, would revert to traditional power politics or espouse instead a policy of mutual obligations within a new international system.[4]

Fourthly, Germany's endorsement of her western frontiers was given on the explicit proviso that the option of territorial revision in the east would remain open. Stresemann offered Poland and Czechoslovakia arbitration treaties to secure the peaceful resolution of mutual differences; in 1926 he also strengthened the co-operation between Germany and the Soviet Union that had begun at Rapallo. Central and eastern Europe proved to be the weak link in the process of international rapprochement.[5]

Fifthly, and generally, the precise trade-off between ends and means, between revisionism and rapprochement, remained unclear. Rapprochement served as a brake on revisionism, inasmuch as it had the effect of binding Germany more tightly into networks of international agreements which a policy of maximalist revisionism would have torn asunder. But by 1928–9 Stresemann's foreign policy had reached a critical stage. It had become apparent that most of the revisionist goals were unlikely to be realized, and there were in practice only two ways forward. Either the revisionist path could be more or less abandoned, or the tactic of rapprochement could be replaced by something tougher. Until Stresemann's death in October 1929, the choice between these two alternatives was still unmade. Afterwards, however, a switch to an altogether more active and militant policy took place. Was this a wilful abandonment of a workable foreign policy that had been true to the spirit of Weimar or was it merely an acknowledgement of the 'failure of the liberal imperialist policy of revisionism'?[6]

Historians still differ in their verdicts on Stresemann's achievements in these five areas.[7] As we consider each of the areas in more detail, we can see that the reason for this is precisely that the policies of Stresemann and the German Foreign Office were marked by the inconsistencies we have outlined. In the final analysis, the question of revisionism and the relationship between revisionist ends and conciliatory means remained unresolved.

REPARATIONS

After Germany's capitulation in the Ruhr crisis of 1923, it was decided that the problem of reparations should be dealt with by an independent advisory commission, which was headed by the American Charles G. Dawes. As a result, the technical problems of Germany's ability to pay and the procurement of foreign exchange were now detached from the tangled political issue of Franco–German rivalry. The Dawes Plan, submitted and ratified in 1924, was underwritten by the United States and was a victory for financial realism.[8] Germany's annual reparations payments were modified to match the economic performance of the Reich, with German property (such as the state railways) serving as security. In Berlin an Allied Agent for Reparations Payments, installed by the Americans, would monitor German finances and the economy and supervise the procurement of reparations funds and their transfer into foreign exchange.

In domestic politics, the Dawes Plan gave the government some ammunition in dealing with the parliamentary right. Although

Stresemann failed in his attempts to get the DNVP to commit itself to outright support for the Dawes Plan, a sufficient number of *deutschnational* members of Parliament voted for the necessary legislation to enable it to be passed. Stresemann secured this result by throwing out hints that there might be a place for the DNVP in the governing coalition and promising that the government would officially repudiate the 'war-guilt lie' in the Versailles Treaty. It was his first step – and, for the present, a successful one – in the dangerous game of playing off rapprochement on the international front against nationalistic rhetoric designed for home consumption.

With the German currency stabilized and reparations payments brought under control, American capital, as predicted, poured into the country. For the moment Germany was able to satisfy her foreign-exchange needs, and the reparations process went into action. But in the medium term a vicious circle developed, as American credits were followed by German reparations payments, which led to French credit repayments, primarily to the Americans, which in turn were followed by new American credits. In late 1929 this whole overblown system collapsed, and the countries involved were sucked into the world-wide recession.

Before this occurred, the relatively smooth flow of payments under the Dawes Plan led to agreement on an ostensibly conclusive settlement of the reparations question in the form of the so-called Young Plan of 1929. By the terms of this plan, Germany would finally discharge her reparations debts by 1987–8. The fact that German financial liability would drag on so far into the future provoked considerable public disquiet and gave far-right agitators against the plan a cheap slogan: 'Three generations of forced labour!' For financial practitioners, however, the much more important point was that the initial annual payment instalments were now fixed at a lower level than those given in the Dawes Plan and that financial supervision by the Allies was to be abolished. Other problems could be dealt with by low-key subsequent legislation.

Under the Young Plan, Germany would initially have to pay 1.6 billion (thousand million) RM per year – a bearable burden, given annual exports of 13.5 billion RM. In the event the plan, ratified early in 1930, soon became a dead letter. In 1931 a one-year postponement was granted under the so-called Hoover moratorium, because of the world recession, and at the Lausanne conference in the summer of 1932 reparations were finally suspended altogether.

All told, reparations were far less of a burden on the German post-war economy than had been feared.[9] Between 1919 and the introduction of the Dawes Plan in 1924 Germany remitted approximately 10 billion RM in reparations. Simultaneously, the inflation led to a devaluation of foreign capital investment in Germany amounting to about 15 billion RM. Under the Dawes and Young Plans annual reparations payments ranged from 0.6 to 2.1 billion RM, giving a total of 11.3 billion RM between 1924 and 1932. During the same period, however, imported capital to the value of about 28 billion RM flowed into Germany, of which the Americans alone lost roughly 8 billion RM as a result of the world economic crisis.

Reparations did not, in fact, bleed the German economy. Indeed, their net effect was to leave the economy in rather better shape. But the psychological effects of reparations were extremely serious, as was the strain that the vicious circle of credits and reparations placed on the international financial system.

GERMANY AND THE WORLD ECONOMY

This last point brings us on to Germany's distinctive position in the world economy.[10] It is true that by 1929 Germany had been able to make up some of the economic ground that had been lost during the war and the immediate post-war period, but several crucial indicators remained below pre-war levels.[11] Between 1926 and 1929, for example, although Germany achieved an 11.6 per cent share of world industrial production, ahead of Britain (at 9.4 per cent) and France (at 6.6 per cent), this was still below her 1913 level of 14.3 per cent and substantially below the United States' share of 42.2 per cent. Similarly, Germany's share of world exports fell from 13.2 per cent in 1913 to 9.1 per cent in the years 1927–9, while the United States, Britain and France achieved shares of 15.7, 11 and 6.5 per cent respectively. In parallel, the proportion of German exports to national income fell from 20.2 per cent in 1913 to 17 per cent in the best post-war year,

1928. There was also a large import surplus, and foreign indebtedness was rising.

Against this background, problems were bound to arise. in view of the fact that the success of the new German foreign policy of rapprochement was closely dependent on Germany's integration into the world economy. With Germany powerless in a military sense and, at first, isolated in her international relations, Stresemann concentrated on mobilizing Germany's economic potential as a way of enhancing her political weight in the world. In this aim he was at first successful, as the boom arrived after 1924. American credits and the short-lived spurt in world economic growth simultaneously fostered international rapprochement and allowed world markets to become more liberalized. But after 1929, with the collapse of the world economy, the interdependence of foreign policy and economic expansion backfired. Economic co-operation, on which the policy of political rapprochement had been founded, went by the board. Inter-state conflict mounted as each country tried to salvage what it could for itself. The liberalization of world trade was halted and was replaced by a rush into national and regional autarky.

Nevertheless, in 1924 Germany had no option but to move towards fuller participation in the world economy and a more conciliatory role in international relations. Fate dictated, however, that this first step towards greater openness, after years of national self-absorption, should have been taken under conditions of only partial economic recovery. There was no time for the new policy to mature and to win acceptability, and after a mere half-dozen years of relative calm it collapsed under the pressure of its own in-built contradictions.

RAPPROCHEMENT IN THE WEST

From the perspective of the present day the Germany policy of rapprochement in the west can thus be seen as a noteworthy, if short-lived, attempt at a new departure. The novelty of the policy should not be underestimated; and it is also worth pointing out that the only way in which the later history of Germany and Europe might have turned out differently is if the policy had been pursued more consistently, as well as under more favourable circumstances.[12]

The ending of the crisis in the Ruhr and the introduction of the Dawes Plan made it particularly important that France's legitimate security interests *vis-à-vis* her potentially more powerful, if temporarily weakened, eastern neighbour should be met. The more Germany was able to count on the goodwill of the Americans and the British, the more unequivocal her guarantees towards France needed to be, if France were not to be driven into isolation and tempted to sabotage Germany's policy of rapprochement. In fact, the true novelty of Germany's foreign policy was that the national tendency towards introversion was sufficiently overcome for France's vital interests to be acknowledged.

Soon after the Dawes arrangements over reparations had been concluded, the German Foreign Office proposed, as a protective measure, a multilateral security pact guaranteeing Germany's western borders. This proposal led to the agreements enshrined in the Treaty of Locarno of 1925. The central provision of the treaty was a guarantee of the western frontiers of 1919, given by Britain, France, Germany, Belgium and Italy. At France's insistence, Germany also signed arbitration treaties with Poland and Czechoslovakia pledging the peaceful resolution of all mutual conflicts, Stresemann having firmly refused to agree to a recognition of the eastern frontier through a multilateral security treaty similar to that agreed in the west. The logic of Stresemann's revisionism had begun to emerge. Rapprochement in the west would lead to an early ending of the occupation of the Rhineland and the withdrawal of the Inter-Allied Military Control Commission, and the Saar would be reincorporated within the Reich. Once these aims had been met – and once the border territories of Eupen and Malmédy, annexed by Belgium, had been returned – Germany might then set about trying to obtain a revision of her eastern frontiers.

Stresemann's western policy was guided by two general considerations. He wanted to present the German public with some dramatic pieces of territorial revision; at the same time, he was pursuing a more cautiously advertised step-by-step plan for restoring the Reich to the status of a great power. In an era of nation states, and in view of Germany's actual weight within Europe, these goals were scarcely surprising ones. What was controversial was Stresemann's choice of methods, and the balance that he struck between preserving national freedom of action and being ready to make international commitments. He came down clearly for a peaceful foreign policy of voluntary agreements, at any rate as far as western Europe was concerned and as long as the Reichswehr remained a 'quantité négligeable'.

The Locarno Treaty of 1925 and Germany's admission to the League of Nations in 1926 were achievements that added considerably to Stresemann's prestige, but they also made further progress in his revisionist policy more difficult. Stresemann, in tandem with German public opinion, pressed for speedy evacuation of the Rhineland as the next step, but the western powers saw little need for haste in making further concessions. At an informal meeting in Thoiry in 1926 Stresemann and the French Foreign Minister Briand tried to sketch out a scheme for resolving all outstanding problems at a stroke. Germany would pay off her reparations ahead of schedule, so relieving France's and Belgium's financial difficulties, and in exchange France and Belgium would accept the evacuation of the Rhineland and the return of the Saar and Eupen. This dramatic scenario, however, failed to win the enthusiasm of the American creditors who would have had to fund the reparations payments or, when the small print of the scheme came to be spelled out, of the governments concerned. Nevertheless, it was remarkable that such a plan could be formulated only three years after the crisis in the Ruhr.

Comprehensive revision having failed, the only alternative was the arduous route of piecemeal change. This yielded some successes, but it was a longer haul than the German Foreign Office and, above all, the German public had hoped for. Allied military administration in Germany ended in 1927, and in the same year a Franco–German trade agreement brought about a liberalization of economic relations. In 1928 the Briand–Kellogg Pact solemnly renounced war as a tool of politics – ten years after the end of the First World War, a highly symbolic gesture. Finally, in 1929–30 the evacuation of the Rhineland was achieved, and the Young Plan brought a conclusive settlement of the reparations question. The period also saw a call for moves towards European unification, led by the French Foreign Minister Briand. Here Stresemann envisaged a form of purely economic union, which would have promoted German economic hegemony, while Briand sought a

political federation which would have put the brakes on G___
drive for territorial revision.

But by the end of 1929, with the world economic crisis and
death of Stresemann, the policy of rapprochement in Europe came to
a halt, its work not yet complete. It is difficult to say whether the
strategy had already run out of momentum, or whether the shift in
German foreign policy in 1930 represented the wilful squandering of
an historic opportunity. Controversy still surrounds this question, the
key to which must be a consideration of Stresemann's policy in the
east.

EASTERN POLICY AND ITS CONTRADICTIONS

For Stresemann, and for German politicians and the German public
generally, the revision of Germany's eastern frontiers was an indispensable aim of foreign policy.[13] The border that had been drawn with
Poland, in particular, was unanimously regarded as 'unjust' and a
'national humiliation', since it divided off East Prussia from the rest of
the Reich by the Polish corridor and brought rather more than a
million Germans under Polish sovereignty. The problem of the
German minority in Poland was, in turn, merely one instance of a
much wider phenomenon. It was reckoned that there were between
10 and 12 million Germans living outside the borders of the Reich: in
Alsace, in the South Tirol (leaving aside Austria itself, whose union
with Germany had been blocked by the Allies in 1919) and in the
various states of eastern, south-eastern and central Europe. The two
broad issues at stake in German eastern policy – the question of frontiers
and the question of minorities – thus encompassed a whole range of
highly thorny specific problems that had arisen as a result of the new
political dispensation in the region. Over the centuries the pattern of
settlement in central, south-eastern and eastern Europe had caused
different national groups to become inextricably interspersed among
one another. The central heartlands of the different nationalities – to
the extent that such territories could be clearly defined at all – were
surrounded by wide areas of mixed nationality, with the result that
any drawing of frontiers inevitably led to the creation of minorities.

Furthermore, Germans and Jews, in particular, were scattered in rural or urban communities throughout eastern Europe, forming enclaves even in regions where the definition of a core national territory was least problematical.

With the rise of nationalism in the nineteenth century, this patchwork pattern of settlement had generated increasing tensions, but for ethnic Germans, at any rate, the situation had remained reasonably acceptable as long as the three great empires in eastern Europe formed a framework of supra-national states within which different groups could live together. The new system of nation states established in 1919–20, in the lands of the old tsarist and Habsburg monarchies and the ceded German territories in the east, brought the problems of nationality into the forefront of public attention and led, in all the newly created states, to frontier disputes with neighbouring countries or to inter-ethnic conflicts within the newly drawn boundaries. Germany herself was no exception: the old eastern frontier of 1914 had included roughly as many Poles within the Reich as the new frontier now incorporated Germans within Poland. What was new, however, was that both Germans and Jews now formed minorities within a large number of independent nation states, instead of within the small number of great supra-national empires.[14]

As early as 1919–21 the conflict over Upper Silesia showed that these problems could not be fundamentally resolved if national self-determination were the sole criterion to be applied. Originally the whole of Upper Silesia was to have been ceded to Poland, but in the Versailles Treaty, at the insistence of the German delegation, this provision was dropped in favour of a plebiscite, which was eventually held in March 1921. The vote went 68 per cent in Germany's favour, but, as was only to be expected in a region of mixed settlement, the effect would have been the incorporation of a substantial Polish minority within the Reich, with many areas having local Polish majorities, especially in the east. It was therefore decided that Upper Silesia should be partitioned, but this in turn threw up intractable problems about where precisely the boundary lines should be drawn, particularly since, in addition to the question of mixed settlement, control of the Upper Silesian industrial region was at stake. In this atmosphere of tension, Polish volunteer corps attempted to resolve the issue by force, but were repulsed when German Freikorps stormed the Annaberg in May 1921. It was not surprising that the partition of Upper Silesia that followed Allied arbitration left neither party satisfied.

The example of Upper Silesia ought to have served as a warning against the belief that the future of German eastern policy lay in frontier revision, since exactly the same set of problems would be likely to arise in the Polish corridor. Stresemann's position on the frontier question, however, in essence remained quite unshakeable, but he did adopt a more realistic view about the possible procedures of revision than was taken by the circle around von Seeckt, the head of the German armed forces, who wanted to use the Rapallo Treaty of 1922 as a stepping-stone towards the complete extinguishing of Poland by Russia and Germany. Stresemann, for his part, was looking for a negotiated solution, backed by the agreement, or at least the tacit consent, of the western powers, although he knew that Poland would be prepared to strike a bargain only if she were on the brink of economic and political collapse. Germany, accordingly, not only had to keep the frontier question open but had to contribute to the internal destabilization of Poland. Similarly, the logic of the policy dictated that Germany had to work through the League of Nations while simultaneously undertaking a series of public and secret initiatives in support of German nationals in Poland.

Offering her eastern neighbours arbitration treaties and espousing purely peaceful methods of frontier revision could not alter the basic fact about Germany's eastern policy, which was that support for Germans outside the Reich and calls for frontier changes in an already unsettled eastern and central Europe were bound to be destabilizing. The policy could not be a truly constructive one, since the inter-mingling of nationalities in eastern and central Europe meant that a solution based on national self-determination that was 'just' to all concerned was impossible in principle. Any readjustment of frontiers would create at least as many grievances as it removed.

The situation bred, both in the small nation states and in Germany, a variety of schemes for achieving radical 'final solutions' of the nationality question. These schemes included the forcible assimilation and resettlement of ethnic minorities, the drawing of national frontiers favouring one group at the expense of others and the establishment of broader forms of hegemony based either on traditional ideas of empire or on new racialist principles.

It was a telling limitation of German foreign policy in the Stresemann era – for all the realism of the process of rapprochement in the west – that these difficulties in the east were never dealt with constructively. Certainly, for that to have happened, the painful decision to abandon the hope of frontier revision would have had to be made. But stability would then have been brought to a region where latent nationalistic conflict always carried the danger of violence and war.

Part and parcel of the intellectual rigidity of German eastern policy was the failure of contemporaries, until fairly late in the day, to perceive a change that had occurred in Germany's circumstances since the First World War. In comparison with the pre-war period, Germany's long-term prospects in central and eastern Europe had fundamentally improved, now that post-revolutionary Russia had been driven back on itself and had entered on a protracted bout of internal change. The new nation states in the 'cordon sanitaire', from Finland in the north to Romania in the south, were in need of a degree of economic consolidation and political support which France and Britain would not be able to provide on more than a temporary basis. Germany, if she had made the difficult decision to drop the policy of frontier revision in the east, would have been able to offer a zone of security and co-operation similar to that created in the west, and would in all likelihood have assumed the informal role of dominant power in the region, thanks primarily to her economic strength. The political conflicts and upheavals that took place in central Europe in the 1930s show just how far the balance of forces in the region had begun to shift in Germany's favour. If Germany's eastern policy had been based on co-operation, the Stresemann era would have bequeathed an incomparably more precious legacy for the future.

Eastern policy was the latent flaw in German international relations in the 1920s. Its manifest inconsistencies and shortcomings entail a measure of scepticism, in turn, in any assessment of the western policy's chances of survival after 1929.

THE SHIFT TO CONFRONTATION AND *GROβRAUM* POLICY IN 1930

Death spared Stresemann from witnessing the collapse of his policy of rapprochement. Even under the Great Coalition that continued to hold office until March 1930 there were signs of a new and harder line in foreign policy. After the coalition's fall, the new Reich Chancellor Brüning then accelerated the shift towards a policy of national self-assertion, not shunning open confrontation and a loosening of international economic and political links in favour of the creation of a protected *Groβraum* or supra-national region in central Europe. We shall survey briefly the main aspects of the new policy, which contained elements of continuity as well as marking a new departure.[15]

The world economic crisis led to the adoption of more strongly protectionist policies in most countries, and this undermined a vital pillar of the international order for which Stresemann had been striving. The early evacuation of the Rhineland, for which Stresemann had prepared the way, deprived France of her last means of direct leverage and gave Germany a free hand to pursue a policy of confrontation and calculated risk. Brüning at once set his sights on bringing about the termination of reparations payments, exploiting the distress caused by the world slump as a means to this end. He achieved the result he wanted, but in the process destroyed the possibility of continued political and economic co-operation.

This became apparent when in 1931 Germany and Austria announced a plan to establish a customs union, a scheme which was seen as a first step towards political union and was also intended to lead to German economic expansion in central Europe, directed towards Czechoslovakia, the Danubian basin and Poland. The plan miscarried, owing to opposition by the western powers, and it also helped trigger the Austrian and German banking crashes of 1931, which seriously exacerbated the economic crisis.

In addition, the Reichswehr and the German Foreign Office were pressing for Germany's armed forces to return to a position of parity with other countries, as a prelude to a new round of rearmament. The fruits of these various policies would in due course be reaped by the Third Reich, the foreign policy of which, at least until 1937–8, continued along the path inaugurated by the revisionist offensive of 1930.

The qualitative differences between Stresemann's policy, the change of direction initiated in 1930 and the foreign policy pursued by the National Socialists until 1937–8 should not be ignored. Whatever one's overall judgement of Stresemann's gradualist form of revisionism, in practice he confined himself strictly to peaceful means of agreement and rapprochement, and his aim of restoring Germany to the status of a great power was always counter-balanced by a commitment to international links and obligations. On the other hand, his policy of rapprochement was marred by ambiguities and inconsistencies, notably as far as eastern Europe was concerned, and it is not at all clear how the policy might have been continued in the changed international circumstances that came about in 1929 and 1930.

Whether or not Germany's foreign policy between 1923 and 1929 was an authentic expression of republicanism, Stresemann's achievement was a significant one, both in its design and as a symbol of greater international understanding. This remains true despite the fact that by failing to adjudicate between revisionist alternatives, it helped pave the way for a revisionism that brooked none.

11. THE ILLUSION OF DOMESTIC STABILITY

===

In describing the years between 1924 and 1929 as ones of relative stability, we should not forget that they seem stable only by contrast with the periods of crisis that preceded and followed them.[1] The period 1924–9 was itself marked by a good number of smaller and greater crises that were indicators of deeper structural tensions in German society. The structural problems created by the peace treaty and the establishment of the Republic in 1918–19 had not been properly solved; nor had those which had built up during the years of inflation and which had been only temporarily alleviated in 1924. All of these tensions and frustrations were carried over into the period of 'stabilization', as were other unresolved problems in the economy and the welfare state, to say nothing of the challenges thrown up by the headlong rush into modernization.

In this sense, it may be said that the unresolved contradictions which were to be the undoing of the Republic from 1930 to 1933 had actually been gathering strength during the years of 'stabilization'. The Republic had already been heading for the crossroads before the immediate crisis of 1929–30 occurred. Everything had been pointing towards a possible crash.

And yet the destruction of the Republic was not an automatic outcome. When all was said and done, it was astonishing how often the Republic had survived crises since 1918. This suggests that even in this apparently darkest hour a solution, or at least a 'shabby' compromise, might have been found which could have postponed the Republic's demise or – who knows? – even have prevented it.

If we look at the domestic politics of the years 1924–30, we find a highly variegated picture: efforts to create stability and efforts to subvert it; attempts to strengthen the legitimacy of the Republic and attempts to vilify the new order whatever the cost; and searches for mechanisms of political decision-making that would enable a course to be steered between the competing claims of constitutionality, the demands of the electorate and the manipulative schemes of those who wanted to usher in a different sort of state altogether.

THE ELECTORAL LANDSCAPE: TRENDS AND PROBLEMS

The elections held between 1919 and 1924 established the characteristic pattern of Weimar party politics. The elections of 1919 and 1920 represented a two-stage transition away from the party-political land-scape of the monarchy into that of the Republic. The victory of the centre-left (SPD, Centre and DDP) in 1919 made possible the promulgation of the constitution; a year and a half later the Weimar Coalition of the constitution's founding fathers failed to secure a parliamentary majority. The important features of this second election were the growth in support for the anti-republican right, notably the DNVP, and the split in the socialist vote. (For these and other election results, see figure 8.)

The right, after making further gains in the first election of 1924, then fell back again as the political and economic situation stabilized at the end of the year; on the left, the Communists also lost votes. But the tripartite division of the party spectrum into a radical left, a radical right and a centre group of parties from which governing coalitions were made up had become firmly established and it continued to operate in essentials until 1932. After 1924 the main shift of balance was within the right and on the margin between the right and the centre, whereas the KPD, SPD and Catholic Centre retained, with comparatively little fluctuation, the levels of support they had already achieved. Between 1924 and 1930 the electoral popularity of the liberal centre continued to decline, at first mainly to the advantage of splinter parties. Then, between 1930 and 1932, the right-hand side of the political landscape was transformed by the surge of support for the NSDAP, which took votes from the splinter parties, the remnants of

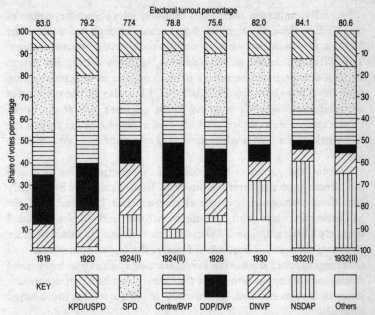

Figure 8 Reichstag elections during the Weimar Republic (1919, National Assembly elections)

Source: compiled from J. Falter *et al.*, *Wahlen und Abstimmungen in der Weimarer Republik*, Munich, 1986, p. 44

the liberal parties, the other parties of the right and previous non-voters.[2]

Analysing these continuities and changes in voting behaviour in broad terms we can pick out several general trends, including a number of problems which made it unlikely, even from the beginning of the 'stabilization' period, that the pattern of party politics in the Republic would remain fixed.

First, the pro-republican parties were always under pressure from the radical parties on the left and the right. Even so, it was not until the period 1930–32 that the electoral arithmetic actually ruled out the construction of some form of pro-republican governing coalition. Before this time, the instability of Weimar governments cannot be ascribed to a 'pincer movement' by the far right and far left.[3]

Secondly, although radical-left opinion, which was the source of the KPD's electoral strength, was sizeable enough to weaken the SPD, it was itself too weak to underwrite a revolutionary strategy. The KPD was aware of this dilemma, not only during the period when it was prepared to offer a limited amount of concerted action with the SPD (between 1925 and 1927) but also in the subsequent ultra-left phase when it went on to the offensive against the Social Democrats – a shift of tactics which won it added support among the distressed working class when the world economic crisis descended in 1929.[4]

Thirdly, the parties in the middle of the spectrum, the SPD and the Centre (and the latter's offshoot in Bavaria, the BVP), broadly held their own: indeed, in the elections in late 1924 and 1928 the SPD recorded clear gains. On the other hand, both parties remained strangely paralysed. The SPD could not make up its mind whether to plump for being a broad-based party, sharing in government and attracting support across class boundaries, or to cleave to a course of strictly socialist opposition, while the Centre was afraid that its constant presence in government served only to efface its already blurred image.[5]

A fourth feature of Weimar party politics was that the two liberal parties, the DDP and the DVP, turned out to be the real 'problem children' of the system, steadily losing votes in succeeding elections, then trying to hold their own as small splinter parties and finally succumbing to the advance of the NSDAP. It was during the 'stabilization' period, in fact, and not later that this crucial element in the parliamentary pattern – a liberal bloc, which, although somewhat battered, had weathered all the turmoils of the age of Bismarck, the Wilhelmine era and the revolution, holding on to one-fifth or so of the popular vote – began to collapse. The electoral decline of the liberals was the decisive event of Weimar politics, because it undermined the pro-republican centre from within.[6]

Fifthly, this decline helps explain the intellectual short-sightedness and the reluctance to take responsibility for difficult decisions that were displayed by all the parties in the centre of the political spectrum, from the SPD to the DVP, when they came together to form a Great Coalition in 1928. Viable government and convincing programmes could not be built on such shaky foundations (though we should exempt Stresemann's non-partisan foreign policy here). Hopes of catching the public imagination with enterprising domestic policies were thwarted not only by growing tensions between the employees' camp, represented by the SDP, and the employers in the DVP, but also, to an equal if not greater degree, by the prolonged mood of profound uncertainty that had been generated by the electoral collapse of the liberal bloc. The result was that politicians began increasingly to talk about the possible abandonment of the parliamentary system, and there was mounting support for some form of presidential regime that would recast the state along authoritarian lines.[7]

But sixthly, and paradoxically, a new right-wing mass movement was building up, in the form of the National Socialist Party. Its rapid electoral surge united the fragmented right, supplying the cause of anti-republicanism with votes which the supporters of an authoritarian presidential system were unable to muster. This is not yet, however, the moment to discuss the distinctive dynamism of the National Socialist movement. The NSDAP was not relevant to the crucial move away from parliamentarism and towards an authoritarian presidential system that was taken during the 'stabilization' period.[8]

VARIETIES OF COALITION

Governing coalitions were formed and re-formed in bewildering sequence during the Weimar Republic, and we shall not list the changes in detail here; in practice there were only a small number of basic, recurring combinations.[9]

Each government included the Centre Party – a phenomenon most graphically brought out by the fact that the post of Minister for Labour and Social Affairs was almost permanently held by the Centre politician Heinrich Braun. Furthermore, the Catholic party supplied the Reich Chancellor (Wilhelm Marx) on four occasions between 1923 and 1928. One political combination was for the Centre to be joined by one or more of the other middle-class parties, such as the BVP, the DDP and the DVP, to form a minority government. This government, depending on parliamentary numbers, would then look for parliamentary support either from the right (from the DNVP and the splinter parties) or from the left (from the SPD).

After the Reichstag elections at the end of 1924, two rightward-leaning cabinets were formed which, enlarged to include the DNVP, commanded a parliamentary majority. These *Bürgerblock* (Bourgeois Coalition) governments, in other words, were made up of the two liberal parties, the DDP and the DVP, the Catholic Centre and BVP, and the Protestant, conservative DNVP.

The elections to the fourth Reichstag, held in 1928, saw gains by the SPD and losses by the DNVP, and led to the formation of a Great Coalition consisting of the SPD, the Centre, the BVP, the DDP and the DVP. This combination, however, was so broad that, although agreement could be reached on foreign policy, no comparable consensus over social policy could be sustained.

There was something unnatural about all these political permutations, since deep-seated regional tensions and ideological differences had to be glossed over for the sake of making the parliamentary arithmetic come out right, and there was no real meeting of minds on political goals. For similar reasons, the mere fact that a given party was a member of a governing coalition did not induce any special sense of loyalty to the government. Parties frequently disavowed the policies of ministers of governments to which they belonged, setting greater store by the long-term identity of their own political organization than by any short-term commitment to a particular coalition.

Frequent changes of government, then, made parties reluctant to share in power, and this reluctance, in turn, bred frequent changes in government. Both phenomena were deplored by contemporaries, and have been deplored by historians since. The charges are hard to deny, and yet the syndrome was not the product of a failure on the politicians' part to grasp the rules of the game of parliamentary democracy, or of a survival of the tradition of powerless, *Weltanschauung*-based parties from the days of the monarchy. Rather, the post-war German political system was hampered by two sets of structural factors. In the first place, the depressed state of the economy left no scope for trade-offs between different interest groups, and indeed led to painful cuts in living standards in the crises of 1923 and 1929 to 1932. This meant that the chances of maintaining stable coalition agreements would have been extremely slim even if all the various party groupings had been models of democratic self-restraint, which they were not. On top of this, the electoral collapse of the middle-class centre left the relevant politicians little option but to keep trying to come up with new ways of projecting themselves to their potential supporters, which did nothing to halt the rise of splinter parties simply representing special-interest groups. Thus the crumbling of the middle-class centre also led inexorably to political fragmentation in parliament and government.

There was one gleam of light amid all this political gloom. In Prussia, the biggest of the *Länder*, the Weimar Coalition of Social Democrats, liberals and Centre remained in power until 1932, demonstrating, under conditions that were scarcely any more propitious than elsewhere in Germany, that continuity of government was still possible.[10]

It is also worth remembering that the experience of other countries – France under the Third Republic, say, or Italy after the Second World War – shows that a rapid turnover of governmental coalitions need not, of itself, lead to the collapse of democracy. On the contrary, democracy may actually flourish in a time of protracted institutional crisis, provided that the system itself retains the respect of a majority of voters and politicians. Drawing the 'lessons of Weimar' is a popular sport among commentators, but changes in Weimar's political institutions or constitutional procedures would not necessarily have been to the point. The problem which the Weimar Republic faced was one of political culture. The Republic not only had to struggle with the crises of the post-war period, but had to fight to assert its very legitimacy.

THE INGREDIENTS OF PRESIDENTIAL SUPREMACY

This question takes us on to a sore point in Weimar constitutional history, namely the division of power between the two directly elected seats of supreme authority in the Republic, the Reichstag and the Reich President. On this matter, again, international comparisons may be drawn: for example, with the United States, or with France under

the Fifth Republic. A constitution weighted in favour of a strong
presidency need not, as such, lead to a collapse of constitutionalism.
In the early post-war crises of the Weimar Republic the relative
strength of the position of the President served, if anything, to stabilize
democracy rather than undermine it. This applied even to Ebert's
frequent exercise of the right to issue emergency decrees, as well as to
the assumption of extraordinary powers by the executive during the
internal and external threats posed to the state in 1923.

Despite all its weaknesses, even the notorious Article 48 of the
Weimar constitution[11] contained an effective safety device in the form
of Parliament's right to override presidential emergency decrees at any
time by means of a majority vote. Article 48 could certainly be applied
as a way of evading the effort of seeking parliamentary consensus on
particular measures, but it could not be misused to prop up an anti-
parliamentary government for any length of time if Parliament were
able to muster a majority to nullify the emergency decrees. Even the
presidential weapon of parliamentary dissolution soon became blunted,
as the events of 1932 showed. A sustained exercise of authoritarian rule
was possible only through an open breach of the constitution.

The founding fathers of the constitution had favoured a strong
presidency because they were fearful that political decision-making
would become paralysed if it were totally dependent on alliances and
manoeuvring in Parliament. In practice, however, the directly elected
presidency functioned as a stabilizing rather than a dynamic force,
since there was no shortage of instability in the party system. The
election of a new Reich President in 1925, made necessary by the death
of Ebert, accordingly took on great significance. The presidency had
become a key political institution, and the political affiliation of the
incumbent mattered considerably. Jarres, the candidate of the right
(the DVP and DNVP), obtained 10.4 million votes in the first ballot,
but it seemed likely that he would be defeated in the decisive second
ballot when the Centre and the SPD, whose candidates had received
3.9 and 7.8 million votes, would put forward a joint candidate. Under
these circumstances the right agreed to support the 78-year-old Paul
von Hindenburg, victor of Tannenberg, joint head of the Supreme
Command in the First World War and object of undeservedly high
public esteem. This symbol of the Wilhelmine age that had so recently

met its inglorious end only just got in ahead of the wholly uncharismatic pro-republican Centre Party candidate, Wilhelm Marx, by 14.6 million to 13.7 million votes – thanks to the fact that the KPD, as an electoral exercise, insisted on fielding Ernst Thälmann (he picked up 1.9 million votes) and because the BVP, despite being a Catholic party, came out in favour of the north German Protestant Hindenburg.

The election of Hindenburg was undoubtedly a severe setback for the cause of democracy in the Republic, although the narrowness of the result should serve as a warning not to view it fatalistically. The Republic could still count on strong popular support. It would be political events in the coming years that would decide whether republican sentiment or a rising nostalgic tide of authoritarianism would finally triumph.

Contrary to the hopes of many of those who had voted for him, Hindenburg adhered to the terms of the constitution. But there had been a shift in the political balance, in two respects.

In the first place, the senior representative figure of the Republic was now a man who owed his reputation entirely to his links with the Wilhelmine past. While he did not let himself be carried away again into making such untruthful and defamatory allegations about the causes of Germany's defeat in the war as he had done before the commission of inquiry of the National Assembly in 1919, he nevertheless personified a different Germany. On that occasion he and Ludendorff, quoting a putative British general, had claimed, 'The German army has been stabbed in the back.' One of the most infamous anti-republican myths had been given currency by the man who now, in 1925, stood at the head of the Republic.

Secondly, Hindenburg and his advisers, in particular the State Secretary Otto Meißner and the new strong man of the Reichswehr, General Kurt von Schleicher, systematically set about exploiting the weaknesses in the process of forming governing parliamentary coalitions in order to build up the office of the Reich President as a competing centre of power. From now on repeated attempts were to be made, both open and covert, to shift the political centre of gravity of the Republic to the right, to strengthen authoritarian features in the process of government and thus to create the conditions for an eventual rewriting of the constitution. Significantly, Hindenburg blocked all legislative attempts to circumscribe the use of emergency powers under Article 48, so as to retain a free hand for himself.

THE REPUBLIC'S LEGITIMACY AT STAKE

The presidential election of 1925 and the Reichstag elections of 1928 demonstrated, despite all the tensions and structural weaknesses within the party system, that the forces sustaining the Republic were capable of holding their own, even when, as in the Hindenburg election, they confronted a roughly equal-sized bloc of right-wing anti-republican opinion. The much quoted saying that Weimar was a 'republic without republicans' was very far from being true.

These two broad groupings engaged in a number of political trials of strength in the mid-1920s which, while not ending in victory for the republicans, did not end in their defeat either. One such event involved the minority cabinet formed in January 1926 under the non-party Reich Chancellor Luther, which consisted of the two Catholic and the two liberal parties. Anxious to assure the right that it was a government of 'national responsibility', the coalition issued an edict allowing the German navy and missions abroad to fly the traditional Prussian black, white and red flag of the Wilhelmine monarchy. This slighting of republican symbolism led to a heated public debate and a parliamentary motion of no confidence, which was carried by the combined votes of the parties of the left and the DDP. The left, admittedly, was unable to turn this victory to much account. The Centre politician Wilhelm Marx formed a new minority government which, mindful of the presence of Hindenburg, avoided taking decisive action on the question of the flag. All the same, it had been clearly asserted that certain acts of flagrantly anti-republican revisionism were inadmissible.

A campaign in the same year for a referendum on the question of expropriating the former imperial princes gave the left further ammunition in this political confrontation.[12] Years of tug-of-war between the princely families and the national and provincial authorities had not established a satisfactory way of distinguishing between the families' personal property and the possessions which they had held in their capacity as ruling houses. The right bitterly contested all attempts to tamper with dynastic privileges, while the left was in favour of expropriation. The middle-class centre parties spent so long wavering between the two positions that the SPD and KPD finally plumped for a referendum. They mustered 14.4 million voters, or 36.4 per cent of those entitled to take part – not enough to get the legislation passed, but well over 3 million votes more than they had obtained in the previous Reichstag elections.

This exceptional moment of unity between the two working-class parties, however, was not to lead to any longer-lasting co-operation, particularly since the KPD, with the Comintern's switch to an ultra-left line in 1928, now began to vilify the SPD as 'social fascists', while the Social Democrats, by forming part of a Great Coalition between 1928 and 1930, became committed to a path of compromise with the right. Republican sentiment was still widespread enough in the mid-1920s to yield, in principle, an electoral majority. But the republican cause was prosecuted without energy and with a growing lack of conviction. Anti-republicanism, on the other hand, had begun to thrive on the passionate sense of rancour felt by a growing number of people in German society, and was profiting from the political indifference of other groups.

These disputes over republican symbolism, over the deposed ruling houses and over the suitability of a Wilhelmine Field Marshal as Reich President show that the Republic was hard put to it to establish itself as a legitimate source of authority. Political conflict did not take place within a constitutional framework that commanded broad loyalty or acceptance; rather, it was a contest between different, sharply competing conceptions of legitimacy altogether.

If we follow Max Weber and distinguish between three ideal-type forms of social legitimation of authority – traditional, rational and charismatic – it is apparent that the Weimar Republic was unable to establish its legitimacy in any of these three ways. The Republic had, by definition, set itself against traditional legitimacy of the sort that had attached to the monarchies that had gone before it. Support for the old order still survived, however, and this created a reservoir of resentful and defiant right-wing opposition. Furthermore, the attempt by republicans to mobilize nationalist sentiment for their own cause, to appeal to the 'German concept of the state' in the hope of tapping the traditions of the integrationist nationalism of the period before 1918, was bound to backfire. If liberals, say, attacked the 'diktat of Versailles', the effect was to cast the republicans, *qua* perpetrators of the *Dolchstoß*, as guilty by association.

It might well have been expected that the Weimar state would have enjoyed a considerable degree of rational legitimation, now that the ideals of parliamentary democracy had been officially promulgated and a catalogue of basic social rights had been enshrined in the constitution. But a form of constitutional patriotism signally failed to emerge. The compromise deals that had had to be negotiated did not carry much glamour and, although the basic social rights were symbols of social integration, they could not be fully implemented because the economy was too weak. A certain degree of rational legitimacy attached to the civil service, but for members of the bureaucracy itself, for example, loyalty was owed to the state as such and not specifically to the Republic. Indeed, this loyalty was liable to be invoked as a way of disparaging the Republic, the detached, business-like behaviour of *Beamten* being favourably contrasted with the 'bickering' of the political parties.

Charismatic legitimation of the Republic, finally, was out of the question. The disappointing failure of the revolutionary mass movement was deeply etched into the minds of many of those who had taken part in it. Charisma was scarcely the salient characteristic of the elderly survivors of the Wilhelmine parliamentary system, and even the personal prestige that attached to certain political figures, such as Stresemann, was insufficient to create any great reserve fund of republican sentiment. There was a widespread desire for charismatic renewal and legitimation, but this worked against, rather than for, the Republic. Its principal beneficiaries were the parties of totalitarian integration, the KPD and the NSDAP.

The totalitarian temptation, however, was by no means confined to the two anti-Weimar parties at the extremes of the political spectrum.[13] Indeed, in Europe generally and not just in Germany, although liberal democracy was apparently triumphant and self-determining constitutional states had been widely established after the First World War, democratic institutions were imperceptibly entering on a very severe crisis. The resurgence of 'bourgeois Europe'[14] and the defeat of left-wing movements immediately after the war were followed either by a nostalgic return to the pre-war 'good old days' or, if conditions made that impracticable, by a fundamental questioning of liberal bourgeois traditions and a demand for the masses to be integrated within a system of authoritarianism. It was not only radicals who talked about a 'strong man'. Stresemann, for example, declared:

The supplanting of the individual by the organization is the prime evil of modern political life. A person is not only the representative of a professional organization, a local association or a mass body of one sort or another: his significance lies in himself ... We must strive to achieve reform of the parliamentary system. We must demand that the spirit of party be confined to what is vitally required for Germany's development, that Parliament itself exert the pressure to produce a real and not merely formal majority. But if that fails in the present situation, because of the parties themselves, then let the cry go up, 'Res venit ad triarios!' and let responsible individuals find the courage to govern – that is, to assume leadership.[15]

Stresemann's call for a reform of Parliament and for the emergence of 'responsible' personal leadership reflected an unease with democracy that had long assailed democrats themselves. In the SPD, younger right-wingers associated with Haubach, Leber and Mierendorff argued for a shift towards a new populist form of socialism with charismatic leadership and a mass militant base.[16] Among the liberals, Stresemann's DVP was not the only party to flirt nervously with the mystique of 'leadership' and the notion of a broad-based middle-class mass movement (not that the party's dignitaries had the appropriate political talents for such a change of direction).[17] The DDP, too, plunged into the adventure of an alliance with the esoteric 'Jungdeutsche Orden' (Young German Order), but after retitling itself the 'Deutsche Staatspartei' (German State Party) it went on to lose votes more heavily than ever.[18] Even the Centre Party tried to submerge its internal differences by promoting a leadership personality in Prelate Kaas and, taking its cue from the militant Catholic youth organizations,[19] toying with ideas of building up an authoritarian mass movement. Under Brüning the Centre became the parliamentary platform for the bypassing of Parliament itself and its replacement by a presidential regime.[20]

The DNVP, although it had been formed in fierce opposition to the Republic, had in some measure complied with the rules of the parliamentary game during the 'stabilization' period. In the late 1920s, however, it made a sharp turn to the right after a split by more moderate *Deutschnationale*[21] cleared the way for the demagogic politics of the party's dictator, Alfred Hugenberg.[22] But, like all the other middle-class parties, the DNVP was forced to discover that root-and-branch right-wing opposition to the Republic, once aroused, could be exploited very much more effectively by the NSDAP.

By the end of the 'stabilization' period, then, most of the political movements of the Weimar Republic had tasted failure. Revolutionary socialism had been defeated in 1919–20; the Communists, for all their radical rhetoric, were still suffering from the trauma of the abortive October putsch of 1923; the Social Democrats and liberals, once the Weimar Coalition had lost its majority, were effectively on the defensive, the liberals in particular losing electoral ground; and the Centre, its support crumbling away at the edges, was retreating into isolation. Only for the conservative preachers of authoritarianism did failure still lie in the future; and they would have their turn in the years 1930–32.

As the parties had failed, so too had the central compromises on which the Republic had been built:

– the constitutional compromise of 1919 had evaporated into a bitter competition of party ideologies

– the corporatist compromise on social policy reached in 1918 had been severely shaken in 1923–4, and in 1928 it collapsed as the retreat from the welfare state began

– the compromise on foreign policy that had been secured in 1924 failed to survive the ending of the favourable climate in international relations and the international economy that had originally made it possible.

To sum up: in the course of little more than twelve years the Republic tested to destruction an array of modes of political action which had taken decades to evolve. The variety and the dynamism of the political movements and social programmes which make the

Weimar period unique in recent German history, and which still exert their fascination on us today, were also uniquely corrosive of the political process itself. The result was disillusionment and a recoil from democracy. Naturally, the totalitarian temptation was most clearly apparent on the right and left extremes of the political spectrum. But it had pervaded the political system, exerting its influence on almost everyone who played a part within it. 'Republik – das ist nicht viel – Sozialismus unser Ziel' (A Republic isn't good enough – what we want is socialism), the young socialists chanted. Young Catholics sang, 'Es zittern die morschen Knochen' (The brittle bones are shaking). Before long the craving for a total solution, for mass submission to authoritarian control, would be satisfied by the NSDAP, endowed with a dynamism the older parties would be unable to match. Another song would be heard; and instead of the words 'Denn heute, *da hört* uns Deutschland ...' (Today Germany hears us ...), there would be a slight but important alteration, and a million voices would roar, 'Denn heute *gehört* uns Deutschland und morgen die ganze Welt!' (Today Germany belongs to us, and tomorrow the whole world).

It is misleading, none the less, to sum up this complex process – involving the breakdown of political consensus, the crumbling of the central compromise formulas on which the Republic was based and the growing attractiveness of the totalitarian temptation within the political culture – in the phrase 'the self-destruction of a democracy'.[23] Indeed, it is precisely if we reject monocausal explanations that it becomes all the more pertinent to ask just how much room for manoeuvre the republicans really had. The constraints on the behaviour of the actors within a situation can be extensive even if they are not absolute. And, although a republican solution to the crisis of the Republic may never have been entirely out of the question, the fragmentation of the political culture threw up a further set of obstacles which made such a solution steadily less likely.

12. THE FRAGMENTATION OF THE POLITICAL CULTURE

The rise of the mass National Socialist movement between 1930 and 1933 and the transfer of power to a cabinet of 'national concentration' in January 1933 could not have occurred if the political culture of the Republic had not disintegrated earlier, leaving the fragments to be reassembled into a new combination that was susceptible to the exercise of force. The political culture had begun to break down before the full onslaught of the political and economic crisis that heralded the end of the Republic. It had already fallen victim to the contradictions that remained unresolved by the process of relative 'stabilization'.

THE CHALLENGE FROM THE ÉLITES

A key role in the long-drawn-out process of fragmentation was played by the élites that had traditionally been responsible for the functioning of the state: civil servants and judges, the armed forces, employers, and large landowners and farmers. None of these élite groups could have challenged or defeated the Republic on its own. In combination, however, their attitudes and actions posed a growing threat to its survival.[1]

The role of the judiciary provides a clear example of the gulf between the republican state and the élites responsible for its working.[2] The effective civil war of the years 1919–23 had repeatedly inspired judges to hand down explicitly political verdicts.[3] When passing sentences for acts of insurrection and politically motivated violence, they demonstrated unambiguously that they viewed political crimes committed for 'patriotic' reasons as venial or meriting only mild punishment, while left-wingers who had challenged the bourgeois order were awarded draconian penalties. Quite often, proceedings against the anti-republican right were delayed or quashed. Even the leader of the beer-hall putsch, Adolf Hitler, was given only a mild sentence of fortress detention rather than a jail term. It is true that after the murder of Rathenau in 1922 the Law for the Protection of the Republic provided democrats with a means of acting against enemies of the constitution.[4] But even the use of this measure during the 1920s was outrageously one-sided: a Communist, for example, was sentenced to four weeks' imprisonment for libelling the Weimar state as a 'robber's republic', while a *völkisch* activist who called it a 'Jew's republic' merely received a fine of 70 marks.[5]

National and provincial governments tried, notably at the urging of Social Democrats and left-wing liberals, to rectify such obvious political abuses of the judicial system, but they made only partial headway, as did the massive censure of the judiciary in the liberal and left-wing press and the criticisms that were mounted by the 'Republican Association of Judges'. The fact that this latter body was a lonely minority within the German judiciary pointed up the root of the problem, which was that as long as the overwhelming majority of German judges remained unsympathetic to the new state, all legislation and public scrutiny of the legal system was bound to be engaged in a losing battle. Judges, indeed, had become even more isolated socially than other public officials, notably as a result of the system whereby the future judges of the younger generation were required to do years of unpaid work as *Assessoren* (assistant judges).

Under the monarchy the judges had felt no clash between, on the one hand, the positivistic, literalist conception of the law which their training had instilled in them and, on the other, the basic structure of the authoritarian state and the hierarchical nature of the bourgeois social order. After the revolution their clear sense of the fitness of things was challenged, both from above and from below. A saddler (Ebert) could become Reich President. Party coalitions representing a philosophy other than the judges' own middle-class nationalism could begin to pass laws which would have to be enforced despite the judges' own views of their demerits. Above all, the floodgates of criticism had been opened, not only by the press but – seldom enough, yet still too frequently for comfort – by state bodies authorized to supervise the legal system. With the onset of inflation, these challenges to the judges' status and values were reinforced by a palpable decline in their material living standards. This strengthened the nostalgic, resentful anti-republicanism of the older judges and advocates, and radicalized the nationalistic, anti-revolutionary attitudes of the younger lawyers, already predisposed in this direction by their university experience.

These changes, together with a shift in an academic debate that had long been under way among jurists, began to undermine the hitherto dominant school of legal positivism and increased the pressure for the administration of justice to take on a more substantive character again and for 'content', rather than merely formal criteria, to be given greater weight.[6] Such ideas were not confined to the right, where the call was for 'national feeling' on moral questions to be made a legal category; on the left, too, although the arguments could be somewhat tortuous, there were demands for rehabilitation and for the personality of the criminal to be taken into account in sentencing. In either case, the aim was to increase the discretionary power of the judiciary, re-emphasizing conceptions of natural law as against the mere execution of legal prescriptions. The 'revaluation dispute' of 1923–4 was something of a turning-point here, a debate which centred on the question of whether it was right, in view of the galloping inflation, to uphold the basic legal concept of the continuing identity of the currency: the principle 'Mark = Mark' was valid on formal grounds, but in terms of 'content' it had become absurd.

The dilemma facing the Republic's policy-makers, therefore, was not just that new legislation (labour laws, for example) had to be implemented by committed representatives of the old social order and the old politics: an even greater problem was that the partial eclipse of legal positivism, which the reformers themselves welcomed, opened up new areas of judicial discretion which the judges might then exploit to attack the Republic.

The inevitable result was that the legitimacy of the Weimar legal system, in the eyes of the population, was severely undermined. People on the right were offended by the horse-trading over new legislation that went on in Parliament and by the attacks on the judiciary that were staged in the press, to say nothing of the attempts, however modest, to use the law to promote social justice for the underprivileged. On the left, conversely, legal reforms were seen as inadequate piecemeal measures: rigorous enforcement of the law, it was argued, was politically one-sided, judicial decisions continued to reflect the attitudes of the judicial caste and decisions on matters of labour law, in particular, threw up unambiguous instances of class justice in favour of the properties.

On the whole, the same analysis can be extended to the civil service generally. *Beamten*, like judges, acted professionally in a formal sense and, in the case of the Kapp putsch of 1920, for example, retained a sceptical detachment from events. In this respect they were not active opponents of the Republic. But in their day-to-day dealings and decisions civil servants let it be known that, where their discretion permitted, the solutions they favoured sprang from social and political ideals other than those for which the Republic stood.[7]

The Weimar constitution had expressly guaranteed the privileged status of *Beamten*, but had earned little credit among them for doing so. If, then, the civil service were to be reformed so as to become a true instrument of the republican policies, the process – assuming that it could succeed at all – was going to be a protracted one and would entail systematic personnel changes in national, provincial and local government. In Prussia, in fact, there was some increase in the proportion of members of pro-republican parties in the bureaucracy. In general, however, there was not enough time for thorough-going reform to be achieved, and in any case the senior officials responsible for employing junior personnel often themselves had no loyalty to the Republic.

Above all, the public service was subject to swings between periods of expansion, as new functions in social policy, for example, were undertaken, and periods of job freezes and redundancies when the financial situation became straitened. *Beamten* had already been badly hit by the failure of their salaries to keep up with inflation and by the loss of their savings, and they were affected again by cuts in jobs in 1924–5 and by further redundancies and salary cuts in the period 1930–32. The result was a perceptible radicalization of opinion among civil servants and public employees, which, after 1930, began to benefit the

NSDAP, though outward loyalty and fear of sanctions stemmed the big surge into the Nazi party until March 1933.

As long as civil servants merely stuck outwardly to the letter of their obligations, while remaining privately disaffected, the democratization of the apparatus of state was clearly going to be a lengthy business, and hopes would have to rest largely on the rising generation of state officials. But the younger generation was by no means promising material.[8] After 1919 the German universities were strongholds of anti-republicanism. Even 'Vernunftrepublikaner' ('rational' republicans), who had not originally wanted a new state but had come to terms with it now that it was in being, were in the minority within the universities. Committed republicans, on the other hand, had to endure acts of provocation by student fraternities and nationalist associations and face the aloofness of their colleagues. Anti-Semitism had also taken possession of the academic world long before the Nazi movement made its political breakthrough. This underlying animosity towards the Republic was further sharpened (as it was in many other sections of the middle class) by the inflation, which was falsely laid at the door of the Republic rather than of the military adventurism of the Wilhelmine empire. In addition, employment prospects in the academic labour market had been badly depressed since the early 1920s, and growing numbers of students had begun to pin their faith on a radical transformation of a 'system' which offered them no future. In this climate the National Socialists made rich pickings. By the end of the 1920s they had built up a fanatical following among students, advancing more rapidly and thoroughly here than with any other group in society.

The armed forces similarly went through a process of evolution between the middle and late 1920s which resulted in a redefinition of their relationship with the Republic.[9] After the immediate post-war turmoil, when they had protected the Republic against attacks from the left while proclaiming their neutrality in face of attacks from the right, they had proceeded to seal themselves off as a state within the state under General von Seeckt. In 1926, with Seeckt's dismissal, a new debate on the future of the Reichswehr, both within the Republic and with regard to the Versailles Treaty, began to gather pace.

While officially adhering to the disarmament conditions of the treaty, Seeckt had effectively reorganized the remaining cadres and had made secret arrangements with the Red Army to acquire certain categories of weapon. When the collusion was revealed in 1926 and Seeckt fell from grace, General Kurt von Schleicher, head of the political bureau of the Reichswehr, assumed a dominant role within the military. The Reichswehr at once began to advance from merely reorganizing surviving units to making long-term preparations for rearmament. For this reason alone it inevitably became more active politically, as it sought to square these plans with the revisionist foreign policy of the government. In addition, the planners in the military had learned from their experience in the First World War that armed forces could no longer enjoy any real measure of autonomy in an age of mass conscription and modern technology. A future war was, in this sense, bound to be a total war. War plans would have to reckon on the total mobilization of society.

Military leaders like Schleicher and Groener were quite ready to contemplate a variety of means of reaching what they regarded as the vital long-term objective of a merger between the military and society. At first, indeed, they tried to reach a greater degree of rapprochement with republican institutions and parties. Public controversy over the construction of new battle cruisers in 1928, however, convinced them that the SPD would never countenance the sort of expansion of the armed forces they wanted. Schleicher therefore began to look with urgency for a form of government that would bypass the need for parliamentary consent. Presidential rule was necessary, in his view, and the constitution would have to be adapted in favour of greater authoritarianism and militarism. By 1929–30, accordingly, the opponents of the Great Coalition were able to count on the backing of the Reichswehr.

The armed forces' withdrawal of support for the Republic, then, did not spring from conservative animosity on the part of older monarchist officers, but was the logical outgrowth of a highly modern, dynamic military doctrine calling for the militarization of society. As it turned out, even the Brüning cabinet would only partially meet the political aims that flowed from the army's long-term rearmament programme of September 1928. Be that as it may, the implications of the 1928 programme were clear: there would have to be an intensification of revisionism in foreign policy, including, especially, an insistence on military sovereignty, and there would be pressure for political change at home. On the army's plans, by the end of 1932 at the latest the tight limits on numbers of military personnel imposed by the Versailles Treaty would be exceeded; by then, if not earlier, far-reaching decisions on the remilitarization of society would have to be taken.

The Reichswehr's rearmament programme thus not only gave crucial pointers to the nature of the military's disaffection but implied a timetable. Nevertheless, the plan did not lead directly and inexorably to the final denouement of 30 January 1933. Schleicher's behaviour, in particular, shows as much: his about-turns during the year 1932 not only bewildered the politicians but, in the end, also left him isolated. His flirtation with the labour movement in 1928–9 and then again in late 1932 demonstrated that those pushing for rearmament were keeping their tactical options open. But it also indicated that they would inevitably gravitate towards the right if they were rebuffed by the left; and such a rebuff, in turn, could scarcely be reckoned unlikely, given the implications of a policy of rearmament.

The revolutionary period in 1918 had symbolically ended with the making of three fundamental compromises: the constitutional compromise of 10 November, which led to the formation of the Council of People's Representatives; the compromise on the role of the military, reached by Ebert and Groener on the same day; and the compromise on social policy between trade unions and employers that was reached on 15 November. The three compromises only just managed to weather the series of post-war crises that erupted between 1918 and 1923, and at the beginning of the 'stabilization' period they were upheld only by dint of various omissions and provisos. Despite this, various elements of the compromises continued to hold good, and amid mounting difficulties they retained a measure of influence until the fall of the Great Coalition in 1930. Up to this point, the central landmarks of the political system constructed in 1918 remained standing. All the same, in the mid-1920s changes began to occur, and by the end of the 'stabilization' period even the foundations of the compromise structure had been undermined and its retaining walls had started to cave in.

The process of demolition was considerably accelerated by German industrialists and employers, notably the leaders of heavy industry, who staged a dress-rehearsal revolt against republican legality in the Ruhr iron and steel disputes of 1928.[10] Even before the onset of the world recession, the accumulating structural weaknesses of the German economy had begun to breed a mood of gloom and crisis, and there were mounting cries that the burdens of the welfare state and the shackles of the 'trade union state' would have to be cast off if the economy were to recover.

While the onslaught on the socio-economic compromise of 1918 was mounted primarily by entrepreneurs in heavy industry, those in secondary manufacturing and exporting remained more disposed towards moderation, and they preserved a powerful influence within the Reich Association of German Industry (Reichsverband der Deutschen Industrie). But the moderates also fell in behind large parts of the programme to cut back the welfare state, reduce wage levels and weaken the system of collective-bargaining agreements. There were attempts to come to an understanding with Social Democracy and the trade unions, not only during the period of the Great Coalition but after the disastrous election results of September 1930, but these attempts were ultimately doomed to fail, since even those employers who were prepared to compromise expected the unions to agree to tough austerity measures that would hit workers, while the militant wing of the industrialists favoured imposing the programme by excluding employees' organizations from the process altogether. It is clear that for all the differences over tactics that existed within the employers' camp, in practice the assumptions which employers shared in their search for a resolution of the crisis – set out, for example, in the memorandum of the Reich Association of German Industry, *Aufstieg oder Niedergang*, in December 1929 – led to a steady shrinking of the political options. A few industrialists continued to dream of bringing Social Democracy back into the fold and of reanimating the old *Arbeitsgemeinschaft* with the trade unions, since – realistically enough – they could not see how, in the long run, economic policy in a modern mass society could be conducted without being grounded in mass consent. But the call for retrenchment of welfare benefits, wage cuts and the dismantling of the system of collective bargaining

was virtually tailor-made to suit the political aims of the right. It was
no surprise that, despite differences of emphasis, the authoritarian line
pursued by the presidential cabinets after 1930 coincided closely with
the industrialists' strategy. On top of this, the effect of the world
recession was to redouble the efforts of those who wanted to strengthen
German economic autarky and to build up central and eastern Europe
as a protected economic region. And heavy industry, which had been
particularly badly hit by the economic crisis, was anxious to recover
by winning armaments orders, and therefore had a vested interest in
a new rearmament drive.

The aims and interests of industrialists were thus virtually sufficient
in themselves to render the policies of a republican coalition unworkable and to make some form of authoritarian, anti-parliamentary
regime more likely. In 1932 German employers almost unanimously
welcomed the formation of the Papen cabinet; at this stage only a
small number of them backed Hitler. Indeed, even in January 1933 we
can perhaps speak of a 'divided front' as far as the response of industrialists to the National Socialists' bid for power was concerned. On
the other hand, there can be no denying that the employers were united
in their hostility to the Republic, to the fundamental compromises of
1918 and to the welfare state.

REVOLT IN THE PROVINCES

The Republic perished not only because its ruling élites undermined
it but because its middle-class citizens had become alienated from it.
There were basic differences between the two phenomena, but also
ominous similarities. The crucial difference, which we shall describe
in greater detail shortly, was that as the middle classes became more
and more disenchanted with and hostile towards the Republic, their
energies ceased to be channelled into the proto-political associations
and party-political organizations of the centre and the right which the
old élites had traditionally headed. Increasingly, the radicalized troops
of the middle classes deserted these organizations and their leaders.

Nevertheless, these contrasting forms of radicalization also had features in common. Both groups, the authoritarian élites and the radical-

ized masses, engaged in a similar process of demonization. They might not want the same things, but they agreed about what they did not want. They shared a hatred of 'the system', the republican political and social order; a hatred of the working-class reformist movement, which was seeking to protect and increase its share of society's resources; a hatred of the revolutionaries who had 'turned the world upside down' for a brief moment in Germany in 1918–19 and for a longer, more threatening period in Russia from 1917; and, not least, a hatred and a fear of protests 'in the streets' which expressly challenged the familiar, hallowed way of doing things.

Accordingly, real and imagined dangers became ever more indissolubly blurred as the general political and social situation became more disturbing and racked by crisis. The wildest ideological and quasi-mystical notions took root among the middle classes, among members of the lower classes who did not belong to the workers' movements and even among the upper echelons of society. The air was heavy with crisis and apocalypse. Racism and nationalism, anti-Marxism and anti-Bolshevism, anti-liberalism and cults of 'leadership' flourished.

National Socialism was the beneficiary of all of these hatreds and anxieties; but it had not created them. Both among rank-and-file voters at the 'bottom' of the middle-class scale and among the élites at the 'top', rejection of Weimar clearly antedated the surge of support for Hitler. Symptoms of the collective retreat from the republican consensus began to accumulate in the mid-1920s, at first and most noticeably in the provinces, in the patchwork of countryside and small towns where the majority of Germans still lived. It was here that ideological doubts about unbridled modernization were most readily voiced, and that metropolitan Berlin was most often condemned as the habitat of 'mass man' and the scene of party-political 'bickering'. But events in the provinces in the later 1920s were not merely a conservative backlash against 'Berlin'. On the contrary, their significance was that they actually constituted a form of revolt against traditional attitudes and constraints.[11] We have already described this phenomenon as it manifested itself on the political plane: the electoral decline of the traditional parties of the centre and right, and the short-term success of diverse smaller interest-group parties, such as the

Wirtschaftspartei (Economic Party) and various peasant parties. Underlying these political shifts, though, were deeper social changes.

Gustav Stresemann touched on an important feature of these changes when he complained in 1926:

What is regrettable about current developments is the excessive emphasis being placed purely on considerations of economics and profession in the political battle. If the idea behind the Economic Party is victorious, then the political life of the German people will eventually break up into an agricultural interest and into industrial groups, civil-service and white-collar interests – but unfortunately there will be no common spiritual bond.[12]

Events unfolded as Stresemann feared. Panic set in within the two liberal parties and also, after its electoral defeat in 1928, in the conservative DNVP, which then underwent a drastic shift to the right. Middle-class and rural voters no longer felt that these traditional parties represented their interests. But as the world economic crisis deepened, the appeal of voting for the small interest-group parties also soon wore off. These parties, with their narrow programmes, were an authentic expression of the disintegrating political situation, but they were also trapped within it. In 1932 the electorate escaped from the sterility embodied in the interest-group parties by turning to the NSDAP. Although the National Socialist Party was itself an assemblage of highly diverse interest groups, it brought these separate groups together under the banner of its demagogic, uncompromising struggle against 'the system', promising them that their different aims would all be fulfilled once the age of the 'Third Reich' had dawned.

There was more, however, to events in the provinces than the decline in influence of the traditional middle-class parties and the rise of modern pressure-group bodies representing purely sectional interests. A more fundamental change was a general loss of authority on the part of the traditional leading figures in provincial society: people who had been prominent not only in the major political parties but in local associations and local politics.

It is difficult to generalize here, since the regions of Germany were so diverse in their social and denominational make-up. Each part of the country had its own traditions and socio-political pattern. In the Catholic areas of the south and west, especially, older social and political mechanisms of integration were still largely intact, though they were slowly beginning to weaken. In the Protestant areas – whether those with a strong peasantry or the East Elbian region of large landowners – the influence of traditional institutions of authority was waning dramatically during the 1920s, and this process created the conditions for the dramatic swing to the NSDAP that took place in 1929–30.

In *Mittelstand* associations and farmers' organizations, younger members were starting to rebel against the old structures of leadership. The effects were evident in various ways: radicalization within the established associations, a growth of membership in new, competing organizations, spontaneous outbreaks of protest action (as in Schleswig-Holstein) and mounting support for the NSDAP. The National Socialists had at first paid less attention to the provinces than to the big cities. In the Reichstag elections of 1928 they suffered widespread setbacks, especially in the cities, but they also made small yet conspicuous gains in Protestant small towns and rural areas. The NSDAP's subsequent rural campaign fell on fertile ground, for two overlapping reasons. First and foremost, the socially underprivileged of the countryside now gave it their support. The growth of the NSDAP after 1929–30 was, in this sense, the expression of a profound revolt against traditional social ties, and the party both profited from and served as a catalyst for modernization in the provinces. In addition, leading figures in local society and local *Mittelstand* associations increasingly began to look towards the NSDAP, thereby helping it shed its reputation as an outsiders' party, though in many cases this process was not completed until long after the Nazis' seizure of power in 1933.[13]

The waning of the influence of prominent middle-class liberal and conservative provincial party figures, which accelerated radicalization among middle-class interest groups, and the channelling by the National Socialist movement of the growth of social mobility and protest in the provinces were vital factors in the general crisis of the Weimar Republic. The 'panic of the *Mittelstand*' and the Nazis' appropriation of social discontent among the rural lower classes signalled the painful arrival of modernization in the provinces, as localism and leadership by long-established élites faded and national pressure groups and a dynamic, broad-based political organization took their place. At the same time, it was not surprising that this revolutionary change was cloaked in an exaggerated display of antiquated ideological vocabulary. The figures who had been dominant in provincial politics found their traditional integrationist language being commandeered and taken to extremes by the new movements, which projected themselves as the sole trustworthy and consistent representatives of the beliefs for which the older generation had previously been the acknowledged spokesmen. This process was seen particularly clearly in the way in which the NSDAP displaced the DNVP. The further the DNVP conservatives moved to the right, the more they found that they were producing arguments for persuading people to make the full switch to their younger, more dynamic and more radical rivals.

The revolt of the provinces was thus directed in the first instance against those who had hitherto been the dominant figures in local community life. Under other circumstances it might have led to forms of more representative democracy, to a modernized system of local representative organizations and to a pluralistic, nationally integrated party system. This route was cut off, however, once the Republic became associated with the social decline of the middle class and the smothering of the provinces by parasitical metropolitan Berlin. The inflation years had played a part here,[14] but the crisis in agriculture in the 1920s delivered the Republic's legitimacy the *coup de grâce*.

The relatively steady expansion in German agriculture before the First World War disguised a number of structural problems whose impact was not felt until the post-war period – or, more accurately, until after the inflation, which also worked to the agricultural producers' advantage.[15] These internal structural problems came to a head at a time of world-wide agrarian crisis. Surpluses caused the international wheat price, for example, to fall by 40 per cent between the periods 1919–22 and 1927–30: that is, before the arrival of the world recession. The big East Elbian grain producers, in particular, were seriously affected.

But small and medium-sized farmers were also hit by the agricultural crisis. They were caught in a trap between rising prices for manufactured goods, which they needed to buy in order to modernize their farms, and falling prices for their own products. Capital income in agricultural enterprises, averaged over the years 1925–32, fell to a negative value: the figures for losses in agriculture were greater than comparable data in industry, even during the world economic crisis. Given these income trends, German farmers' debts, which had already been oppressive enough, took on nightmarish dimensions.

The sense of doom in agriculture was symbolized by a growing number of compulsory auctions of debt-ridden farms – events which were often the occasion for spontaneous outbursts of protest. Political attitudes in the countryside rapidly became radicalized, reflecting the falling price curves of grain, milk and meat after 1927–9 and the rising number of bankruptcies. For the mass of the population dependent on agriculture – not only farmers and agricultural labourers but shop-keepers and craft tradesmen in villages and small towns – the effect of this political radicalization was simple: after a short spell spent taking their bearings, they went over to the NSDAP.

For the political leaders of the farmers' organizations and the spokes-men for the big East Elbian estates, the agricultural crisis was the final shove that propelled them into coming out for a system of authoritarian presidential rule. Agrarian politicians such as Schiele entered the Brüning cabinet; Junkers backed Hindenburg in his drive against parliamentary democracy. On the other hand, large landowners and farmers were looking not only for radical political changes in general but for an immediate improvement in their own position in particular; and the Brüning cabinet had not got the means to bring this about. Between 1930 and 1932 Hindenburg and the Junkers were given, on paper, a gigantic amount of so-called *Osthilfe* (eastern aid), but the scheme had a major shortcoming: a lack of resources to fund it. Brüning's clumsy attempt to break up heavily indebted estates and divide them into peasant smallholdings was promptly denounced as 'agrarian Bolshevism' and eventually provoked the big landowners into coming out against his presidential cabinet in early 1932.

The agricultural crisis, then, at first led to different political reactions at the 'top' and 'bottom' of the rural social scale. While growing numbers flocked to join the National Socialist mass movement, the rural upper class, notably the East Elbian Junkers, favoured the idea of presidential dictatorship. It was only after the latter became dis-enchanted by a lack of financial support that many of them, in the course of the year 1932, changed their minds and also threw in their lot with the NSDAP.

We have anticipated later events here and elsewhere in this chapter because the processes which began during the 'stabilization' period, and were then intensified by the world economic crisis, continued to obtain until 1933. Despite variations and some shifts in attitudes, one common factor underlay all these processes of change: the dramatic growth of the NSDAP.

THE DYNAMISM OF THE NATIONAL SOCIALIST MOVEMENT

Although the National Socialists suffered their greatest electoral setback in 1928, when they obtained only 2.5 per cent of the vote, it was nevertheless during the years of relative stability that they laid down the foundations for their later success. Furthermore, while the elections of 1930 – which gave the NSDAP a sensational breakthrough with over 18 per cent of the vote – took place during an economic crisis, the country appeared to be at a stage of the trade cycle analogous to that of 1926, when the crisis was quickly overcome, so that in a sense even the Nazis' coming of age as a mass movement can be said to have occurred during the closing phase of the era of 'stabilization'.

After his release from Landsberg prison in December 1924, Hitler set about reorganizing his party with remarkable energy.[16] During the following years the basic elements of the leader-centred structure were laid down, and all the techniques of the modern communications media were put to good use. The style of the party's mass gatherings was established, with their mixture of sacramental ritual and military parade and their transformation of the 'party comrades' into a kind of ornamental regimented mass. Uniting all these features was the tireless drive to recruit and organize that was the NSDAP's true hallmark. The party's rationale was constant movement: movement for its own sake, movement that served as a perpetual confirmation of the party's onward march.

Ideologically speaking, on the other hand, the NSDAP stood for a *mélange* of ideas and grievances that were far from original and indeed were common to much of the German right; all that was new was the passion and single-mindedness with which the separate ingredients of this ideological mixture were combined on behalf of the struggle against 'the system'. This demonized image of 'the system' was a projection of attitudes that were by no means identical: anti-Semitism, anti-liberalism and anti-Marxism. And on many issues the party accommodated sentiments that flatly contradicted one another: anxieties aroused by rapid modernization and the impatience of a younger generation with the ossified world of its elders; indignation at the loss of social cohesion and aggressive opposition to cramping convention; provincial resentment of the big city and a new spirit of quasi-egalitarianism as people submerged their regional differences within the nation-wide mass movement.

Some of the Nazis' specific political arguments were certainly borrowed from the attacks on modernization that had been mounted by conservative *Kulturkritiker*. But the Nazis' cult of dynamism and the movement's utopian appeal to a future 'Volksgemeinschaft', or 'national community', outrivalled the conservatives' attempts to restore the old order. Although the fact that they had some political aims in common encouraged the old élites in the illusion that they would be able to 'tame' the NSDAP and make it serve their own ends – this was later the fragile basis for the deal that was negotiated in January 1933 – the NSDAP made it clear that it was something other than a more radical version of anti-republican conservatism. The movement's dynamism and its use of modern means of propaganda and self-projection gave it the image of a fresh new force.[17]

The party's newness was also apparent in the types of people who belonged to it and voted for it. It was the first 'Volkspartei', or broad-based 'people's party'.[18] According to official party statistics, in 1930 it had a disproportionately high number of members in the following social categories, compared with the population as a whole: white-collar workers (25.6 per cent of members), farmers (14.1 per cent), craftsmen and tradesmen (9.1 per cent), small businessmen and shop-keepers (8.2 per cent), self-employed professionals (3 per cent), teachers (1.7 per cent) and other *Beamten* (6.6 per cent). Workers, although they certainly constituted a substantial share of party membership, at 28.1 per cent, were far less heavily represented than in society generally.

The NSDAP, then, was a 'Volkspartei' in a significantly skewed sense. It attracted workers, but it made little headway in the paradigmatic working-class milieu which the SPD and KPD represented. It spread to all corners of the Reich and created a denser and more complete organizational network than any of the other parties had been able to achieve, yet it had difficulty establishing a foothold in the Catholic west and south. By being disproportionately composed of members of the middle classes, it embodied the tangle of very disparate griev- ances and fears that exercised the middle classes in the twenties. Its middle-class members included impoverished and embittered small shopkeepers and crafts tradesmen, but also small and medium-sized employers; civil servants and white-collar workers fearful of losing their relatively privileged status, but also young academics and teachers who saw themselves as lacking professional prospects altogether.

This complex picture becomes further confused if we examine the sorts of life-story that lay behind the bald employment categories given in the party's statistics. A 'small businessman' might be a door- to-door salesman; a 'worker' might be a *déclassé* ex-serviceman from a 'good' family, or an East Elbian farm labourer. Furthermore, during the ups and downs of the war and the post-war period NSDAP members were quite likely to have taken part in all sorts of activities that did not fall within the 'normal' categories of employment. The times themselves had scarcely been normal. A man might have been a fighting soldier at the front, then have served in the Freikorps and later have become a member of a nationalist paramilitary organization during the period of the crisis in the Ruhr, before finally finding his niche in the SA.

A close analysis of the careers of individuals in the SA and in the party organization itself suggests that the National Socialists belonged, as it has been put, 'between' social classes.[19] They included more people who were downwardly, rather than upwardly, mobile, though both categories were represented. In particular, as we have said, they included men who could not, or would not, be assigned to the standard social categories of employment. This diagnosis is borne out if we study the age composition of the NSDAP. In 1930 more than one- third of the membership was aged 30 or under – they were born, in other words, at or after the turn of the century (Heinrich Himmler, for example, was born in 1900) and as a rule had therefore had no combat experience during the war. Among those who joined the party between 1930 and 1933 this age-group exceeded 40 per cent. A further 27 per cent of the new members were aged between 30 and 40, the generation that had fought in the war. Most of the leaders of the NSDAP belonged to this age-group: Hitler himself was only 41 years old in 1933. In comparison with all the other political parties of the time, apart from the KPD, the NSDAP thus stood out clearly as a movement of the 'younger generation'. The party's age make-up was a central factor in creating the image of dynamism, mobility and focus on the future that attracted mass support for the Nazis during the years of crisis after 1929–30. But it also provides further confirmation that Nazi members fell 'between' social classes. A majority of them were still at an age when their life and career patterns had not yet been set, while mass unemployment, which affected the 18- to 30-year-old group most severely, also served to prolong their adolescence in this sense, as well as imbuing it with a quality of hopelessness.

If the NSDAP can be said to have been a 'Volkspartei' in terms of membership, the same was true as far as its electoral support was concerned.[20] The party's breakthrough in the countryside and small towns, at any rate in the Protestant regions of Germany, happened between 1928 and 1930; after 1930 it also gained ground in larger towns and cities, and even in a number of Catholic areas. In 1932–3 the NSDAP was the only party to have a substantial presence in all regions of the country. This did not mean it was without its clear strongholds and its areas of relative weakness. The NSDAP occupied a leading position in Protestant areas, in the countryside and in the middle-class residential suburbs of towns; after 1930 it also became much stronger in upper-middle-class suburbs, where the comfortably-off had at first favoured the conservative parties which were pressing for presidential government. By contrast, the National Socialists had less influence in the traditional centres of the labour movement, where if anything the KPD was recording gains, though the SPD was still broadly managing to hold its ground. The Nazis made least headway in areas loyal to the Centre and its fellow Catholic party in Bavaria, the BVP.

Despite these regional, social and denominational variations in electoral popularity, however, the NSDAP may rightly be seen as the first political party in Germany to bring together people from across class boundaries. It was both a totalitarian party and a 'Volkspartei'. More important still, it was able to pull in the votes of the disaffected in all different groups in society while also projecting the charismatic appeal of a young, fresh, compelling and dynamic alternative to 'the system'. In place of the paralysis and conflict that beset the republican parties in the twenties and the high-level intrigues that marked the period of presidential regimes at the beginning of the thirties, the NSDAP seemed to offer an entirely new start.

The NSDAP's ability to appeal across class lines and its unparalleled dynamism were due to two originally separate phenomena. One was the growth of a profound and widespread sense of anxiety and crisis, and the concomitant desire to be released from it; the other was the way in which the National Socialist Party was built up around the cult of a charismatic leader. In 1923 Hitler's popular appeal, often attested by contemporaries, had not been sufficient to disguise the grotesque amateurism of the 'Führer's' handling of the beer-hall putsch. Even in the later 1920s the leadership cult served primarily as a means of cementing internal reorganization, and was not translated into notable electoral success. It took the enormous political vacuum that had been created by the decline of the traditionalist liberal and conservative parties, as well as the intensification of people's fears for their future livelihood and their longing for some sort of release from uncertainty as the shaky Republic was buffeted by its most serious crisis, to induce mass sections of the population to begin to pin their hopes on the promises offered by the 'Führer'. It was not until the combined political, social and economic crisis seemed to be leading the country into despair that large numbers of people became ready to listen to charismatic offers of redemption, and that the 'Führer' acquired his following.

Even so, the fact that this charismatic leader could attract more than one-third of German voters in 1932 – and, it should not be forgotten, a majority of all Germans after 1933 – may still seem difficult to explain, unless we bear in mind that in the twenties German society had already been increasingly exposed to many aspects of the totalitarian temptation, and had rapidly become less able to withstand them.

THE TOTALITARIAN TEMPTATION

In the 1920s, as we have seen earlier, German politicians began to experiment with new ways of shaping public opinion and staging public events and to consider the possibility of promoting personalized 'leader' figures. In civil society generally, the totalitarian option came to look more and more tempting as a way out of the conflicts and impasses created by the process of modernization.

In many areas of society – among academics, specialists in social policy, educationists, writers and artists – there began a subtle shift in the debate about modernization and whether it should be welcomed or rejected. Glimmerings of a new, totalitarian consensus, clearly transcending party-political divisions, became apparent. The shift was not a uniform one: on the contrary, some specifically political differences became even more pronounced. But there was a definite readiness to give credence to various ideas which then gained significant political influence in the early thirties and eventually became central to the National Socialists' drive to regiment society after their seizure of power in 1933. These ideas were to find sufficient resonance, except among the groups who were their targets – the left, Jews and the avant-garde – that it is fair to assume that a totalitarian consensus had already been some time in the making.

It was during the crisis of the late 1920s, and then during the world economic crisis, that the new perception of the nature of the country's problems began to crystallize. Established political methods were failing, the old sources of authority were no longer a unifying force and a sense of dissatisfaction with 'the system' was becoming more widespread. People did not know what the future would hold, but they had become convinced that a change of direction was necessary.

The new totalitarian mood was expressed in various different ways: in a desire for highly personalized leadership; in the wish that middle-class privileges should be restored; in the drive to dismantle the egalitarianism of the welfare state; and in a realization that the mass media could be used to shape public opinion and the public domain generally.

Part and parcel of the new mood was an abandonment of the ideal of progress through technology that had originated with the Enlightenment but had become perverted into a merely materialistic utilitarian ideology in the course of the economic expansion of the nineteenth century. By the turn of the century and the time of the First World War it was clear that, although Germany professed, in theory, to be a Christian state, secularization had spread to wide sections of the population and Christian values and traditions were no longer universally accepted. This process of secularization had, of course, repeatedly been deplored in the nineteenth century, but the steady improvements in material well-being, health and security that people could observe in their daily lives had seemed to offer compensating advantages. During the First World War and the subsequent years of distress, however, the materialistic promise of progress began to lose much of its plausibility.

It was during the Weimar period, therefore, that secularization and the 'disenchantment' of the Christian outlook were first really brought up short by a failure of the secular progressive ideal. There was a widespread search for new foundations and new values, a hunger for strong feelings and grand objectives. The search took several different forms of political expression: authoritarian conceptions of an autocratic state administered by experts; left-wing visions of class dictatorship; a longing for a 'Volksgemeinschaft'. And another important political by-product was the sort of racialist utopia that played a central role in National Socialist ideology, though such ideas had actually enjoyed intellectual respectability in many academic disciplines since the late nineteenth century. The old century's great reformist causes – education, health, law and order, and social welfare – had increasingly come to be regarded as inadequate, in view of the imperfect nature of the 'human material' with which they had to operate. If human beings were not sufficiently adaptable, then what was more natural than to discard these environmentalist ideas and turn instead to theories of race, diagnoses of hereditary defects and new methods of 'breeding'? By no means all those who dreamed of totalitarian 'final solutions' for the great problems facing humanity were National Socialists; but they helped to create an intellectual framework on which the state-sponsored racial policies introduced after 1933 were then able to build.[21]

As part of this broad change in the climate of social thought, new idealized images came increasingly to the fore: images which were discordant with republican ideals but found a ready place in the ideology of totalitarian dictatorship. One such image was that of the engineer, the tireless benefactor of mankind, the brilliant inventor of technologies that would turn age-old dreams into concrete and steel. Another was that of the leader: go-ahead, a good comrade, and yet owing his legitimacy solely to his charisma, a man whose visions and commands his followers would obey as in a dream. There was the image of the strong, healthy man, hard-working and loyal, without blemish in body or mind, Aryan or Bolshevik revolutionary or youth-movement paragon, the propaganda model of the strong, healthy *Volk* of the future. And there was his close cousin, gaining in prominence as politics became more polarized: the heroic fighter, the man who would unhesitatingly lay down his life for 'das Ganze' (the whole) – the soldier, the storm trooper or the Communist *Rotfront* militant.[22]

These images and ideas cannot be sweepingly dismissed as 'fascist'. Not everyone who promoted or responded to them was a Nazi or a Nazi sympathizer. But as well as entering popular thinking and discourse, and influencing social policy and academic research, they helped create a climate in which traditional political solutions were jettisoned and new, totalitarian ones could be proposed. Modern historians may be exercised by the question of whether the Republic could have been saved from extinction, but for people living at the time the main issue was what was going to replace the Republic when it was gone. They believed they were shot of its illusions, and they could see the glittering *fata Morgana* of a new order taking shape before their eyes.[23]

As the economic crisis was a world-wide structural phenomenon, so the crisis of liberal democracy affected all the countries of Europe. The anxieties and the challenges to traditional ideas and practices that had been generated by modernization were evident across the continent. Why, then, was it only in Germany that the mass exodus from reality into the promised land of totalitarianism took place?

There is no single answer to this question. Several distinct factors combined to shape the situation in which Germany found herself at the start of the 1930s.

Germany was more badly hit by the economic crisis than were most other countries. In France, for example, the crisis did not arrive until

1931, and its impact was less severe. The Germans therefore became more despairing about the ability of the system to right itself and placed their faith in a totally new political departure. This explanation, however, is not a sufficient one, since the United States, for example, despite very severe economic setbacks, found a solution that did not involve abandoning constitutional democracy. A further contributory factor in the German case was that the country, as contemporaries saw it, had been in a state of crisis since 1918 and there seemed less and less likelihood that this crisis was ever going to be overcome. The German people, in other words, had seen the whole course of their lives undermined and all their hopes for the future thrown into question.

Furthermore, before the end of the century the process of modernization in Germany had already begun to accelerate at a pace and with a dynamism that clearly outstripped the social changes in other European countries. Until the First World War the transformation of German society had been viewed with a mixture of bombastic, imperialistic enthusiasm and submerged unease. With the traumatic events of the war and the post-war period, the whole process of modernization began to be seen in a darker light, and during the twenties people became very sharply aware of the drawbacks that came with modern life. The chronic economic and social weaknesses and recurrent acute crises of the twenties and early thirties led to a questioning of, and a retreat from, many of the achievements of modernization. With the deepening of the crisis, the mirage of radical 'renewal' and a re-created 'national community' became increasingly attractive: an image that was the more lustrous for being ill-focused. Similar processes were at work in other countries, but change there was less rapid and it was not accompanied by the additional factors that jointly led to catastrophe in Germany.

A further ingredient in the German situation was the decisive breach of political continuity that took place in 1918 and became allied, in the popular imagination, with the decline in social morality that occurred in the war years and during the inflation. A crisis of political legitimacy had, in fact, already begun to build up in the years before the war, but the dramatic upheavals of the decade 1914–24 caused people to forget this challenge to the late-Wilhelmine system of authority. Certainly, nostalgia for the pre-war era was not so profound as to tempt a majority of Germans to wish for a return to the Wilhelmine order. The crucial new feature of the counter-revolution against the Weimar Republic was that it was itself subversive and revolutionary and was not an attempt to restore the past.

The Weimar Republic had failed to build on the fundamental compromises achieved in 1918 and to use them to create a deep-rooted legitimacy of its own: it had lost the struggle for the hearts and minds of the people. This vacuum of political authority was the vital factor that caused a growing section of the population to seek its salvation in the promises of the National Socialists. What undermined the Republic was not, primarily, the resistance to modernization put up by the old élites who wanted to cling to traditional attitudes and practices: it was the peculiarly crisis-prone nature of the process of modernization itself. Yet the dynamism of modernization did impel the old élites into making a head-on assault on the fundamental compromises of 1918, an assault that was to help destroy themselves as well as the Republic. And the same experience of crisis drove the mass of the population into the arms of the National Socialist movement.

What made the crisis a peculiarly German crisis, which led eventually, in Friedrich Meinecke's phrase, to the 'German catastrophe', becomes clearer if we again draw comparisons with other countries. In Great Britain, for example, the economy also went through difficult times. There was no dearth of social conflict, as the General Strike of 1926 shows, and there were far-reaching changes in party politics, the upshot of which remained unclear until the Labour Party finally inherited the position of its Liberal rivals. Nevertheless, the basic prevailing social mood remained traditionalist. Compare the Germany of 1930 with the portrait of England that George Orwell painted as late as 1940:

More than either it resembles a family, a rather stuffy Victorian family, with not many black sheep in it but with all its cupboards bursting with skeletons. It has rich relations who have to be kowtowed to and poor relations who are horribly sat upon, and there is a deep conspiracy of silence about the source of the family income. It is a family in which the young are generally thwarted and most of the power is in the hands of irresponsible uncles and bedridden aunts. Still, it is a family. It has its private language and its common memories, and at the approach of an enemy it closes its ranks.[24]

'Still, it is a family': could this have been said about German society after the First World War, or indeed at any time after the turn of the century? Germany had long since torn itself loose from the traditions which still served to legitimize the social system in Britain into the 1940s. In Third Republic France, too, political activity might be highly agitated on the surface, but local élites and the middle-class centre on which they were based still throve and provided continuity. The Germans had been plunged into the rough seas of modernization and were searching for dry land on which to gain a footing. The more fiercely the crisis raged, the more frantic their search became. In the end they succumbed to National Socialism's beckoning promise of salvation, and were swept away to their destruction.

V. TOTAL CRISIS, 1930–33

═══

We're living a makeshift life; the crisis will never end.

Erich Kästner, *Fabian*

13. THE WORLD ECONOMIC CRISIS

With the onset of the world economic crisis in late October 1929 and the fall of the last parliamentary government under the Social Democrat Chancellor Hermann Müller in March 1930, the real question, both for professional politicians and for the mass of the population, was no longer whether the republican constitutional system could be saved or restored: it was what would come in its stead. The main general outlines of this changed attitude had, as we have seen, first begun to emerge during the period of relative stability after 1924.

The economic crisis now acted as a trigger, occasioning the abandonment of a political system that had already lost its legitimacy. In Germany, in other words, unlike most other countries, the economic crisis was first and foremost a political event: it signalled the collapse of a political experiment. Although Germany was also the country worst hit by the crisis in an economic sense, the crisis was significant primarily for its political consequences. The crisis was international, but it affected Germany in a unique way.

That said, on the purely economic plane Germany was certainly the victim of exceptionally severe setbacks. There had been the catastrophic hyperinflation of 1922–3, and there was disastrous mass unemployment between 1930 and 1933. Economic distress had also put the basic legitimacy of the political system under repeated strain.

The fact that a structural economic crisis coincided with a crisis of political legitimacy should warn us against any monocausal explanations of the collapse of the Weimar Republic. At the same time, the historian must make every effort to keep an open mind about the possibility of alternative courses of action that may have been available until the last moment, notwithstanding all the constraints that undoubtedly existed. The path to economic and political downfall was precipitous, but the final destination was not utterly pre-determined, even though the options became progressively fewer. Recent debate on the impact of the international economic crisis has tended to revolve around these two key questions of freedom and constraint: the amount of short-term political room for manoeuvre that was permitted by the crisis in the economy and the extent to which the course and severity of the crisis were determined by a long-term accumulation of causes.[1]

CAUSES OF THE WORLD ECONOMIC CRISIS

The international economic crisis cut short the process of post-war reconstruction, which had not yet been completed.[2] It was the product of a number of factors: unsolved structural problems of the post-war period, more specific difficulties induced by measures of consolidation and reconstruction that had been pursued in the 1920s, and a downward movement in the trade cycle. It is difficult to disentangle all the separate strands of the crisis, but we can pick out the principal ones in summary form.[3]

The stabilization achieved in Germany in 1924 was followed by a period of expansion, but this was soon interrupted by the short yet serious international economic crisis of 1926. The fact that this crisis was speedily overcome may have played a crucial part in influencing perceptions of events after 1929.[4] Furthermore, the upturn between 1927 and 1929 showed tell-tale signs of imbalance, even though important economic indicators had, for the first time, regained pre-war levels. Unemployment remained extremely high, new investment was exceptionally low and the war of attrition over the relative shares of wages and profits became increasingly bitter.[5]

The obstacles to expansion in the domestic economy were matched by difficulties on the international front. The rebuilding of world markets after the war had been achieved only at the cost of accepting some deep-seated contradictions. The new dominant power in the world economy, the United States, while generally in favour of an open system of world trade, sealed off her own territory behind high protective tariffs. The dollar effectively became the new leading currency to which other currencies, with the return to the gold exchange standard, had to adjust. Simultaneously, however, the French franc and the British pound remained in a state of unresolved rivalry with the dollar, so that the international financial system was trapped in a three-way tension across the London, Paris and New York currency markets. A further problem arose from the inflationary international financial roundabout created by American credits, German reparations payments and French credit repayments to America. For Germany this meant an especially heavy degree of dependence on foreign credits, particularly from the USA, at a time when the financial consolidation of 1924 was limiting the Reich's budgetary room for manoeuvre. Disruptions of the financial system such as those which followed the Wall Street crash of October 1929 therefore inevitably hit Germany particularly hard.

With recession, structural crisis and domestic and external burdens all acting in concert, it was a foregone conclusion that the effects of the world economic crisis of 1929 would prove extremely damaging.

THE COURSE OF THE CRISIS IN GERMANY

In the course of the crisis, production in Germany fell so dramatically that many observers expected the capitalist system in the country to break down altogether.[6] Between 1928 and 1929 the index for capital-goods production had increased slightly (from 100 to 103), but by 1930 it had already fallen to 81, and between 1931 and 1932 it sank to below half its pre-war level (from 61 to 46). The capital-goods sector was, naturally, particularly badly affected by the crisis, since there was little prospect that new machinery would be manufactured while so much plant was lying idle, but consumer-goods production, with its more elastic demand, had actually fallen earlier (reaching only 97 per cent of its 1928 level in 1929), though it then declined much less sharply as the depression reached its lowest point (falling from 91 in 1930 and 87 in 1931 to 74 in 1932). Prices of consumer goods, admittedly, dropped further than output (from an index of 100 in 1928 to 98 in 1929, 91 in 1930, 80 in 1931 and 67 in 1932, fully one-third lower than the pre-crisis level). During the same period wages were severely depressed, partly because contractual rates were lowered by state emergency decrees, partly because employers engaged in wage under-cutting. The fall in money wages, which achieved the 'adjustment' in wage costs for which employers had repeatedly been calling, was so enormous that despite the simultaneous falls in prices, real wages also dropped substantially (to 87 per cent of the 1928 level).

As far as most employees were concerned, however, the level of real wages was of no significance, since they were on short-time work or were unemployed. Mass unemployment, indeed, was by far the most conspicuous feature of the crisis.[7] On the basis of yearly average figures (that is, allowing for the difference between high unemployment figures in winter months and lower figures in summer months), unemployment had remained high even after the crisis of 1926, at 10 per cent of the workforce. The level sank to 6.2 per cent in 1927 but then rose continuously, to 6.3 per cent in 1928, 8.5 per cent in 1929, 14 per cent in 1930, 21.9 per cent in 1931 and 29.9 per cent in 1932: this last figure represented 5.6 million registered unemployed. An unknown number of unemployed were not even registered: probably over a million. Among unionized workers the proportion of unemployed was especially high. In 1929 the figure was 13.1 per cent, and in 1932 it reached 43.7 per cent; on top of this, 22.6 per cent of unionized workers were on short-time work.

Apart from the unemployed themselves, of course, their family dependents were also directly affected. Furthermore, white-collar public employees, while they did not lose their jobs, were forced to accept massive salary cuts, small shopkeepers and tradesmen were hit by the falls in prices and purchasing power, and the crisis in agriculture was at its most acute phase. With all these groups being affected by the depression, immiseration and loss of security penetrated virtually every area of German society.

*

THE EXPERIENCE OF CRISIS

Nevertheless, it was blue- and white-collar workers who suffered the greatest hardship.[8] Among them, in turn, workers in the building trades and in heavy industry fared worst. As whole collieries and plants were shut down, industrial communities often lost their sole source of employment. In addition to these sectoral differences, and closely linked with them, were differences between regions. Areas such as the Thüringer Wald, in which working at home was prevalent, and which were already severely deprived, presented an image of despair.

If we look at the age make-up of the unemployed, the striking fact is that while unemployment in the group under 18 was relatively low, it rose sharply among those in the early years of adulthood. For men aged between 18 and 30 unemployment was considerably above the average. Those in this group who still lived with their families were also debarred from receiving unemployment benefit, so that they were affected in several ways at once, losing their jobs, forfeiting any other source of income and seeing the collapse of all their hopes for a working future.

Unemployment among women was also high, though less high than among men of corresponding age-groups. This led to campaigns against women who were 'Doppelverdiener'.

The average length of time that a person spent unemployed increased steadily. By 1933 many people could look back on five years without work. During this time both their social status and their income declined, the latter soon falling to subsistence level. Neither unemployment insurance, which had been established in 1927, nor the emergency relief that supplemented it provided benefits on more than a fairly short-term basis. Thereafter a person had to fall back on local welfare services, which paid out niggardly sums determined by a subsistence minimum (though also by the emptiness of local community coffers); and even this meagre relief was subject to degrading means-test procedures. The unemployed were made to climb down the ladder, step by step, until they had reached the very bottom. Moreover, the state's repeated recourse to economy measures and its unavailing attempts to cope with the massive numbers claiming relief led to great confusion about people's actual entitlements. Few people, not even the lowly officials who actually operated the welfare services, were able to pick their way through the jungle of perpetually changing regulations. Many of the long-term unemployed, as well as suffering poverty and loss of status, felt that they had forfeited all self-respect and had been delivered over to the anonymous power of officialdom. If there had ever been a hope that the Weimar Republic would gain acceptance by virtue of its constitutional guarantees of a welfare state, the economic crisis stood this hope on its head. The failure of the welfare state played a large part in robbing the Republic of its legitimacy.

Daily life for the unemployed was not merely a matter of material deprivation and anxiety for the well-being of their families. They also bore the psychological burdens, difficult to overstate, of knowing that they were excluded from the production process – of having to spend the day without being able to perform any useful tasks. The rhythms of work, the time-discipline of the working day, had given shape to their lives and had made leisure all the more precious. All contemporary studies of the daily life of the unemployed were agreed that even their leisure activities gradually withered away, that a general loss of a sense of time set in and that the long-term unemployed, in particular, increasingly lost all initiative and hope for a better future.

The remedies provided by the state, through the welfare authorities and in the form of relief works, were actually of less avail than the help the unemployed could provide for themselves by joining organized or *ad hoc* groups formed from their own ranks. These groups ranged from young people's *wilde Cliquen* and the hosts of social clubs and leisure organizations to the various militias which fought one another for control of 'the street'.

These fighting organizations, of both left and right, not only offered comradeship but gave the unemployed a way of filling up their empty day. Military discipline took the place of work discipline. Non-stop campaigning enabled the members of the Communist *Rotfront*, the Social Democratic *Reichsbanner* and the SA to perform tasks that seemed to give them a new sense of purpose. Street fighting became an integral part of the power struggle, and hence of the battle for a new political order in which the individual dreamed of being able to make a new start. In an age of personal, social and political dislocation the paramilitary organizations, and the radical parties with which they were associated, took on the role of collective sources of meaning that gave shape to their members' everyday lives. Men without hope attached themselves to a dynamic political movement that rekindled hope by promising revolutionary change.

By 1932, in fact, the KPD had become purely a party of the unemployed, while the NSDAP was also recruiting among the young unemployed as well as mobilizing the bewildered millions 'between' the social classes, the panicking members of the *Mittelstand*, farmers and agricultural workers.

The world economic crisis thus hastened the final crisis of the Republic on two levels of society simultaneously. The masses whose hopes for the future had been blighted by the crisis became radicalized; the old élites and the politicians of the right, for their part, believed that the moment had come when they could dismantle, once and for all, the structures established in 1918.

THE GOVERNMENT'S RESPONSE

It has been debated ceaselessly whether the extraordinary severity of the impact of the world economic crisis on Germany might somehow have been mitigated, and whether the collapse of the Republic and the National Socialists' accession to power might thereby have been prevented. These are hypothetical questions, but they are essential ones all the same. They cannot be answered to everyone's satisfaction, but a discussion of them may serve to clarify particular aspects of the actual events of the crisis and to suggest to what extent alternative courses of action might have been feasible.[9]

The events of the crisis themselves show that we are dealing not with blind automatic processes, but with a volatile mixture of economic phenomena and political decisions. Even before the onset of the crisis, during the period of boom in which structural problems became more acute and the portents of danger became ever more apparent, certain decisions had been taken whose consequences proved to be of crucial significance. Employers, for example, had mounted their campaign against the 'trade union state', causing such a deterioration in the political atmosphere that all attempts to sustain the Great Coalition in a united effort to stave off the crisis were doomed to fail.

During the first year and a half of the crisis proper, up to the spring of 1931, politicians comforted themselves with the hope that, despite the alarming rise in unemployment, the recession would be overcome as quickly as that of 1926 had been. In early 1931, in fact, some indicators suggested a possible recovery, and it is certainly true, as the Munich historian Knut Borchardt has pointed out, that we should not judge the Brüning government's handling of the crisis up to this time in the light of our knowledge of the subsequent downturn of 1931–2. On the other hand, the government behaved passively not only because it lacked the gift of second sight but because it wished to use the crisis to secure its objectives in domestic and foreign policy. If Germany became insolvent, she would find it easier finally to shake off the burden of reparations; the exclusion of the Social Democrats and the bypassing of Parliament would provide the foundation for the new political dispensation the government wanted; and the employers' drive against wages and collective bargaining would 'straighten out' the social and political scene generally. The restoration of sound finance by draconian cuts and fiscal reforms would follow later. On this ordering of political priorities, no 'premature' measures to deal with the economic crisis could be expected. It would just have to be accepted that things would get worse before they got better.

On the international front, however, the Brüning government took the more active step of proposing a customs union with Austria. This ostentatious act of revisionism provoked financial counter-reactions from the French which finally set in train the breakdown of the world financial system. The immediate casualty of the customs union dispute was the Austrian Kreditanstalt, which collapsed in May 1931. The failure of the German Danat Bank followed in July, and the collapse of the Bank of England in September 1931 was averted only by Britain's abandonment of the gold standard. In a chain reaction, the international financial system began to break down, nations tried to seal themselves off from world markets, the German financial system became badly crippled and Germany, along with the rest of the world, braced herself for a further, disastrous slump in production.

By the end of 1931 all manner of proposals for combating the crisis by reflationary measures and work-creation schemes had been put forward.[10] It is doubtful whether such programmes would actually have begun to bear fruit during 1932, but they would at least have been symbols of hope for the mass of the population as the depths of the slump were plumbed in the summer of that year. Indeed, in 1933 the Hitler government was able to avail itself of the civil service's detailed advance preparations for work-creation programmes and thus claim undeserved credit for the recovery when it came. The Brüning government would have been able to profit from the same goodwill had it not refused, because of its priorities in foreign policy, to take action to combat the slump until reparations had been finally abolished in July 1932. Its rigidity meant that the country had to suffer the unemployment and hardship of 1932 without being given a glimmer of light at the end of the tunnel. The swing to the radical parties that did offer hope, the KPD and the NSDAP, was therefore only to be expected.

Germany's exceptional 'solution' to the international economic crisis – the accession to power of the National Socialists – was not, then, the product merely of the country's exceptionally severe economic situation: it arose out of the specific nature of Germany's political response to that situation. Although the economic crisis struck more harshly in Germany than it did in, say, France or Great Britain, its scale and its social effects were no greater than they were in the United States. It is true that the German people were now confronted with a collapse of their economy for the second time in less than a decade and that they had still scarcely come to terms with the military failure of 1918 and the political upheavals that had followed. But the real scale of the economic crisis was perhaps less important than the symbolic meaning of the crisis as Germans perceived it. Economic catastrophe seemed to furnish conclusive proof that the chronic instability of the post-war period had brought about the devaluation of old certainties without creating new social and political values to take their place. The crisis deprived the nation of all hope of returning even to the living standards of before the war, and millions of people saw themselves as powerless to shape their own destinies. The answer seemed obvious: to join the headlong rush to abandon the Weimar 'system' altogether.

14. THE EROSION OF OPTIONS

The months between the fall of the Great Coalition in March 1930 and the confrontation between the new government and Parliament in the summer of the same year, which led to the Reichstag elections of 14 September, saw the demise of parliamentary politics in Weimar Germany.[1] The Brüning cabinet had been approved by the Reich President Hindenburg on the explicit understanding that it would govern without Parliament and would combat Social Democracy. With these long-term goals in view, Brüning made no attempt to win the Social Democrats' support for the budgetary programme he announced in the summer of 1930; the measures were promulgated by emergency decree. When the decree was reversed by a majority vote in the Reichstag, Brüning dissolved the Reichstag and the decree was reissued, with trivial changes, a few days later. Irrespective of whether this act was itself a breach of constitutionality in a technical legal sense, it was clearly a fundamental attack on the basic principle that animated the constitution. It abrogated the bipartite division of power between Reichstag and Reich President by effectively crippling the former; the legislature's principal means of resisting presidential power under Article 48 was neutralized. This was the political change of direction that Brüning and Hindenburg had sought, and it was to be merely the prelude to a further strengthening of presidential authority later.[2]

The government was also prepared to countenance the dissolution of the Reichstag two years before the expiry of its full term, despite the fact that results in *Länder* and local-government elections in the preceding months pointed to an alarming surge in support for the National Socialists. The rise of the far left and far right has subsequently been blamed for the weakness of Parliament, but this is to put the cart before the horse. Parliament was perfectly capable of effective action and could have continued to provide a clear majority in favour of democracy until 1932. It was deliberately sidelined so that presidential rule could be imposed.

In the Reichstag elections held on 14 September the NSDAP gained over 18 per cent of the vote, the non-radical parties ceased to constitute an overall majority and the right-wing conservative DNVP suffered a catastrophic defeat, causing it to go into implacable opposition even to Brüning's presidential cabinet. Now the Reichstag had indeed become incapable of taking decisive concerted action. Even so, Brüning could still count on the SPD to display its traditional sense of national political responsibility and desist from making common cause with the extremist parties to assemble a wrecking anti-government majority. The result was a curious hybrid: an undisguisedly anti-parliamentary presidential government upheld by an acquiescent parliamentary majority. But Brüning's tactical reliance on the remnants of parliamentarism should not be misconstrued: it was certainly not his intention to seek to preserve democracy through a temporary recourse to authoritarianism.

THE PATH TOWARDS AUTHORITARIANISM

The general direction of the political change which Brüning brought about was by no means clear to people at the time, thanks partly to Brüning's own shrewdness and skill in keeping his cards close to his chest but also to the numerous political fluctuations that occurred between 1930 and 1932. It was difficult simply to keep track of the domestic political situation, since there were all manner of conflicts among the various parties and interest groups, rapid changes in tactical alliances and confusing ideological arguments among policy-makers. We can map the path that led to authoritarianism by giving a schematic account of its main elements.

Politically speaking, the immediate issue was the freeing of government from dependence on the process of decision-making in Parliament. Policy-making became increasingly concentrated within the

Reich Chancellor's office, but it derived its legitimacy solely from the President and its crucial instrument was the emergency decree. With the elimination of any countervailing constitutional locus of power, the executive no longer had its own separate power base but became ever more dependent on the camarilla around Hindenburg.

In the longer term the presidential regimes hoped to bring about a twofold change in the constitution: *Reichsreform* would strengthen the power of the national government *vis-à-vis* the *Länder*; and Parliament would be confined to a purely supervisory function, with the state being governed along authoritarian lines on the Bismarckian model. Brüning actually nurtured the far-fetched idea of restoring the Hohenzollern monarchy, while Franz von Papen envisaged a 'new state' in the Italian mode. Although Brüning wished to maintain constitutionality and Papen was looking for a new corporatism run by the old élites, and although both rejected Hitler's extremism on grounds of sheer political self-preservation, neither of them wanted to preserve the status quo, let alone return to the Weimar system.

On the social front, the crisis enabled the government finally to start unravelling the achievements of 1918. The weakening of the trade unions, the abolition of the hitherto accepted system of collective wage bargaining, the marginalizing of the SPD and the reduction of wage and salary levels were all part of this strategy. Welfare benefits were cut back, and financial measures were taken to pare down public expenditure and the machinery of state. Once again, the crisis did not so much force the government to act as provide the occasion for the introduction of reactionary policies which it wanted to implement in any case.

The main thrust of Brüning's policies, however, lay in the field of international relations. Here too the crisis provided a convenient pretext for accelerating the revision of the Versailles settlement. First and foremost, Bruning wanted to achieve a final cessation of reparations payments, and to that end he was prepared to tolerate increasing poverty in Germany. At the same time, the new leadership at the Foreign Office was pushing for Germany to regain a free hand in international relations and, in the wake of the international economic collapse, was preparing a switch to a policy of hegemony in central

Europe designed to lead in the medium term to the establishment of economic autarky in the German *Großraum*.

These projected moves closely complemented the aims of the military. The Reichswehr's plans entailed an extensive programme of rearmament and a rise in numbers of army personnel: policies which could be pursued only if the Versailles Treaty were revised. But although treaty revision along these lines was entirely consistent with the thinking of the presidential cabinets, the demand was at odds – crucially so by 1932 – with Brüning's belief that the solution of the reparations question should take priority. This was one reason why Brüning lost the favour of the Reichswehr. The other reason was a clash of attitudes towards the SA and the Stahlhelm: the Reichswehr wanted to incorporate the two mass paramilitary organizations as part of the nation's military forces, while Brüning and his Minister for the Armed Forces and the Interior, Groener, were worried about the SA's capacity to cause havoc in domestic politics and therefore resolved to ban it. Nevertheless, in general the armed forces and the Chancellor were united in the desire to transform the state along authoritarian lines, partly on the grounds that this would make for discipline and order in the event of a new outbreak of war.

The decision by Hindenburg and his Chancellors Brüning and Papen to embark on the path of authoritarianism had the widespread approval of the old governing and social élites. Despite differences over tactics, there was a broad consensus in these circles that the fundamental compromises which had underlain the founding of the Republic in 1918 should be repudiated. The presidential cabinets did not adopt this policy under the pressure of the economic crisis: they used the crisis to further their political aims, and they were quite prepared to let the effects of the crisis become more acute if they thought it would help.

The policy of authoritarianism took priority not only over dealing with the economic crisis but also over responding to the rising threat of National Socialism. When the Reichstag was dissolved in 1930, the predictable growth in the National Socialist vote was regarded as an acceptable price to pay for bringing nearer the achievement of the primary goal, the bypassing of Parliament. Between 1930 and 1932, likewise, Brüning, Papen and Schleicher sought to use the NSDAP as a tool with which to realize their vision of a restructured state. The difficulties confronting the presidential cabinets were due in no small part to the fact that Hitler flatly refused to let himself be used in this way. It would be quite wrong to conclude from the fact that the tactic of 'taming' Hitler failed that the ploy was an anti-fascist one. Its purpose was to secure hegemony within the projected 'new state': not to defend the Republic against National Socialism.

ACTIONS AND REACTIONS, 1930–32

Brüning's dissolution of the Reichstag and calling of elections in the summer of 1930 set the pattern for the rest of his chancellorship.[3] The institutional balance of power created by the Weimar constitution, which had already come under serious strain, was now overturned. Parliament had effectively been eliminated, though it could still be called on to give its 'consent' to government policies. The way had been cleared for a purely cabinet-based form of government dependent on the confidence of the Reich President. Brüning at once began to weave a subtle and intricate web of political tactics. One of the main reasons, indeed, why he was the arch-exponent of a presidential form of government was that he was still able at this stage to count on the backing of a substantial number of leading politicians.

His ability to secure the active co-operation of the middle-class parties (with the exception of Hugenberg's DNVP) and the passive consent of the Social Democrats; the fact that he enjoyed, at one and the same time, the confidence of Hindenburg and his cabal and of the leaders of the Reichswehr; his skill in negotiating with the major interest groups and the representatives of the *Länder*; the courteous manner that cloaked his toughness on the international stage – all of these assets made him, at the outset, indispensable. But as time went by Brüning's secretiveness and taste for intrigue bred considerable public coolness, mistrust and disillusionment. He was reluctant to spell out the logic and ultimate aims of his policies – assuming, that is, that they were as clear to him at the time as they were when he came to write his memoirs in exile, and assuming too that he was not, in the last analysis, a mere victim of circumstances rather than, as he claimed to be, their master.[4]

Be that as it may, in pursuit of his policies Brüning eroded his own position. The more impotent Parliament became, the less need there was for a middleman of his sort. The more deeply his administrative and financial reforms cut into the bureaucracy, the more he forfeited the loyalty of the officials who had to implement them. As a settlement of the reparations question drew closer, there was less need for a Brüning figure on the international front, especially as the Reichswehr began to press for a show-down on the issue of rearmament. And the longer the economic crisis continued, the nearer came the inevitable moment when the man who had been responsible for the unpopular cuts in prices, wages and welfare benefits would be discharged, leaving the 'new state' that he wanted and the reflationary measures that were urgently needed to be ushered in by a politician with an untainted record.

Misjudging the true alignment of political forces, Brüning believed that he had been halted 'a hundred metres away from the finishing line'. He fell victim to the dialectic between authoritarian politics and what Bracher has called the 'disintegration of power'. Virtually all the important countervailing sources of authority had been excluded from the political process, leaving the Reich President as the sole focus of legitimacy in the state. And the presidential cabal was not a reliable custodian of power. As the authoritarian tide advanced, so the crumbling of the power of the professional politicians accelerated. The more talk there was of a 'new state' governed by the old élites, the more impotent the small number of surviving wire-pullers around Hindenburg actually became.

The year 1932 brought the death-agony of presidential government; the disintegration of power was followed by a power vacuum. Until this time the economic and political crisis had been useful to Brüning in his drive to destroy the Weimar Republic, but it now backfired on the exponents of authoritarianism themselves. In 1930 the Republic's enemies had assumed power and pursued a politics of crisis designed to serve their anti-republican goals. By 1932 the crisis that they themselves had aggravated was wrecking all their calculations and manoeuvrings.

The presidential election of March and April 1932 was a presage of the political confusion that was to follow. If Hindenburg were to defeat Hitler, at least on the second ballot – when Hitler in fact won over 13 million votes, or 36.8 per cent of the electorate – then the old Field Marshal would need support from, of all parties, the Social Democrats. Clearly, in a highly mobile and politicized modern society such as Germany was in the early 1930s, a move towards authoritarianism could not be carried out without a broad basis of electoral support. The only possible sources of such support, however, were the democratic parties, notably the SPD – parties which had been driven into isolation over a period of years and were fearful that they could not retain their popular followings – or the National Socialist mass movement on the right. But the democratic parties had been banished to the sidelines by the very shift towards authoritarianism, while the National Socialists threatened, if they were once allowed to share power, to take advantage of the newly installed apparatus of authoritarian rule for their own much more ambitious ends.

For the rest of 1932 the presidential cabinets remained caught in this self-laid trap. The attempt by Brüning and Groener to stem the advance of the National Socialists by banning the SA came too late and merely had the effect of earning the opposition of Hindenburg and Schleicher, who wanted to co-opt the paramilitary organization's mishandled but useful 'patriotic loyalty'.

The new Chancellor installed on 1 June 1932, Franz von Papen, enjoyed the confidence of Hindenburg and his entourage, brought the field-grey eminence of the Reichswehr, Schleicher, into the cabinet and could properly regard himself as a quintessential representative of the old élites, employers and large landowners. But he lacked the one thing indispensable in modern politics, despite the fact that the parliamentary heads of the hydra of democracy were now supposed to have been cut off: a popular following. As a result, all talk of a 'new state' remained hollow, as did plans for a *coup d'état*. The dry run for a coup that took place in Prussia, when the SPD-led *Land* government was deposed on 20 July 1932, proved to be a Pyrrhic victory. So also did the two dissolutions of the Reichstag and the bitter elections that followed, which provoked intensified street fighting and merely raised the political temperature higher still. The Papen government certainly succeeded in ridding itself of institutional opposition, in the form of Parliament and the federal states, but the election of 6

November 1932 conveyed the inescapable message that its electoral support remained stubbornly below 10 per cent. In these elections, too, the National Socialists fell back perceptibly for the first time, gaining only 33.1 per cent of the vote as compared with 37.4 per cent in the elections held in the preceding July.

With Papen's gentlemen's club of a cabinet at a loss how to act and with the NSDAP showing signs of weakening, the kingmaker Schleicher was induced to try his own hand at leading the government. His gamble that he could achieve mass cross-party support from the trade unions and the Strasser wing of the NSDAP proved to be as misconceived as Papen's flirting with the idea of a *coup d'état*. Schleicher's failure merely underscored what had been perfectly obvious since the spring of 1932.

The policy of authoritarianism had been successful to the extent that the Republic had been destroyed, but it failed in its aim of enlisting the support of the mass anti-republican movement, which went instead to Hitler and the NSDAP. By the end of 1932, accordingly, all options but one had been eroded. The democratic option had been deliberately blocked since 1930; the Communists remained trapped in their ghetto of protest; presidential government was running aground for lack of mass support; and a coup by the Reichswehr, given the high degree of politicization in the country and the swarms of extremist militias on the streets, might have unleashed civil war with incalculable consequences.

That left the NSDAP. The Nazis' losses in the November election showed that they lacked sufficient electoral backing to assume power on their own. At the same time, the forces which had sustained the presidential regimes until now could not continue to do so without mass support. So far, though, each side had rightly viewed the other with mistrust. Hitler did not wish to be 'tamed' by the old élites and used as a tool to further their own political ends. The old élites, in turn, had not destroyed Weimar democracy in order to be ousted by Hitler's radical mass movement from the leadership role they had only just resumed. Until late in 1932 these contradictory aims barred the way to any mutual accommodation. By the end of the year, however, it seemed that both sides were in urgent need of a deal. Hitler needed power, and the old élites needed mass support. There was no love lost between the two parties, but an engagement was finally about to be announced.

THE END OF THE WEIMAR REPUBLIC

The end of Weimar did not happen overnight and was not the product of any single set of causes. We can distinguish four separate processes which together destroyed the Republic and which led in three separate chronological phases to the events of 1933.

In the first place, the Republic was badly weakened by the chronic economic and social crisis. The scope for building on the fundamental compromises of 1918–19 gradually diminished. This *destabilization* placed a severe strain on the Republic, though it was not sufficient to destroy it, as the crisis of 1923 proved.

Secondly, in the course of the 1920s the popular legitimacy of the Republic, never secure at the best of times, underwent a steady decline. The Republic's *loss of legitimacy* reflected the collapse of the fundamental compromises of 1918; it was the expression of a widespread lack of faith in the future, in both a personal and societal sense; and it was symbolized, notably, by the electoral attrition of the moderate liberal and conservative parties, though the split in the labour movement also prevented the left from functioning as an effective political force. The loss of legitimacy was already alarmingly far advanced by 1930, when the international economic crisis set in: the Weimar constitution had become unworkable and unwanted. Nevertheless, this process too was insufficient in itself to bring about the Republic's downfall.

A third necessary condition, then, was the avowed determination of the old anti-republican élites to destroy Weimar's already battered parliamentary and democratic institutions. The *reversion to authoritarianism*, the policy pursued by the presidential cabinets of the years 1930–32, finally brought the political and social order of Weimar to an end. Moves towards a conservative and authoritarian system were, of course, a common response in Europe to the crises of the 1930s, but the German version of this response was distinctive in two ways. Nowhere else in Europe had both traditional values and new political and social reforming ideas been so called into question as they had been in post-war Germany; and nowhere else had public life become so politicized and polarized. The one phenomenon reduced the chances of an accommodation between liberals and conservatives and threatened the very survival of the fundamental compromises of 1918. The other deprived the old élites of the mass support they needed in their search for a return to authoritarianism, while at the same time ruling out the possibility of any authoritarian solution that did not rest on such support. Finding themselves in an impasse of their own making, the old élites plumped for an alliance with Hitler.

Fourthly, even Hitler's broad-based *totalitarian movement* was not capable of toppling the Republic on its own, despite the fact that it had attained an astonishing level of political dynamism and had become the voice for the anxieties of a good one-third of Germans as the crisis deepened. By the end of 1932 the NSDAP had plainly reached the limits of its electoral potential and was showing signs of falling back once again. It was only thanks to the consortium of élite representatives which became the new government on 30 January 1933 that Hitler was given the chance of translating the destructive dynamism of the National Socialist movement into the *Machtergreifung*, the seizure of power.

Freedom died, if not by inches, then in three main chronological phases. In the years leading up to 1930 an increasing number of republicans disavowed the Republic, and the fundamental compromises of 1918 evaporated. This was the end of 'Weimar' proper. After 1930 the presidential regimes destroyed what was left of the republican constitution and created a power vacuum which their own moves towards authoritarianism proved unable to fill. Any feasible alternative to the Weimar 'system' was thereby also extinguished. In 1933, finally, the new governing élite consortium, in partnership with the National Socialist movement, released the destructive energies of the 'Third Reich'. The German crisis had become the German catastrophe; its ultimate result was to be the devastation of Europe.

*

ANTI-FASCISM PARALYSED

The National Socialist mass movement had grown by recruiting followers from all social groups and regions within Germany, but it had made no substantial inroads either into Catholic society and the Centre Party or into the organized labour movement represented by the SPD and the KPD. In the Reichstag elections of 6 November 1932 the Centre (and BVP) retained 15 per cent of the vote and the KPD and SPD 37 per cent. In other words, in the last free elections held before Hitler assumed power the proportion of the electorate that remained immune to the appeal of both National Socialism and the right-wing radicalism of the German nationalists still constituted a numerical majority.[5]

There was, of course, no prospect that this statistical majority could be converted into a unified political force. The KPD and SPD were embroiled in bitter fratricidal conflict, the KPD being engaged in no less implacable a struggle against the Republic than were the anti-democratic forces on the far right. The Centre had become ground down by the troubles of the Brüning and Papen governments – both Chancellors, it should be remembered, were from the Catholic camp – and had gradually slipped into a more authoritarian frame of mind, so that it no longer had the energy to offer resistance.

Many workers, all the same, put up a fight against the NSDAP, and to some effect, even though they had no chance of ultimate victory.[6] During 1932 an assault by the SA against working-class residential districts, club premises and workers' organizations and meetings was repulsed. The political campaigns of the KPD and SPD at least had the result of immunizing their rank-and-file supporters against the blandishments of the National Socialists.

Yet the anti-fascist opposition on the left had telling weaknesses. In general, because its thinking rested on an economistic Marxist tradition, the left underestimated the dynamism of the NSDAP, its ideological radicalism and its relatively high degree of political autonomy. There were some acute analysts among the socialist intelligentsia who took the new phenomenon of National Socialism seriously and whose insights remain instructive today, but they did not find a wide hearing within their parties, where the day-to-day flurries of election campaigning understandably took precedence.

A more decisive weakness, however, was that the long-term strategy and short-term tactics of both the KPD and the SPD were strait jacketed by the effects of the period of revolution and the subsequent years of internecine hostility. In accordance with the line laid down by the Comintern in 1928, the KPD devoted most of its energies to combating 'social fascism'. This inflationary extension of the term 'fascism' had the consequence, temporarily at least, of relegating the real enemy, the NSDAP, to the background. The SPD, because of the competition from the Communists on its left flank, was unable to espouse a moderate policy for dealing with the political and economic crisis. Each party refused to contemplate joint action with its rival, and the few hesitant attempts that were made to overcome the mutual antagonism – at moments of acute crisis such as 20 July 1932 or 30 January 1933, for example – were quickly reversed.

The trade unions, likewise, were paralysed as an anti-fascist force. The employers' campaign, falling membership and high unemployment had all reduced their capacity for action, and the weapon of the general strike, which had been wielded successfully back in 1920, had become of questionable usefulness.

The formation of the Hitler cabinet on 30 January 1933 provided the labour movement with a last chance of issuing a call for collective action, however slim the prospects of success. But by now the leaders of the KPD, the SPD and the General German Trade Union Federation had become resigned to the outcome. Separately, each section of the movement had proper and legitimate reasons for holding back; once the moment for action had gone, however, the initiative had passed to other hands, where it was to remain.

30 JANUARY 1933

By the end of 1932 it had become clear that a deal between the governing politicians, the old social élites and Hitler's NSDAP was possible. The political establishment lacked sufficient popular backing to be able to continue to govern on its own, and the NSDAP had reason to fear a haemorrhage of its own supporters if it did not deliver the promised spoils of victory soon.

In addition, the political clique surrounding the Reich President, while not abandoning its goal of containing Hitler, now dropped its hitherto crucial objection to a Hitler chancellorship in the hope that Hitler would be 'framed in' by reliable right-wing leaders. Papen as Vice-Chancellor, Hugenberg as Economics Minister, Blomberg as Reichswehr Minister and leader of the Stahlhelm and Seldte as Minister of Labour would, it was believed, be strong enough to neutralize the National Socialists Frick and Goering, who became Minister of the Interior and Minister without Portfolio respectively.

Hindenburg offered the 'government of national concentration' that was formed on 30 January 1933 the opportunity of calling new elections to obtain a parliamentary majority. The machinery of state would be put at the government's disposal and a generous flow of funds would be assured. In so doing, Hindenburg set in train the 'national revolution' which, in the space of a few months, was to see the complete collapse of the old politicians' scenario. Instead of being 'tamed' by being given a share of power, Hitler would demand all power for himself.

In point of fact, the consortium of élite interests that had now been formed by industry, the army and the NSDAP was little affected by this revolution. Sharing the aims of destroying the labour movement, setting up a 'leadership state' and pressing forward with rearmament, these institutions became the central components of the new power structure of the 'Third Reich' and played a central part in its future evolution. The months of the *Machtergreifung* were dominated by the use of terror to eliminate the real or alleged 'enemies' of National Socialism. Social Democrats, Communists, Jews and loyal democrats were imprisoned, tortured, murdered and sent into exile. The terror was accompanied by a wave of *Gleichschaltungen* (measures of 'co-ordination'), both imposed and self-imposed, and also by a surging new sense of national reawakening, now extending to an active majority as people came to believe that the removal of the last vestiges of the Republic and the creation of the promised 'Volksgemeinschaft' would bring an end to the protracted economic and social crisis.

Only seven years were to lie between the final crisis of the Weimar economy and state and the outbreak of a second world war. In the space of these seven years the National Socialist movement advanced from offering a totalitarian pledge to banish the discontents of modernity to that unique combination of destructiveness and moral indifference which led to the 'final solution'.[7]

It would certainly be wrong, in the light of what we now know about the machinery of murder that came to embody the true meaning of National Socialism, to argue that those who were responsible for the destruction of the Weimar Republic after 1930 and for the transfer of power to the National Socialists in 1933 were, by the same token, directly responsible for all the Nazi crimes that were to follow. Nevertheless, whatever emphasis one chooses to place on the facts, it is undeniable that after the nation's political and social leaders had cast off the republican institutions and the democratic settlement of 1918 like a worn-out garment, Germany then consciously decided, in an attempt to find a way out of the crisis it had itself deliberately exacerbated, to give a free hand to the destructive force of National Socialism.

It has often been concluded from this that the collapse of the Republic and the assumption of power by the National Socialists are the supreme and culminating demonstration of the existence of a 'deutscher Sonderweg', a 'special German path of development': that is, of a process of modernization peculiarly burdened by traditionalism, illiberality and a yearning for powerful authority. On closer consideration, however, it is clear that even the anti-republican governments' abandonment of parliamentary democracy was not so much a reversion to outmoded tradition as an attempt to combine technocratic efficiency with authoritarian methods of social control in order to resolve the tensions that had been created by modernization and heightened by the chronic crises of the 1920s. The growth of mass political movements and the politicization of rival interest groups had advanced much too far for any purely reactionary solution to these problems to have been feasible. If the Brüning and Papen regimes had been successful, there might perhaps be some justification for enlisting their traditionalism as evidence in favour of the hypothesis of a 'Sonderweg'. But their very failure shows that the dynamic thrust of the process of modernization could no longer be held in check. Hitler, for his part, succeeded in creating a broad-based totalitarian movement by mobilizing the masses whom the crisis of modernity had alarmed into political visibility. The tensions of a mass society which had come so dramatically to a head at the end of the 1920s could, in fact, be resolved only in one of two ways: either by democracy or by totalitarianism. The historical responsibility which must be borne by the old élites that governed Germany between 1930 and 1932 is, therefore, likewise twofold: first, that they repudiated democracy; and then, when the authoritarian road proved to be a dead end, that they threw in their lot with Hitler.

VI. REVIEW: THE CRISIS OF CLASSICAL MODERNITY

═══

The concept of progress is founded on the notion of catastrophe. The fact that 'things move on' *is* the catastrophe.

Walter Benjamin

1. It is unfair to assess the history of the Weimar Republic solely in the light of its ending: that is, in light of the fact that it issued into the 'German catastrophe'. None the less, any attempt to explain the history of Weimar must of necessity include an analysis not of the National Socialist dictatorship itself, but of the conditions that made such a dictatorship possible. Weimar has its own history, which must be judged on its own terms, but it is also proper to judge Weimar against the history that followed its downfall.

2. The years between 1918 and 1933 fall within two independently definable historical periods, each extraordinarily dramatic in its own terms. They form, on the one hand, the nucleus of the period of world war and world crisis that stretched from 1914 to 1945. The feverish succession of events that marked this period, the vast convulsions and the violent changes in political culture and society, were not incidental to it but of its essence. They generated a deep-seated sense of unease and disorientation, an awareness that the conditions underlying everyday life and experience were in flux, and a questioning of many inherited assumptions, such as those concerning the relationships between the sexes and the generations. The hallmark of the period was uncertainty.

3. At the same time, the years of the Weimar Republic constitute a crucial phase, set into greater relief by crisis, of the period of social and cultural innovation beginning around the turn of the century which we call the era of 'classical modernity'. It was during the Weimar years that the main features of the contemporary world took shape

and that modern ideas and movements in social policy, technology, the sciences, the humanities, art, music, architecture and literature achieved their breakthrough. In less than a decade and a half virtually every social and intellectual initiative we think of as modern was formulated or put into practice. And yet, even as this happened, classical modernity was also moving rapidly towards its own point of crisis. No sooner had modern ideas been put into effect than they came under attack, were revoked or began to collapse.

4. Germany's experiment in modernity was conducted under the least propitious circumstances. For over thirty years the world economic and political system was in a state of structural crisis, the lowest points of which were the Great Depression of 1929–33 and, later, the Second World War of 1939–45. The exceptionally severe check to Germany's economic growth that followed the First World War reduced the scope for compromises and trade-offs which would have made the Weimar Republic's innovations in politics and welfare provision acceptable to a wide range of groups within the country. With little or no growth in wealth to distribute, or with real reductions in living standards having to be carried out, disputes over wages and benefits became increasingly embittered and social fragmentation and polarization became more pronounced. Society crystallized into opposing camps, each of which was incapable of working with the others and none of which was capable of sustaining effective political action on its own. The regression from reform to political stalemate and, finally, to the undoing of such gains as had been achieved was particularly evident in the field of social and economic policy, though that was not the only example. In 1919 the welfare state was, for the first time, enshrined in the constitution, and in the following years reformist legislation was introduced dealing with important matters ranging from education to unemployment insurance. And yet as soon as these reforms began to be implemented in full, problems and external obstacles started to accumulate, and there were calls for the 'limits of the welfare state' to be recognized. The world economic crisis, when it came, served as little more than a pretext for work to start on dismantling the system of welfare provision. There was a similar evolution in economic and industrial policy. In the immediate post-war

period there were several important innovations: the *Arbeitsgemeinschaft* agreement, moves towards co-determination in industry and the creation of a state-guaranteed system of collective wage bargaining. But by the time that the inflation had been contained, or even before, the scope for further reform had narrowed here too, and the premise on which the compromise settlement of 1918 had rested was beginning to crumble. Bitter disputes over wages induced the employers to go on to the offensive against the 'trade union state' and the welfare state; working-class wages and living standards were cut. Under the remorseless pressure of the economic crisis, the basic social compromise on which the Republic had been grounded had become the principal threat to the Republic's continued existence.

5. The years before the outbreak of the First World War had already been marked by the challenges of modernization, by a questioning of previously undisputed assumptions about society and culture, and by a popular mood oscillating between enthusiasm and anxiety, hopes of national reawakening and fears of national extinction. After the war these phenomena took centre stage, stripped of the familiar reassuring veils of national mythology which had still disguised them during the Wilhelmine era. The world of the new could no longer be ignored, and it was not an entirely attractive sight. The Janus-faced nature of the process of modernization became a fact of everyday life; it dominated cultural discourse. In a breathless whirl of change the Weimar Republic tried out every cultural fashion that modernity had to offer, scarcely having time to don one idea or style before discarding it for the next.

6. The 'golden twenties' were seen, at the time, as the culmination of a process of rationalization and efficiency, not only in technology and the economy, but in the social structure and in people's daily lives. A substitute religion of social and technological utilitarianism and a euphoric faith in progress inspired a cult of 'Americanism', but optimism was dispelled by the brute realities of the economic crisis. The dream of modernity set off searching and harsh counter-reactions, which sprang in part from a desire to go back to traditional values and assumptions, but were partly inspired, too, by prefigurations of a

critique of modernity we can now call 'post-modern'. This twofold reaction explains the unusual ideological hybrid that was the 'conservative revolution'.

7. The Weimar Republic was born out of national defeat. Whatever form the peace treaty might have taken, the millenarian hopes which the First World War had aroused were bound to have been disappointed. That, rather than the severe yet ultimately tolerable terms of the peace settlement, was the root cause of the revanchist Versailles myth. Given this starting-point, the achievements of the policy of rapprochement that was pursued between 1923 and 1929 can scarcely be exaggerated. They created the basis for a modern internationalist foreign policy committed to political co-operation and economic integration. But it was precisely the modern aspects of the policy that became the inevitable casualty when the world economy collapsed and policies of autarky and national self-interest took root among the ruins. The persistence of the mystique of nationalist integration and the desire to reassert Germany's position as a great power also helped inspire the revanchist shift in foreign policy that began in 1929–30 as the international and political crisis set in.

8. The Weimar experiment in democracy may have been an 'unfinished revolution', but the significance of the experiment should not be minimized. Every revolution is an unfinished revolution. On a sober assessment the constitutionalist movement, which carried forward the parliamentary traditions of Social Democracy, liberalism and political Catholicism, can be said to have achieved all of its important goals, at least in a preliminary sense. Its aspirations were enshrined in the fundamental compromise settlement reached in 1918–19. The Weimar constitution established an open, pluralistic framework and looked ahead to a wide-ranging programme of domestic and social reform, the details of which were to be fleshed out later. The compromise agreement between trade unions and employers on social and industrial policy survived the period of demobilization, though the ending of the inflation took away the economic room for manoeuvre and accommodation that was needed if it was to be sustained. Altogether, what undermined the Weimar experiment was the continuous shrink-

ing of freedom of manoeuvre in the social and economic spheres that occurred not only during the domestic and external post-war crises but during the years of relative stability in the mid-1920s. A less 'unfinished' revolution would have had to battle against the same difficulties. The crisis-ridden nature of the whole period prevented the new political system and welfare structure from becoming consolidated and gaining real legitimacy in the eyes of the German people. It is all very well to take the political parties to task for being insufficiently prepared to compromise in the interests of democracy, but the material and economic basis for compromise was not available in the first place. The proliferation of ideological and interest-group splinter parties merely reflected the profound divisions within society itself. The fundamental compromises of 1918–19 were undermined rather than reinforced, and the parties to the settlement eventually retreated from the disintegrating structure of the Republic, leaving the old élites to bring the condemned ruin tumbling to the ground.

9. The Weimar Republic was destroyed by four distinct processes, each of which might well have been withstood on its own.

– From a starting-point of structural socio-economic crisis, the continuous shrinking of the economic room for manoeuvre that was needed to strengthen the settlement of 1918–19 led to a fundamental *destabilizing* of the Republic's political and social system.

– The steady retreat from the original settlement also played a part in bringing about the new Republic's *loss of legitimacy*. Even before the onset of the world slump, the political system of the Republic had reached a point of crisis, evidenced particularly by the sustained decline in support for the old liberal and conservative parties. As the centre-right parties declined, they were driven into increasingly bitter competition with the Social Democrats, who in turn were prevented from acting as an effective force by the presence of the Communists on their left.

– The *reversion to authoritarianism* which the old élites hoped to effect at the start of the 1930s was an attempt to undo the compromise settlement of 1918 and to restore the power relations of the Bismarckian

Reich. But while the presidential cabinets were strong enough to destroy the Weimar constitutional order, they were too weak to cope with the mass movements and mounting politicization that had meanwhile transformed German society. They failed to halt the defection of centre-right voters to the National Socialists, and without mass support their own position was doomed to become untenable.

– The *National Socialist movement* benefited in two ways from the failure of the old élites and the traditional liberal and conservative institutions that had supported them. First, the protracted crisis of the years 1930–33 gave the Nazi movement a prime opportunity to present itself as a dynamic, modern totalitarian mass party. Secondly, at the beginning of 1933 the Nazis were handed over the keys of power by the old élites who had been all too successful in destroying the Republic but too feeble to restore the pre-war order. All other political alternatives having been exhausted, a final, extreme alternative presented itself, and was accepted.

10. Each of the various ingredients of the crisis in Germany was also to be found in other modern industrial societies at the time. The German crisis was, in that sense, a representative one. But the process of modernization took a more brutal, uncompromising form in Germany in the twenties than it did in other countries. The glamour of modernization exerted a special fascination on the Germans, but its dark side, too, had a profound effect on lives that were also shadowed by war, military defeat, a loss of confidence in old values, the bewilderments of hyperinflation and the blight of world recession. The way in which the separate ingredients of crisis converged to form a single comprehensive crisis of political legitimacy and social values was unique to Germany in the period. It seemed to Germans that there was no sure path leading out of this all-embracing crisis. The familiar processes of social and political action offered no solution, nor did the individual's pursuit of his private destiny. Comparative statistics of suicides provide dramatic evidence of this helpless state of mind. In 1932 there were 85 suicides per million inhabitants in Great Britain, 133 in the United States and 155 in France. In Germany there were 260.

11. There is no need to invoke the hypothesis of a 'deutscher Sonderweg' in order to explain why Hitler's accession to power was
possible. On the contrary, the *Machtergreifung* of 1933 occurred not
because the traditional élites remained excessively influential, but
because they had become critically weaker as the masses had become
increasingly politicized. What was 'special' about Germany between
1918 and 1932 was, on the one hand, the sudden and uncompromising
manner in which modernization arrived and, on the other, the simultaneous presence of several different elements of crisis. It was a unique
conjuncture, and yet one which at the same time demonstrates how
easily the processes of modernization which we are accustomed to
regarding as part of our normal experience can tip over into catastrophe. To use a metaphor of our own times, the normal operating
state of a nuclear power station is certainly not the same as the 'worst
case' of a melt-down, but the 'worst case' arises as the result of a simple
succession of critical events that represents one possible outcome of
the normal operating state. In a similar way, the crisis in Germany at
the start of the 1930s made the 'German catastrophe' possible because
it set off an escalation of the contradictory pressures that were inherent
in classical modernity.

POSTSCRIPT

Borrowing the three famous categories of historical writing proposed
by Nietzsche in his essay 'The Use and Disadvantage of History for
Life', we can offer some final thoughts on the significance of the history
of the Weimar Republic.

From the *monumentalist* point of view, Weimar may serve as an
archetypal instance of the history of democracy: a compendium of
democracy's virtues as well as its vices. The history of Weimar can
encourage us to refine and elaborate our own traditions of democracy,
and can deepen our understanding of the range of democratic pre-
cedents to be found in the past. At the same time, we must also be
alert to the danger of excessive ritual invocation of the past in the
day-to-day struggles of politics in the present. 'Weimar' may easily
degenerate into a catch-all term of political abuse.

From the *critical* point of view, the history of Weimar demonstrates that the methods of democratic compromise are fragile, that the process of modernization is rife with contradictions, that normality can contain the seeds of catastrophe and that hopes and deals count for little in the face of straitened material circumstances. And yet a preoccupation with crisis and catastrophe may also blind us to the fact that people survived and that life went on. The dangers of an exclusively critical view are cynicism and fatalism: against them, we should stress the value conferred by any new opportunities – large and small, taken and untaken – for personal growth and social change.

From the *antiquarian* point of view, the 1920s, in assuming the features of classical modernity, also reveal to us the emergence of the world we inhabit today. They show us a society on the threshold between what has since become our familiar present and what has turned into a strange and shadowy past – a society which shared our own hopes and anxieties, but one whose fantasies and phobias also present us with a bewildering caricature of what is now our normal everyday life. And yet, even in this respect, the shadowy figures that look out at us from the tarnished mirror of history are – in the final analysis – ourselves.

CHRONOLOGY

===

1914

4 August — Reichstag parties approve war credits; Wilhelm II announces 'Burgfrieden' (party 'truce')

1916

29 August — Hindenburg and Ludendorff form new Supreme Army Command

1917

19 July — Peace Resolution passed by Reichstag (SPD, Centre and left liberals)

1918

3 March — Peace Treaty of Brest-Litovsk with Soviet Russia

29 September — Supreme Command accepts defeat and calls for an armistice and parliamentary government

4 October (–9 November) — Prince Max von Baden Reich Chancellor (government includes SPD, Centre and liberals)

28 October — October reforms: constitutional monarchy established

3–9 November — Sailors' revolt in Kiel; soldiers' and workers' councils (or soviets; *Räte*) spread

9 November	Proclamation of the Republic
10 November	'Council of People's Representatives' formed by SPD and USPD representatives; pact agreed between Ebert and military leadership under Groener
11 November	Armistice signed
15 November	Agreement between heavy industry and trade unions to form a *Zentralarbeitsgemeinschaft*
16–20 December	Reich Congress of Councils meets in Berlin
29 December	USPD leaves Council of People's Representatives

1919

1 January	Founding congress of KPD
5–12 January	'Spartacus uprising'
19 January	Elections to National Assembly
11 February	Friedrich Ebert Reich President
13 February (–20 June)	Scheidemann (SPD) cabinet: Weimar Coalition (SPD, Centre, DDP)
7 April–2 May	Munich *Räterepublik* (Soviet Republic)
21 June (–26 March 1920)	Bauer (SPD) cabinet: Weimar Coalition (SPD, Centre, DDP)
28 June	Versailles Peace Treaty signed
11 August	Weimar constitution signed

1920

| 13–17 March | Kapp putsch and general strike |
| March/April | Fighting between 'Red Ruhr Army' and Freikorps/Reichswehr |

19 March	US Senate fails to ratify Versailles Treaty
27 March (–8 June)	Müller (SPD) cabinet I: Weimar Coalition (SPD, Centre, DDP)
6 June	Reichstag elections: Weimar Coalition defeated
25 June (–4 May 1921)	Fehrenbach (Centre) cabinet: Centre, DDP, DVP
4–7 December	Left wing of USPD joins KPD

1921

20 March	Plebiscite in Upper Silesia
2 May	Fighting breaks out in Upper Silesia
5 May	London ultimatum on German reparations payments
10 May (–14 November 1922)	Wirth (Centre) cabinets I and II: SPD, Centre, DDP
26 August	Matthias Erzberger murdered

1922

16 April	Germany and Soviet Russia sign Rapallo Treaty during world economic conference at Genoa
24 June	Walther Rathenau murdered
18 July	Law for the Protection of the Republic
12 November (–12 August 1923)	Cuno (non-party) cabinet: Centre, DDP, DVP

1923

| 11 January | France occupies Ruhr |
| 13 August | Stresemann (DVP) cabinet I: Great Coalition until |

(–23 November)	3 November (SPD, Centre, DDP, DVP); II: rump cabinet (Centre, DDP, DVP)
26 September	'Passive resistance' in Ruhr called off
22 October	Reichswehr units moved into Saxony; attempted Communist uprising in Hamburg
9 November	Abortive Hitler putsch in Munich
15 November	Rentenmark introduced to end inflation
30 November (–15 December 1924)	Marx (Centre) cabinets I and II (Stresemann remains Foreign Minister until 1929): Centre (BVP), DDP, DVP
30 November	Dawes Commission on reparations established

1924

9 April	Dawes Plan published
29 August	Dawes Plan legislation approved by Reichstag
7 December	Radical parties lose ground in second Reichstag elections of the year

1925

15 January (–12 May 1926)	Luther (non-party) cabinets I and II: *Bürgerblock* (Centre, BVP, DDP, DVP [DNVP])
27 February	NSDAP refounded
28 February	Death of Reich President Ebert
26 April	Hindenburg elected Reich President
14 July	Evacuation of Ruhr
5–16 October	Locarno conference

1926

12 May	Luther cabinet resigns over 'flag dispute'

16 May (–12 June 1928)	Marx (Centre) cabinets III (Centre, BVP, DDP, DVP) and IV (Centre, BVP, DVP, DNVP)
20 June	Referendum on expropriation of princely families
8 September	Germany becomes a member of League of Nations
17 September	Stresemann and Briand hold discussions in Thoiry
8 October	General von Seeckt dismissed as chief of Army Command

1927

16 July	Labour Exchanges and Unemployment Insurance Law

1928

20 May	Reichstag elections (gains by working-class parties, losses by conservatives and liberals)
28 June (–27 March 1930)	Müller (SPD) cabinet II: Great Coalition (SPD, Centre, BVP, DDP, DVP)
October	Ruhr iron and steel dispute: mass lock-out
20 October	Alfred Hugenberg becomes head of DNVP
8 December	Prelate Kaas becomes head of Centre Party

1929

7 June	Young Plan to bring about final settlement of reparations is drawn up
3 October	Death of Stresemann
24 October	'Black Thursday' on New York Stock Exchange; beginning of world economic crisis
22 December	Referendum to reject Young Plan fails

1930

12 March	Young Plan ratified by Reichstag
27 March	Müller cabinet resigns
30 March (–30 May 1932)	Brüning (Centre) cabinets I and II: presidential regime
30 June	Evacuation of Rhineland completed
16 July	Reichstag dissolved
14 September	Reichstag elections (gains by NSDAP)

1931

19 March	Plan for German–Austrian customs union announced
11 May	Austrian Kreditanstalt collapses
20 June	Hoover moratorium
13 July	Banking crisis in Germany

1932

2 February	Geneva disarmament conference opens
10 April	Hindenburg re-elected Reich President
13 April	SA and SS banned (until 16 June)
1 June (–17 November)	Papen cabinet: presidential regime
16 June–9 July	Lausanne conference: reparations ended
20 July	Prussian government deposed by Papen
31 July	Reichstag elections: NSDAP largest party
6 November	Reichstag elections: NSDAP loses ground for the first time

3 December (–28 January 1933)	Schleicher cabinet: presidential regime

1933

30 January (–30 April 1945)	Hitler cabinet
28 February	Emergency decree 'for the Protection of the People and the State': basic constitutional rights suspended
23 March	Enabling Law

NOTES

═══

Preface

1. E. Kolb, *Die Weimarer Republik*, Munich, 1984 (trans. as *The Weimar Republic*, London, 1988); cf. also the survey by H. Schulze, *Weimar, Deutschland 1917–1933*, Berlin, 1982; and the recent contributions to *Deutsche Geschichte der neuesten Zeit* by: H. Möller, *Weimar. Die unvollendete Demokratie*, Munich, 1985; F. Blaich, *Der Schwarze Freitag. Inflation und Wirtschaftskrise*, Munich, 1985; M. Broszat, *Die Machtergreifung. Der Aufstieg der NSDAP und die Zerstörung der Weimarer Republik*, Munich, 1984 (trans. as *Hitler and the Collapse of Weimar Germany*, Leamington Spa, Hamburg and New York, 1987); P. Krüger, *Versailles. Deutsche Außenpolitik zwischen Revisionismus und Friedenssicherung*, Munich, 1986; C. Hepp, *Avantgarde. Moderne Kunst, Kulturkritik und Reformbewegungen nach der Jahrhundertwende*, Munich, 1987.
2. For a summary, see H. Grebing, *Der 'deutsche Sonderweg' in Europa 1806–1945. Eine Kritik*, Stuttgart, 1986.
3. J. Habermas, *Eine Art Schadensabwicklung*, Frankfurt, 1987; *'Historikerstreit'. Die Dokumentation der Kontroverse um die Einzigartigkeit der nationalsozialistischen Judenvernichtung*, Munich, 1987.
4. D. Peukert, 'Neuere Alltagsgeschichte und historische Anthropologie', in H. Süssmuth (ed.), *Historische Anthropologie*, Göttingen, 1984, pp. 57–72; L. Niethammer and A. von Plato (eds.), *'Wir kriegen jetzt andere Zeiten'. Auf der Suche nach der Erfahrung des Volkes in nachfaschistischen Ländern*, Berlin, 1985.
5. U. Kluge, *Die deutsche Revolution 1918/1919*, Frankfurt, 1985; G. Jasper, *Die gescheiterte Zähmung. Wege zur Machtergreifung Hitlers 1930–1934*, Frankfurt, 1986.

I. INTRODUCTION

1. The Weimar Republic and the Continuity of German History

1. See H. Heiber, *Die Republik von Weimar*, Munich, 1966, pp. 7ff.
2. Or, alternatively, the revolutionary events that began with the sailors' mutiny at the beginning of November 1918.
3. An example is A. Rosenberg's classic discussion of the 'unfinished revolution'.
4. The staunchest supporter of this thesis is still K. D. Erdmann. See his *Die Weimarer Republik*, vol. 19 of Gebhardt: Handbuch der deutschen Geschichte, Munich, 1973, pp. 28ff.

5. R. Rürup, 'Demokratische Revolution und "dritter Weg". Die deutsche Revolution von 1918/19 in der neueren wissenschaftlichen Diskussion', *Geschichte und Gesellschaft*, 9, 1983, pp. 278–301.

6. This term was used by E. Varga, for example, in the 1920s.

7. Writers of quite different political persuasions have recently argued that the period of stabilization in the mid-1920s was actually the cause of the later crisis. See, for example, K. Borchardt, *Wachstum, Krisen und Handlungsspielraüme der Wirtschaftspolitik*, Göttingen, 1982, esp. pp. 165–205; B. Weisbrod, *Schwerindustrie in der Weimarer Republik. Interessenpolitik zwischen Stabilisierung und Krise*, Wuppertal, 1978.

8. The Great Coalition, made up of Social Democrats, Centre (and BVP), DDP and DVP, collectively approved the new settlement of reparations contained in the Young Plan but then broke up, primarily, over disagreements about rises in unemployment-insurance contributions and cuts in benefits. For a summary of the behaviour of, and choices available to, the SPD and trade unions on this issue, see H. A. Winkler, *Der Schein der Normalität. Arbeiter und Arbeiterbewegung in der Weimarer Republik 1924–1930*, Berlin, 1985, pp. 736–823.

9. For the classic account, see K. D. Bracher, *Die Auflösung der Weimarer Republik* (1955), 6th edn, Königstein, 1978.

10. A classic statement of the contrary view is in W. Conze, 'Die politischen Entscheidungen in Deutschland 1929–1933', in W. Conze and H. Raupach (eds.), *Die Staats- und Wirtschaftskrise des Deutschen Reiches*, Stuttgart, 1967, pp. 176–252.

11. E. Matthias and R. Morsey (eds.), *Das Ende der Parteien 1933* (1960), 2nd edn, Königstein, 1979; K. D. Bracher *et al.*, *Die nationalsozialistische Machtergreifung* (1962), 2nd edn, 3 vols., 1974; see also the bibliography in D. Gessner, *Das Ende der Weimarer Republik*, Darmstadt, 1978.

12. More precisely, state secretary, in imperial terminology.

13. P. Marschalck, *Bevölkerungsgeschichte Deutschlands im 19. und 20. Jahrhundert*, Frankfurt, 1984, pp. 53–71; K. Tenfelde, 'Großstadtjugend in Deutschland vor 1914', *Vierteljahresschrift für Sozial- und Wirtschaftsgeschichte*, 69, 1982, pp. 182–218.

14. These statistical data, and all other data unless otherwise indicated, are taken from D. Petzina *et al.*, *Materialien zur Statistik des Deutschen Reiches 1914–1945, Sozialgeschichtliches Arbeitsbuch III*, Munich, 1978; for longitudinal studies dealing with the question of continuities see W. Conze and R. Lepsius (eds.), *Sozialgeschichte der Bundesrepublik Deutschland. Beiträge zum Kontinuitätsproblem*, Stuttgart, 1983; on questions concerning the city and the countryside, see J. Reulecke, *Geschichte der Urbanisierung in Deutschland*, Frankfurt, 1985, pp. 139–70.

15. The development of the economy as a whole follows the trend of industrial production: see Borchardt, *Wachstum*.

16. ibid., pp. 100–124; D. Petzina, *Die deutsche Wirtschaft in der Zwischenkriegszeit*, Wiesbaden, 1977; B. Lutz, *Der kurze Traum immerwährender Prosperität*, Frankfurt, 1984.

17. R. Wagenführ, 'Die deutsche Industriewirtschaft', *Vierteljahreshefte zur Konjunkturforschung*, Sonderheft 31, Berlin, 1933; E. Varga, *Wirtschaft und Wirtschaftspolitik, Vierteljahresberichte 1922–1939. Konjunktur und Krise in der Analyse der Kommunistischen Internationale*, ed. J. Goldberg, Berlin, 1977.

18. H. Jaeger, 'Generationen in der Geschichte', *Geschichte und Gesellschaft*, 3, 1977, pp. 429–52; M. Doerry, *Übergangsmenschen. Die Mentalität der Wilhelminer und die Krise des Kaiserreiches*, 2 vols., Weinheim, 1986, esp. pp. 30ff; D. Peukert, 'Alltagsleben und Generationserfahrungen von Jugendlichen in der Zwischenkriegszeit', in D. Dowe (ed.), *Jugendprotest und Generationskonflikt in Europa im 20. Jahrhundert*, Bonn, 1986, pp. 139–50.

19. cf. Doerry, *Übergangsmenschen*.

20. R. Wohl, in *The Generation of 1914*, London, 1980, gives a somewhat tighter periodization for purposes of international comparison.

21. T. Koebner *et al.* (eds.), '*Mit uns zieht die neue Zeit*'. *Der Mythos Jugend*, Frankfurt, 1985; M. Martiny, 'Sozialdemokratie und junge Generation am Ende der Weimarer Republik', in W. Luthardt (ed.), *Sozialdemokratische Arbeiterbewegung und Weimarer Republik*, vol. 2, Frankfurt, 1978, pp. 56–117; M. Kater, 'Generationskonflikt als Entwicklungsfaktor in der NS-Bewegung vor 1933', *Geschichte und Gesellschaft*, 11, 1985, pp. 217–43.

II. NEW DIRECTIONS, 1918–23

2. Old Legacies and a New Start, 1918–19

1. Quoted in R. Rürup, 'Entstehung und Grundlagen der Weimarer Verfassung', in E. Kolb (ed.), *Vom Kaiserreich zur Weimarer Republik*, Cologne, 1972, pp. 218–43; this quotation, p. 230.

2. For this, and for secondary literature not specifically referred to in what follows, see the surveys of research in Rürup, 'Demokratische Revolution', and Kolb, *Weimarer Republik*, esp. pp. 153–63 (trans. pp. 138–47), as well as Kluge, *Revolution 1918/1919*.

3. M. Weber, 'Zur Frage des Friedensschlusses', in *Max-Weber-Gesamtausgabe*, vol. I/15, Tübingen, 1984, pp. 54–67; this quotation, p. 65.

4. S. Miller, *Die Bürde der Macht. Die deutsche Sozialdemokratie 1918–1920*, Düsseldorf, 1978.

5. On the *Zentralarbeitsgemeinschaft*, see chapter 5.

6. For a key study written from a conservative viewpoint, see E. R. Huber, *Deutsche Verfassungsgeschichte seit 1789*, vols. 5–7, Stuttgart, 1978, 1981, 1984; for an incisive review, see Rürup, 'Entstehung'; see also G. Schulz, *Zwischen Demokratie und Diktatur. Verfassungspolitik und Reichsreform in der Weimarer Republik*, vol. I (1919–1930), Berlin, 1963; H. Potthoff, 'Das Weimarer Verfassungswerk und die deutsche Linke',

Archiv für Sozialgeschichte, 12, 1972, pp. 433–83; W. Luthardt, *Sozialdemokratische Verfassungstheorie in der Weimarer Republik*, Opladen, 1986.

7. H. Ehni, *Bollwerk Preußen? Preußen-Regierung, Reich-Länder-Problem und Sozialdemokratie 1928–1932*, Bonn, 1975; H. Schulze, *Otto Braun oder Preußens demokratische Sendung*, Frankfurt, 1977.

8. H. Boldt, 'Der Artikel 48 der Weimarer Reichsverfassung', in M. Stürmer (ed.), *Die Weimarer Republik. Belagerte Civitas*, Königstein, 1980, pp. 288–309.

9. U. Heinemann, *Die verdrängte Niederlage. Politische Öffentlichkeit und Kriegsschuldfrage in der Weimarer Republik*, Göttingen, 1983.

10. A central study is P. Krüger, *Die Außenpolitik der Republik von Weimar*, Darmstadt, 1985; see also A. Hillgruber, ' "Revisionismus" – Kontinuität und Wandel in der Außenpolitik der Weimarer Republik', *Historische Zeitschrift*, 237, 1983, pp. 587–621; and L. Haupts, *Deutsche Friedenspolitik 1918–19*, Düsseldorf, 1976.

11. G. Feldman, 'Economic and Social Problems of the German Demobilisation, 1918–19', *Journal of Modern History*, vol. xxxxvii, pp. 1–23; G. Feldman, 'German Big Business between War and Revolution: The Origins of the Stinnes–Legien Agreement', in G. A. Ritter (ed.), *Entstehung und Entwicklung der modernen Gesellschaft. Festschrift für Hans Rosenberg*, Berlin, 1970, pp. 312–41; W. J. Mommsen (ed.), *Die Organisierung des Friedens: Demobilmachung 1918–1920, Geschichte und Gesellschaft*, 9, 1983, vol. 2.

12. Quoted in Feldman, 'Economic and Social Problems', p. 8.

13. M. Geyer, 'Ein Vorbote des Wohlfahrtstaates. Die Kriegsopferversorgung in Frankreich, Deutschland und Großbritannien nach dem Ersten Weltkrieg', in W. J. Mommsen, *Organisierung*, pp. 230–77.

14. H. A. Winkler, *Von der Revolution zur Stabilisierung. Arbeiter und Arbeiterbewegung in der Weimarer Republik 1918–1924*, Berlin, 1984, pp. 19–26.

3. The Post-War Crisis, 1920–23

1. On the state of recent research, see P. Krüger, 'Das Reparationsproblem der Weimarer Republik in fragwürdiger Sicht. Kritische Überlegungen zur neuesten Forschung', *Vierteljahreshefte für Zeitgeschichte*, 29, 1981, pp. 21–47.

2. A basic study is Krüger, *Außenpolitik*.

3. From the wealth of conflicting accounts of Rapallo, see T. Schieder, 'Die Entstehungsgeschichte des Rapallo-Vertrages', *Historische Zeitschrift*, 204, 1967, pp. 545–609; H. Graml, 'Die Rapallo-Politik im Urteil der westdeutschen Forschung', *Vierteljahreshefte für Zeitgeschichte*, 18, 1970, pp. 366–91; K. Hildebrand, *Das Deutsche Reich und die Sowjetunion im internationalen System 1918–1932*, Wiesbaden, 1977; for a summary, see Krüger, *Außenpolitik*, pp. 132–83.

4. K. Schwabe (ed.), *Die Ruhrkrise 1923. Wendepunkt der internationalen Beziehungen nach dem Ersten Weltkrieg*, Paderborn, 1984.

5. W. Link, *Die amerikanische Stabilisierungspolitik in Deutschland 1921–32*, Düsseldorf, 1970.

6. O. Büsch and G. Feldman (eds.), *Historische Prozesse der deutschen Inflation 1914–1924*, Berlin, 1978; G. Feldman *et al.* (eds.), *Die deutsche Inflation. Eine Zwischenbilanz*, Berlin, 1982; G. Feldman *et al.* (eds.), *Die Erfahrung der Inflation im internationalen Zusammenhang und Vergleich*, Berlin, 1984; C. Holtfrerich, *Die deutsche Inflation 1914–1923*, Berlin, 1980 (trans. as *The German Inflation 1914–1923: Causes and Effects in International Perspective*, Berlin and New York, 1986), which also contains the data on wholesale price indices cited below.

7. G. Feldman (ed.), *Die Nachwirkungen der Inflation auf die deutsche Geschichte 1924–1933*, Munich, 1985; C.-D. Krohn, *Stabilisierung und ökonomische Interessen. Die Finanzpolitik des deutschen Reiches 1923–1927*, Düsseldorf, 1974; H. Mommsen *et al.* (eds.), *Industrielles System und politische Entwicklung in der Weimarer Republik*, Düsseldorf, 1974.

8. M. Schneider, 'Deutsche Gesellschaft in Krieg und Währungskrise 1914–1924. Ein Jahrzehnt Forschungen zur Inflation', *Archiv für Sozialgeschichte*, 26, 1986, pp. 301–19.

9. G. Feldman and H. Homburg, *Industrie und Inflation*, Hamburg, 1977; P. Wulf, *Hugo Stinnes. Wirtschaft und Politik 1918–1924*, Stuttgart, 1979.

10. W. Abelshauser, 'Verelendung der Handarbeiter? Zur sozialen Lage der deutschen Arbeiter in der großen Inflation der frühen zwanziger Jahre', in H. Mommsen and W. Schulze (eds.), *Vom Elend der Handarbeit*, Stuttgart, 1981, pp. 445–76.

11. Ignaz Wrobel (i.e. Kurt Tucholsky), 'Preußische Studenten', *Die Weltbühne*, 15, 1919, pp. 532–6.

12. For a survey of militarism, official and unofficial, see the contributions in K. J. Müller and E. Opitz (eds.), *Militär und Militarismus in der Weimarer Republik*, Düsseldorf, 1978; cf. also H. Schulze, *Freikorps und Republik 1918–1920*, Boppard, 1969; on the attitude of the SPD, see Miller, *Bürde*, and Winkler, *Von der Revolution*.

13. J. Dülffer and K. Holl (eds.), *Bereit zum Krieg. Kriegsmentalität im wilhelminischen Deutschland 1890–1914*, Göttingen, 1986; K. Vondung (ed.), *Das wilhelminische Bildungsbürgertum*, Göttingen, 1976; G. Eley, *Reshaping the German Right: Radical Nationalism and Political Change after Bismarck*, New Haven, 1980.

14. E. Lucas, *Märzrevolution 1920*, 3 vols., Frankfurt, 1970, 1973, 1978; J. Gorlas and D. Peukert (eds.), *Ruhrkampf 1920*, Essen, 1987.

15. W. Angress, *Die Kampfzeit der KPD 1921–1923*, Düsseldorf, 1973; S. Koch-Baumgarten, *Aufstand der Avantgarde. Die Märzaktion der KPD 1921*, Frankfurt, 1986; for a survey of research, see H. Weber, *Kommunismus in Deutschland 1918–1945*, Darmstadt, 1983, pp. 74–96.

16. E. Gumbel, *Verschwörer. Zur Geschichte und Soziologie der deutschen nationalistischen Geheimbünde 1918–1924* (1924), Heidelberg, 1979.

17. K. Prümm, *Die Literatur des soldatischen Nationalismus der 20er Jahre 1918–1933*, 2 vols., Kronberg, 1974; K. Theweleit, *Männerphantasien*, 2 vols., Frankfurt, 1977,

1978 (trans. as *Male Fantasies*, 2 vols., Cambridge, 1987, 1989); U. Lohalm, *Völkischer Radikalismus. Die Geschichte des Deutschvölkischen Schutz- and Trutz-Bundes 1919– 1923*, Hamburg, 1970; J. Striesow, *Die Deutschnationale Volkspartei und die Völkisch-Radikalen 1918–1922*, 2 vols., Frankfurt, 1981; for a very vivid picture of the Bavarian situation, see the novel by Lion Feuchtwanger, *Erfolg* (1930), 2 vols., Frankfurt, 1979.
18. For international comparisons, key works include C. Maier, *Recasting Bourgeois Europe: Stabilization in France, Germany and Italy in the Decade after World War I*, Princeton, 1975; D. Aldcroft, *From Versailles to Wall Street 1919–1929*, Harmondsworth, 1977; G. Ziebura, *Weltwirtschaft und Weltpolitik 1922/24–1931. Zwischen Rekonstruktion und Zusammenbruch*, Frankfurt, 1984.

III. MODERNIZATION AND ITS TENSIONS

1. For a critical survey, see H.-U. Wehler. *Modernisierungstheorie und Geschichte*, Göttingen, 1975.
2. Grebing, *Der 'deutsche Sonderweg'*.
3. G. Feldman, 'The Weimar Republic: A Problem of Modernisation?', *Archiv für Sozialgeschichte*, 26, 1986, pp. 1–26.

4. Generation Gaps and Emancipatory Struggles

1. W. Köllmann, 'Bevölkerungsentwicklung in der Weimarer Republik', in H. Mommsen *et al., Industrielles System*, pp. 76–83; Marschalck, *Bevölkerungsgeschichte*, pp. 53–74.
2. Koebner *et al., 'Mit uns zieht die neue Zeit'*; D. Dowe, *Jugendprotest*; M. Mitterauer, *Sozialgeschichte der Jugend*, Frankfurt, 1986; I. Götz von Olenhusen, *Jugendreich – Gottesreich – Deutsches Reich. Junge Generation, Religion und Politik 1928–1933*, Cologne, 1987.
3. J. Reulecke, 'Bürgerliche Sozialreformer und Arbeiterjugend im Kaiserreich', *Archiv für Sozialgeschichte*, 22, 1982, pp. 299–329; D. Peukert, *Grenzen der Sozialdisziplinierung. Aufstieg und Krise der deutschen Jugendfürsorge 1878–1932*, Cologne, 1986.
4. H. Giesecke, *Vom Wandervogel bis zur Hitlerjugend. Jugendarbeit zwischen Politik und Pädagogik*, Munich, 1981.
5. D. Peukert, *Jugend zwischen Krieg und Krise. Lebenswelten von Arbeiterjungen in der Weimarer Republik*, Cologne, 1987; R. Sieder, *Sozialgeschichte der Familie*, Frankfurt, 1987.
6. G. Huck (ed.), *Sozialgeschichte der Freizeit*, Wuppertal, 1980; Deutscher Werkbund (ed.), *Schock und Schöpfung. Jugendästhetik im 20. Jahrhundert*, Neuwied, 1986.
7. D. Peukert, 'Die Erwerbslosigkeit junger Arbeiter in der Weltwirtschaftskrise in

Deutschland 1929–1933', *Vierteljahresschrift für Sozial- und Wirtschaftsgeschichte*, 72, 1985, pp. 305–28 (trans. as 'The Lost Generation: Youth Unemployment at the End of the Weimar Republic', in R. J. Evans and D. Geary [eds.], *The German Unemployed: Experiences and Consequences of Mass Unemployment from the Weimar Republic to the Third Reich*, London and Sydney, 1987, pp. 172–93); P. Stachura, 'The Social and Welfare Implications of Youth Unemployment in Weimar Germany, 1929–1933', in P. Stachura (ed.), *Unemployment and the Great Depression in Weimar Germany*, London, 1986, pp. 121–47; H. Titze, 'Die zyklische Überproduktion von Akademikern im 19. und 20. Jahrhundert', *Geschichte und Gesellschaft*, 10, 1984, pp. 92–121; R. Bölling, 'Lehrerarbeitslosigkeit in historischer Perspektive', *Recht der Jugend und des Bildungswesens*, 34, 1986, pp. 198–211.

8. B. Zymek, 'Perspektive und Enttäuschung deutscher Gymnasiasten 1933 und 1983', *Bildung und Erziehung*, 36, 1983, pp. 335–49; K. Jarausch, *Deutsche Studenten 1800–1970*, Frankfurt, 1984, pp. 117–64; Kater, 'Generationskonflikt', pp. 217–43.

9. C. Fischer, 'Unemployment and Left-Wing Radicalism in Weimar Germany, 1930–1933', in Stachura, *Unemployment*, pp. 209–26; E. Rosenhaft, 'Organizing the "Lumpenproletariat": Cliques and Communists in Berlin during the Weimar Republic', in R. J. Evans (ed.), *The German Working Class 1888–1933*, London, 1982, pp. 174–219.

10. U. Frevert, *Frauen-Geschichte. Zwischen Bürgerlicher Verbesserung und Neuer Weiblichkeit*, Frankfurt, 1986, pp. 146–99; also contains a good survey of the literature.

11. G. Wellner, 'Industriearbeiterinnen in der Weimarer Republik', *Geschichte und Gesellschaft*, 7, 1981, pp. 534–54; Frauengruppe Faschismusforschung, *Mutterkreuz und Arbeitsbuch. Zur Geschichte der Frauen in der Weimarer Republik und im Nationalsozialismus*, Frankfurt, 1981; C. Sachße, *Mütterlichkeit als Beruf*, Frankfurt, 1986, esp. pp. 149–312.

12. K. Hausen, 'Unemployment also Hits Women: The New and the Old Woman on the Dark Side of the Golden Twenties in Germany', in Stachura, *Unemployment*, pp. 78–120.

13. B. Greven-Aschoff, *Die bürgerliche Frauenbewegung in Deutschland 1894–1933*, Göttingen, 1981.

14. U. Linse, ' "Geschlechtsnot der Jugend". Über Jugendbewegung und Sexualität', in Koebner *et al.*, *'Mit uns zieht die neue Zeit'*, pp. 245–310; R. Bridenthal *et al.* (eds.), *When Biology Became Destiny: Women in Weimar and Nazi Germany*, New York, 1984, esp. pp. 66–197; G. Bock, 'Frauen und ihre Arbeit im Nationalsozialismus', in A. Kuhn and G. Schneider (eds.), *Frauen in der Geschichte*, Düsseldorf, 1979, pp. 113–52; M. Janssen-Jurreit, 'Sexualreform und Geburtenrückgang – Über die Zusammenhänge von Bevölkerungspolitik und Frauenbewegung um die Jahrhundertwende', in Kuhn und Schneider, *Frauen in der Geschichte*, pp. 34–55.

15. D. Peukert, 'Der Schund- und Schmutzkampf als "Sozialpolitik der Seele" ', in H. Haarmann *et al.* (eds.), *'Das war ein Vorspiel nur . . .' Bücherverbrennung Deutschland 1933*, Berlin, 1983, pp. 51–64.

16. K. Hausen, 'Mütter zwischen Geschäftsinteressen und kultischer Verehrung. Der

"Deutsche Muttertag" in der Weimarer Republik', in Huck, *Sozialgeschichte der Freizeit*, pp. 249–81; C. Wittrock, *Weiblichkeitsmythen. Das Frauenbild im Faschismus und seine Vorläufer in der Frauenbewegung der 20er Jahre*, Frankfurt, 1983.
17. Quoted in Prümm, *Literatur*, p. 152.
18. Theweleit, *Männerphantasien*; L. Niethammer, 'Male Fantasies: An Argument for and with an Important New Study in History and Psychoanalysis', *History Workshop*, 7, 1979, pp. 176–86.
19. Quoted in Prümm, *Literatur*, p. 152.

5. The Post-War Economy: Rationalization and Structural Crisis

1. Borchardt, *Wachstum*, pp. 73–150; Lutz, *Der kurze Traum*; W. Abelshauser and D. Petzina, 'Krise und Rekonstruktion. Zur Interpretation der gesamtwirtschaftlichen Entwicklung Deutschlands im 20. Jahrdundert', in W. H. Schröder and R. Spree (eds.), *Historische Konjunkturforschung*, Stuttgart, 1980, pp. 45–114.
2. Borchardt, *Wachstum*, pp. 165–205; also K. Borchardt, 'Noch einmal: Alternativen zu Brünings Wirtschaftspolitik?', *Historische Zeitschrift*, 237, 1983, pp. 67–83; K. Borchardt, 'Zum Scheitern eines produktiven Diskurses über das Scheitern der Weimarer Republik: Replik auf C.-D. Krohns Diskussionsbemerkungen', *Geschichte und Gesellschaft*, 9, 1983, pp. 124–37; C.-D. Krohn, ' "Ökonomische Zwangslagen" und das Scheitern der Weimarer Republik. Zu K. Borchardts Analyse der deutschen Wirtschaft in den zwanziger Jahren', *Geschichte und Gesellschaft*, 8, 1982, pp. 415–24; C.-L. Holtfrerich, 'Alternativen zu Brünings Wirtschaftspolitik in der Weltwirtschaftskrise?', *Historische Zeitschrift*, 235, 1982, pp. 605–32; C.-L. Holtfrerich, 'Zu hohe Löhne in der Weimarer Republik? Bemerkungen zur Borchardt-These', *Geschichte und Gesellschaft*, 10, 1984, pp. 122–41; A. Winkler (ed.), *Kontroversen über die Wirtschaftspolitik in der Weimarer Republik, Geschichte und Gesellschaft*, 11, 1985, no. 3; K. Hübner, 'Zwangslagen oder Handlungsspielräume der Wirtschaftspolitik 1929–32?', *Sozialwissenschaftliche Information für Unterricht und Studium*, 13, 1984, pp. 30–45.
3. H. J. Puhle, 'Historische Konzepte des entwickelten Industriekapitalismus. "Organisierter Kapitalismus" und "Korporatismus" ', *Geschichte und Gesellschaft*, 10, 1984, pp. 164–84.
4. C. Duisberg to E. A. Merck, 31 October 1918; quoted in Feldman, 'German Big Business', p. 338.
5. G. Feldman and J. Steinisch, *Industrie und Gewerkschaften 1918–1924. Die überforderte Zentralarbeitsgemeinschaft*, Stuttgart, 1985; H. A. Winkler (ed.), *Organisierter Kapitalismus*, Göttingen, 1974; H. Mommsen, *Klassenkampf oder Mitbestimmung. Zum Problem der Kontrolle wirtschaftlicher Macht in der Weimarer Republik*, Frankfurt,1978.
6. P. von Oertzen, *Betriebsräte in der Novemberrevolution*, 2nd edn, Bonn, 1976; H. O. Hemmer, 'Betriebsrätegesetz und Betriebsrätepraxis in der Weimarer Republik', in U. Borsdorf et al. (eds.), *Gewerkschaftliche Politik: Reform aus Solidarität*, Cologne, 1977, pp. 241–70.

7. F. Eisner, *Das Verhältnis der KPD zu den Gewerkschaften in der Weimarer Republik*, Frankfurt, 1977; M. Martiny, 'Arbeiterbewegung an Rhein und Ruhr vom Scheitern der Räte- und Sozialisierungsbewegung bis zum Ende der letzten parlamentarischen Regierung der Weimarer Republik 1920–1930', in J. Reulecke (ed.), *Arbeiterbewegung an Rhein und Ruhr*, Wuppertal, 1974, pp. 241–74.

8. H. Hartwich, *Arbeitsmarkt, Verbände und Staat 1918–1933*, Berlin, 1967.

9. There is still no comprehensive historical study of rationalization in Germany. Different aspects are dealt with in G. Stollberg, *Die Rationalisierungsdebatte 1908–1933. Freie Gewerkschaften zwischen Mitwirkung und Gegenwehr*, Frankfurt, 1981; P. Hinrichs and L. Peter, *Industrieller Friede? Arbeitswissenschaft und Rationalisierung in der Weimarer Republik*, Cologne, 1976; P. Hinrichs, *Um die Seele des Arbeiters. Arbeitspsychologie, Industrie- und Betriebspsychologie in Deutschland*, Cologne, 1981; Weisbrod, *Schwerindustrie*; E. C. Schöck, *Arbeitslosigkeit und Rationalisierung. Die Lage der Arbeiter und die kommunistische Gewerkschaftspolitik 1920–28*, Frankfurt, 1977; U. Stolle, *Arbeiterpolitik im Betrieb*, Frankfurt, 1980.

10. H. James, *The German Slump: Politics and Economics 1924–1936*, Oxford, 1986.

11. Petzina *et al., Materialien*.

12. Winkler, *Der Schein der Normalität*, pp. 38ff.

13. C. Maier, 'Zwischen Taylorismus und Technokratie', in Stürmer, *Weimarer Republik*, pp. 188–213; G. Schulz, 'Bürgerliche Sozialreform in der Weimarer Republik', in R. vom Bruch (ed.), *Weder Kommunismus noch Kapitalismus. Bürgerliche Sozialreform in Deutschland vom Vormärz bis zur Ära Adenauer*, Munich, 1985, pp. 181–218.

14. Weisbrod, *Schwerindustrie*; D. Peukert, 'Industrialisierung des Bewußtseins? Arbeitserfahrungen von Ruhrbergleuten im 20. Jahrhundert', in K. Tenfelde (ed.), *Arbeit und Arbeitserfahrungen in der Geschichte*, Göttingen, 1986, pp. 92–119.

15. Schöck, *Arbeitslosigkeit und Rationalisierung*; H. Mommsen, 'Die Bergarbeiterbewegung an der Ruhr 1818–1933', in Reulecke, *Arbeiterbewegung*, pp. 275–314; S. Bahne, 'Die Erwerbslosenpolitik der KPD in der Weimarer Republik', in Mommsen and Schulze, *Vom Elend der Handarbeit*, pp. 477–96.

16. See Stolle, *Arbeiterpolitik im Betrieb*; Weisbrod, *Schwerindustrie*.

17. On this, see the literature cited in note 2 to this chapter, above; on unemployment, see D. Petzina, 'The Extent and Causes of Unemployment in the Weimar Republic', in Stachura, *Unemployment*, pp. 29–48; D. Hertz-Eichenrode, *Wirtschaftskrise und Arbeitsbeschaffung. Konjunkturpolitik 1925/26 und die Grundlagen der Krisenpolitik Brünings*, Frankfurt, 1982.

18. Petzina, *Deutsche Wirtschaft*; D. Petzina and W. Abelshauser, 'Zum Problem der relativen Stagnation der deutschen Wirtschaft in den zwanziger Jahren', in H. Mommsen *et al.*, *Industrielles System*, pp. 57–76; W. Fischer, 'Die Weimarer Republik unter den weltwirtschaftlichen Bedingungen der Zwischenkriegszeit', in H. Mommsen *et al.*, *Industrielles System*, pp. 26–50; Aldcroft, *Versailles to Wall Street*; Feldman, *Nachwirkungen*.

19. Ziebura, *Weltwirtschaft*.

20. Fischer, 'Weimarer Republik', pp. 34–9; J. Flemming, *Landwirtschaftliche Interessen und Demokratie*, Bonn, 1978; D. Gessner, *Agrardepression, Agrarideologie und konservative Politik in der Weimarer Republik*, Wiesbaden, 1976; D. Hertz-Eichenrode, *Politik und Landwirtschaft in Ostpreußen 1919–1930*, Cologne, 1969.

21. For this, see the contributions to the Borchardt controversy cited in note 2 to this chapter, above.

22. C. Stephan, 'Wirtschaftsdemokratie und Umbau der Wirtschaft', in W. Luthardt, *Sozialdemokratische Arbeiterbewegung*, vol. 1, pp. 281–353; F. Naphtali, *Wirtschaftsdemokratie*, ed. R. Kuda, Frankfurt, 1966; R. Kuda, 'Das Konzept der Wirtschaftsdemokratie', in H. O. Vetter (ed.), *Vom Sozialistengesetz zur Mitbestimmung*, 1st edn, Cologne, 1975, pp. 253–74; M. Schneider, *Unternehmer und Demokratie. Die freien Gewerkschaften in der unternehmerischen Ideologie der Jahre 1918–1933*, Bonn, 1975.

23. Weisbrod, *Schwerindustrie*, pp. 415–56; U. Hüllbusch, 'Der Ruhreisenstreit in gewerkschaftlicher Sicht', in H. Mommsen *et al.*, *Industrielles System*, pp. 271–89; G. Feldman and I. Steinisch, 'Notwendigkeit und Grenzen sozialstaatlicher Intervention. Eine vergleichende Fallstudie des Ruhreisenstreits in Deutschland und des Generalstreiks in England', *Archiv für Sozialgeschichte*, 20, 1980, pp. 57–117; M. Schneider, *Auf dem Weg in die Krise. Thesen und Materialien zum Ruhreisenstreit 1928/29*, Wentorf, 1974.

24. M. Schneider, *Unternehmer und Demokratie*; R. Neebe, 'Unternehmerverbände und Gewerkschaften in den Jahren der Großen Krise 1929–33', *Geschichte und Gesellschaft*, 9, 1983, pp. 302–30; B. Weisbrod, 'Die Befreiung von den "Tariffesseln". Deflationspolitik als Krisenstrategie der Unternehmer in der Ära Brüning', in Winkler, *Kontroversen*, pp. 295–325; cf. also H. A. Turner, *German Big Business and the Rise of Hitler*, New York and Oxford, 1985.

6. The Welfare State: Expansion and Crisis

1. G. A. Ritter, 'Entstehung des Sozialstaates in vergleichender Perspektive', *Historische Zeitschrift*, 243, 1986, pp. 1–90, with bibliography; V. Hentschel, *Geschichte der deutschen Sozialpolitik 1880–1980*, Frankfurt, 1983; vom Bruch, *Weder Kommunismus noch Kapitalismus*.

2. G. A. Ritter, *Sozialversicherung in Deutschland und England*, Munich, 1983.

3. R. Münchmeier, *Zugänge zur Geschichte der Sozialarbeit*, Munich, 1981; R. Landwehr and R. Baron (eds.), *Geschichte der Sozialarbeit*, Weinheim, 1983.

4. Huber, *Deutsche Verfassungsgeschichte seit 1789*, vols. 5–7; L. Preller, *Sozialpolitik in der Weimarer Republik* (1949), Kronberg, 1978; C. Hasenklever, *Jugendhilfe und Jugendgesetzgebung seit 1900*, Göttingen, 1978.

5. Weimar Reich Constitution, Articles 119–65.

6. Evans and Geary, *The German Unemployed*; Stachura, *Unemployment*; see also the contributions by Faust, Skidelsky, Weisbrod and Wolffsohn in W. J. Mommsen

(ed.), *The Emergence of the Welfare State in Britain and Germany*, London, 1981, pp. 150–244.

7. E. Orthbandt, *Der Deutsche Verein in der Geschichte der deutschen Fürsorge 1880–1980*, Frankfurt, 1980, pp. 174–277; Geyer, 'Ein Vorbote des Wohlfahrtstaates'; S. Leibfried, 'Existenzminimum und Fürsorge-Richtsätze in der Weimarer Republik', in S. Leibfried, *Armutspolitik und die Entstehung des Sozialstaats*, Bremen, 1985, pp. 186–240.

8. K. Epstein, *Matthias Erzberger and the Dilemma of German Democracy*, Princeton, 1959; T. Eschenburg, *Matthias Erzberger – Der Große Mann des Parlamentarismus und der Finanzreform*, Munich, 1973, pp. 369ff; P. C. Witt, 'Finanzpolitik und sozialer Wandel in Krieg und Inflation', in H. Mommsen *et al.*, *Industrielles System*, pp. 395–426, as well as other contributions to that volume; Krohn, *Stabilisierung und ökonomische Interessen*; data are taken from Petzina *et al.*, *Materialien*, pp. 147–52.

9. Statistical data from Petzina *et al.*, *Materialien*, pp. 153–64; see also D. Nadav, J. *Moses und die Politik der Sozialhygiene in Deutschland*, Gerlingen, 1985; A. Labisch, '"Hygiene ist Moral – Moral ist Hygiene" – Soziale Disziplinierung durch Ärzte und Medizin', in C. Sachße and F. Tennstedt (eds.), *Soziale Sicherheit und Soziale Disziplinierung*, Frankfurt, 1986, pp. 265–85; G. Göckenjan, 'Medizin und Ärzte als Faktor der Disziplinierung der Unterschichten: Der Kassenarzt', in Sachße and Tennstedt, *Soziale Sicherheit*, pp. 286–304; K. H. Roth, 'Schein-Alternativen im Gesundheitswesen: A. Grotjahn (1869–1931) – Integrationsfigur etablierter Sozialmedizin und nationalsozialistischer "Rassenhygiene"', in K. H. Roth (ed.), *Erfassung zur Vernichtung*, Berlin, 1984, pp. 31–56; G. Bock, *Zwangssterilisation im Nationalsozialismus. Studien zur Rassenpolitik und Frauenpolitik*, Opladen, 1986; A. Labisch and F. Tennstedt, *Der Weg zum 'Gesetz über die Vereinheitlichung des Gesundheitswesens' vom 3. Juli 1934*, 2 parts, Düsseldorf, 1985.

10. Peukert, *Grenzen der Sozialdisziplinierung*.

11. H. E. Tenorth, *Zur deutschen Bildungsgeschichte 1918–1945*, Cologne, 1985, is a penetrating survey of research; see also H. E. Tenorth and D. Langewiesche (eds.), *Handbuch der deutschen Bildungsgeschichte*, vol. 5: *1918–1945*, Munich, 1989.

12. W. Wittwer, *Die sozialdemokratische Schulpolitik in der Weimarer Republik*, Berlin, 1980; G. Grünthal, *Reichsschulgesetz und Zentrumspartei in der Weimarer Republik*, Düsseldorf, 1968; H. Behrens-Cobet *et al.*, *Freie Schulen. Eine vergessene Bildungsalternative*, Essen, 1986; C. Führ, *Zur Schulpolitik der Weimarer Republik*, Weinheim, 1970; A. Leschinsky, 'Volksschule zwischen Ausbau und Auszehrung', *Vierteljahreshefte für Zeitgeschichte*, 30, 1982, pp. 27–81.

13. H. Röhrs, *Die Reformpädagogik*, Hanover, 1980; B. Huschke-Rhein, *Das Wissenschaftsverständnis der geisteswissenschaftlichen Pädagogik. Dilthey–Litt–Nohl–Spranger*, Stuttgart, 1979.

14. Sachße, *Mütterlichkeit als Beruf*; R. Bölling, *Volksschullehrer und Politik*, Göttingen, 1978; Bölling, 'Lehrerarbeitslosigkeit'; W. Breyvogel, *Die soziale Lage und das politische Bewußtsein der Volksschullehrer 1927–1933*, Königstein, 1979.

15. Peukert, 'Schund- und Schmutzkampf', pp. 51–64 and 156–68.

16. Quoted in Ritter, 'Entstehung', p. 5.

17. H. U. Otto and H. Sühnker (eds.), *Soziale Arbeit und Faschismus*, Bielefeld, 1986; Peukert, *Grenzen der Sozialdisziplinierung*, pp. 240–304.

7. Social Milieux and Political Formations

1. Basic studies include R. M. Lepsius, 'Parteisystem und Sozialstruktur', in G. A. Ritter (ed.), *Die deutschen Parteien vor 1918*, Cologne, 1973, pp. 56–80; R. M. Lepsius, *Extremer Nationalismus. Strukturbedingungen vor der nationalsozialistischen Machtergreifung*, Stuttgart, 1966; K. Rohe, *Vom Revier zum Ruhrgebiet*, Essen, 1986; K. Rohe and H. Kühr (eds.), *Politik und Gesellschaft im Ruhrgebiet*, Königstein, 1979; O. Negt and A. Kluge, *Öffentlichkeit und Erfahrung* (1972), Frankfurt, 1976.

2. The terms 'political camp' and 'social milieu' are not coextensive. The former connotes a social group defined in terms of political allegiance; the latter, the political expression of a socially defined group.

3. J. Falter *et al.*, *Wahlen und Abstimmungen in der Weimarer Republik*, Munich, 1986; T. Geiger, *Die soziale Schichtung des deutschen Volkes* (1932), reprinted Stuttgart, 1967, remains stimulating.

4. C. Kennert, *Entwicklung der Jugendkriminalität in Deutschland 1882–1952*, dissertation, Berlin, 1957; Peukert, *Jugend zwischen Krieg und Krise*, pp. 245–84; R. Scholz, 'Ein unruhiges Jahrzehnt: Lebensmittelunruhen, Massenstreiks und Arbeitslosenkrawalle in Berlin 1914–1923', in M. Gailus (ed.), *Pöbelexzesse und Volkstumulte in Berlin. Zur Sozialgeschichte der Straße 1830–1980*, Berlin, 1984, pp. 79–124; see also the literature cited in notes 6–8 to chapter 3, above.

5. Detailed case studies include W. S. Allen, *The Nazi Seizure of Power: The Experience of a Single German Town 1922–1945* (1965), revised edn, New York, 1984, and London, 1989; G. Plum, *Gesellschaftsstruktur und politisches Bewußtsein in einer katholischen Region 1928–1933*, Stuttgart, 1972; A. von Plato, ' "Ich bin mit allen gut ausgekommen". Oder: war die Ruhrarbeiterschaft vor 1933 in politische Lager zerspalten?', in L. Niethammer (ed.), *'Die Jahre weiß man nicht, wo man die heute hinsetzen soll'. Faschismuserfahrungen im Ruhrgebiet*, Berlin, 1983, pp. 31–66; E. Lucas, *Zwei Formen von Radikalismus in der deutschen Arbeiterbewegung*, Frankfurt, 1976; J. Wickham, *The Working Class Movement in Frankfurt am Main during the Weimar Republic*, dissertation, University of Sussex, 1979; G. Hetzer, 'Die Industriestadt Augsburg. Eine Sozialgeschichte der Arbeiteropposition', in M. Broszat *et al.* (eds.), *Bayern in der NS-Zeit*, vol. III, Munich, 1981, pp. 1–234; K. Tenfelde, 'Proletarische Provinz. Radikalisierung und Widerstand in Penzberg/Oberbayern 1900–1945', in Broszat *et al.*, *Bayern in der NS-Zeit*, vol. IV, Munich, 1981, pp. 1–382.

6. For surveys of the literature, see G. A. Ritter, *Staat, Arbeiterschaft und Arbeiterbewegung in Deutschland*, Berlin, 1980; D. Lehnert, *Sozialdemokratie zwischen Protestbewegung und Regierungspartei 1848–1983*, Frankfurt, 1983; J. Mooser, *Arbeiterleben in Deutschland 1900–1970*, Frankfurt, 1984.

7. Key studies include Winkler, *Von der Revolution*; Winkler, *Der Schein der Normalität*.

8. E. Lucas, *Vom Scheitern der deutschen Arbeiterbewegung*, Frankfurt, 1983; Koch-Baumgarten, *Aufstand der Avantgarde*; Gorlas and Peukert, *Ruhrkampf 1920*.

9. There is no systematic comparative study of the two membership structures. In addition to the works cited above, pointers can be found in, for example, H. Weber, *Die Wandlung des deutschen Kommunismus*, 2 vols., Frankfurt, 1969; D. Peukert, *Die KPD im Widerstand*, Wuppertal, 1980, pp. 30–71; Schöck, *Arbeitslosigkeit und Rationalisierung*; E. Rosenhaft, *Beating the Fascists? The German Communists and Political Violence 1929–1933*, Cambridge, 1983; H. Mehringer, 'Die KPD in Bayern 1919–1945', in Broszat *et al.*, *Bayern in der NS-Zeit*, vol. V, Munich, 1983, pp. 1–286; H. Mehringer, 'Die bayerische Sozialdemokratie bis zum Ende des NS-Regimes', in Broszat *et al.*, *Bayern in der NS-Zeit*, vol. V, pp. 287–432; B. Rabe, *Der sozialdemokratische Charakter*, Frankfurt, 1978; H. Mommsen (ed.), *Sozialdemokratie zwischen Klassenbewegung und Volkspartei*, Frankfurt, 1974.

10. See the survey by M. Schneider in U. Borsdorf (ed.), *Geschichte der deutschen Gewerkschaften*, Cologne, 1987, pp. 279–446; K. Schönhoven, *Die deutschen Gewerkschaften*, Frankfurt, 1987, esp. pp. 116–76.

11. D. Langewiesche, 'Politik – Gesellschaft – Kultur. Zur Problematik von Arbeiterkultur und kulturellen Arbeiterorganisationen in Deutschland nach dem Ersten Weltkrieg', *Archiv für Sozialgeschichte*, 22, 1982, pp. 359–402; H. Wunderer, *Arbeitervereine und Arbeiterparteien. Kultur- und Massenorganisationen in der Arbeiterbewegung 1890–1933*, Frankfurt, 1980; W. van der Will and R. Burns (eds.), *Arbeiterkulturbewegung in der Weimarer Republik*, 2 vols., Frankfurt, 1982.

12. See chapter 8.

13. Rosenhaft, *Beating the Fascists?*

14. K. Rohe, *Das Reichsbanner Schwarz-Rot-Gold*, Düsseldorf, 1966.

15. R. Morsey, *Die deutsche Zentrumspartei 1917–1923*, Düsseldorf, 1966; R. Morsey, *Der Untergang des politischen Katholizismus*, Stuttgart, 1977; R. Morsey (ed.), *Zeitgeschichte in Lebensbildern. Aus dem deutschen Katholizismus des 20. Jahrhunderts*, 2 vols., Mainz, 1973, 1975; H. Hömig, *Das preußische Zentrum in der Weimarer Republik*, Mainz, 1979; K. Schönhoven, *Die Bayerische Volkspartei 1924–1932*, Düsseldorf, 1972; Götz von Olenhusen, *Jugendreich*.

16. W. Becker (ed.), *Die Minderheit als Mitte. Die Deutsche Zentrumspartei in der Innenpolitik des Reiches 1871–1933*, Paderborn, 1986; K.-E. Lönne, *Politischer Katholizismus im 19. und 20. Jahrhundert*, Frankfurt, 1986.

17. Plum, *Gesellschaftsstruktur*; H. Kühr, *Parteien und Wahlen im Stadt- und Landkreis Essen*, Düsseldorf, 1973.

18. M. Schneider, *Die Christlichen Gewerkschaften 1894–1933*, Bonn, 1982; J. Aretz, *Katholische Arbeiterbewegung und Nationalsozialismus*, Mainz, 1978; F. Focke, *Sozialismus aus christlicher Verantwortung*, Wuppertal, 1978.

19. Morsey, *Untergang*, pp. 14ff.

20. H. A. Winkler, *Mittelstand, Demokratie und Nationalsozialismus*, Cologne, 1972;

for a recent survey of research, see H. G. Haupt, 'Mittelstand und Kleinbürgertum in der Weimarer Republik', *Archiv für Sozialgeschichte*, 26, 1986, pp. 217–38.

21. See notes 6–8 to chapter 3, above.

22. L. Jones, 'In the Shadow of Stabilization: German Liberalism and the Legitimacy Crisis of the Weimar Party System 1924–30', in Feldman, *Nachwirkungen*, pp. 21–41.

23. H. Speier, *Die Angestellten vor dem Nationalsozialismus*, Göttingen, 1977 (trans. as *German White-Collar Workers and the Rise of Hitler*, New Haven and London, 1986); J. Kocka, *Die Angestellten in der deutschen Geschichte 1850–1980*, Göttingen, 1981, pp. 142–70; J. Kocka (ed.), *Angestellte im europäischen Vergleich*, Göttingen, 1981; H. J. Priamus, *Angestellte und Demokratie*, Stuttgart, 1979.

24. S. Kracauer, *Die Angestellten* (1929), Frankfurt, 1971.

25. ibid., p. 97; for the ensuing quotation, see p. 96.

26. M. Prinz, *Vom neuen Mittelstand zum Volksgenossen*, Munich, 1986.

27. M. Richarz (ed.), *Jüdisches Leben in Deutschland 1918–1945*, Stuttgart, 1982; T. Maurer, *Ostjuden in Deutschland 1918–1933*, Hamburg, 1986; H. Knütter, *Die Juden und die deutsche Linke in der Weimarer Republik 1918–1933*, Düsseldorf, 1971.

28. Quoted in Scholz, 'Unruhiges Jahrzehnt', p. 116.

29. This section summarizes the themes of the literature referred to in chapters 7–9 and 11. I am also grateful to Henning Eichberg for stimulating discussions of his 'Lebenswelt und Alltagswissen', in Tenorth and Langewiesche, *Handbuch der deutschen Bildungsgeschichte*.

8. Mass Culture and the Neue Sachlichkeit

1. The following studies and anthologies are central: J. Hermand and F. Trommler, *Die Kultur der Weimarer Republik*, Munich, 1978; W. Laqueur, *Weimar: A Cultural History 1918–1933*, London, 1974; P. Gay, *Weimar Culture: The Insider as Outsider* (1968), 2nd edn, London, 1988; J. Willett, *The New Sobriety 1917–1933: Art and Politics in the Weimar Period*, London, 1978; A. Kaes (ed.), *Weimarer Republik. Manifeste und Dokumente zur deutschen Literatur 1918–1933*, Stuttgart, 1983; *Tendenzen der Zwanziger Jahre*, 15. Europäische Kunstausstellung Berlin 1977, catalogue, Berlin, 1977; Neue Gesellschaft für Bildende Kunst (ed.), *Wem gehört die Welt – Kunst und Gesellschaft in der Weimarer Republik*, Berlin, 1977; Kunstamt Kreuzberg and Institut für Theaterwissenschaft der Universität Köln (eds.), *Weimarer Republik*, Berlin, 1977.

2. B. Hinz, ' "Zweierlei Kultur in Deutschland" ', in Neue Gesellschaft, *Wem gehört die Welt*, pp. 264–8.

3. A. Weber, *Die Not der geistigen Arbeiter*, Munich, 1923.

4. G. Stein (ed.), *Bohemien-Tramp-Sponti*, Frankfurt, 1981, pp. 95–170; E. Schütz, *Romane der Weimarer Republik*, Munich, 1986, esp. pp. 147–59.

5. S. Saenger, review in *Die Neue Rundschau*, 34, 1923, pp. 276–78, quoted in Kaes, *Weimarer Republik*, p. 74.

6. Kaes, *Weimarer Republik*, XXIII.

7. H. Reiser, review in *Die schöne Literatur*, 26, 1925, pp. 10–12, quoted in Kaes, *Weimarer Republik*, pp. 166ff.

8. H. Lethen, *Neue Sachlichkeit 1924–1932*, Stuttgart, 1975; M. Eberle, 'Die neue Wirklichkeit – Surrealismus und Sachlichkeit', *Tendenzen*, 4, pp. 1–272.

9. Kracauer, *Angestellten*, pp. 15ff.

10. The quotations, from Adolf Bahne (1926) and Anton Schirokauer (1929), are taken from Kaes, *Weimarer Republik*, pp. 221 and 202; see also Schütz, *Romane*, esp. pp. 35–51.

11. S. Kracauer, *From Caligari to Hitler: A Psychological Study of the German Film*, Princeton, 1947; for the effects of the new media on people's lives, see also F. Kittler, *Grammophon, Film, Typewriter*, Berlin, 1986.

12. W. Lerg, *Rundfunkpolitik in der Weimarer Republik*, Munich, 1980, from which the cited data are also taken; P. Dahl, *Arbeitersender und Volksempfänger. Proletarische Radiobewegung und bürgerlicher Rundfunk bis 1945*, Frankfurt, 1978.

13. K. Koszyk, *Deutsche Presse 1914–1945*, Berlin, 1972; H. Willmann, *Geschichte der Arbeiter-Illustrierten-Zeitung*, Berlin, 1974.

14. Quoted in Kaes, *Weimarer Republik*, XXXIff.

15. Schütz, *Romane*, esp. pp. 89–102; H. Gallas, *Marxistische Literaturtheorie. Kontroversen im Bund proletarisch-revolutionärer Schriftsteller*, Neuwied, 1971. In 1932, however, the spokesmen of the League of Proletarian Revolutionary Writers themselves fell foul of the official cultural policy of the KPD.

16. Schütz, *Romane*, pp. 184–216.

17. H. Günther, *Die Kunst von morgen* (1930), quoted in Kaes, *Weimarer Republik*.

18. The following data are taken from Lerg, *Rundfunkpolitik*, p. 526; on various aspects of mass consumption and mass culture, see the contributions to J. Boberg *et al.* (eds.), *Die Metropole. Industriekultur in Berlin im 20. Jahrhundert*, Munich, 1986; see also a comprehensive survey of the history of mass consumption and mass culture in S. Giedion, *Mechanisation Takes Command: A Contribution to Anonymous History*, New York, 1948.

19. Schütz, *Romane*, esp. pp. 70–88.

20. Neue Gesellschaft, *Wem gehört die Welt*, pp. 158–360.

21. J. Campbell, *The German Werkbund: The Politics of Reform in the Applied Arts*, Princeton, 1978.

22. Deutscher Werkbund (ed.), *Die Zwanziger Jahre des Deutschen Werkbunds*, Gießen, 1982; for an up-to-date review of the literature, see W. Albrecht, 'Moderne Vergangenheit – Vergangene Moderne. Auf der Suche nach Konzeptionen zur gegenständlichen Umweltgestaltung in Architektur und Städtebau', *Neue Politische Literatur*, 30, 1985, pp. 203–25.

23. G. Huck, *Sozialgeschichte der Freizeit*; Peukert, *Jugend zwischen Krieg und Krise*.

24. K. Strohmeyer, *Warenhäuser. Geschichte, Blüte und Untergang im Warenmeer*, Berlin, 1980, esp. pp. 151ff.

9. *'Americanism' versus* Kulturkritik

1. G. Dehn, *Proletarische Jugend*, Berlin, 1929, p. 39.

2. Schütz, *Romane*, esp. pp. 14ff, 70ff, 164ff; Maier, 'Zwischen Taylorismus und Technokratie'; J. Herf, *Reactionary Modernism: Technology, Culture and Politics in Weimar and the Third Reich*, Cambridge, Mass., 1984; F. Trommler, 'Aufstieg und Fall des Amerikanismus in Deutschland', in F. Trommler (ed.), *Amerika und die Deutschen*, Opladen, 1986, pp. 666–76; G. Schwan, 'Das deutsche Amerikabild seit der Weimarer Republik', *Aus Politik und Zeitgeschichte*, 26, 1986, pp. 3–15.

3. Doerry, *Übergangsmenschen*; J. Boberg et al. (eds.), *Exerzierfeld der Moderne. Industriekultur in Berlin im 19. Jahrhundert*, Munich, 1984; Boberg et al., *Metropole*, esp. pp. 16–101.

4. Trommler, *Amerika und die Deutschen*.

5. Quoted in Schütz, *Romane*, p. 72.

6. F. Giese, *Girlkultur. Vergleich zwischen amerikanischem und europäischem Rhythmus und Lebensgefühl* (1925), quoted in ibid., p. 164.

7. Polgar (1926), quoted in ibid.

8. Quoted in Kaes, *Weimarer Republik*.

9. K. Bergmann, *Agrarromantik und Großstadtfeindschaft*, Meisenheim, 1970; U. Linse, *Zurück o Mensch zur Mutter Erde*, Munich, 1983.

10. Reulecke, *Geschichte der Urbanisierung in Deutschland*, pp. 139–69; H. Poor, 'City versus Country: Urban Change and Development in the Weimar Republic', in H. Mommsen et al., *Industrielles System*, pp. 111–27.

11. Boberg et al., *Metropole*.

12. Neue Gesellschaft, *Wem gehört die Welt*, pp. 38–157; *Tendenzen*, 2, pp. 1–208; Campbell, *The German Werkbund*; L. Benevolo, *Geschichte der Architektur des 19. und 20. Jahrhunderts*, vol. 2, Munich, 1984; L. Niethammer (ed.), *Wohnen im Wandel*, Wuppertal, 1979; A. von Saldern, 'Sozialdemokratie und kommunale Wohnungsbaupolitik in den 20er Jahren – am Beispiel von Hamburg und Wien', *Archiv für Sozialgeschichte*, 25, 1985, pp. 183–238.

13. Quoted in Albrecht, 'Moderne Vergangenheit', p. 212; for a critical view of architectural historiography, see V. Lampugnani, 'Die unehrliche Geschichte', *Frankfurter Allgemeine Zeitung*, 11 December 1985; D. Peukert (ed.), *Lebensräume und Disziplin, Journal für Geschichte*, vol. 2, 1987.

14. See note 9 to this chapter, above; on Franz Oppenheimer's theory of agrarian co-operatives, see also Doerry, *Übergangsmenschen*, pp. 143ff.

15. B. Brecht, *Gesammelte Werke*, vol. 4, Frankfurt, 1967, pp. 316ff.

16. Quoted in Schütz, *Romane*, p. 73.

17. See the new edn of the 'Protestantische Ethik' in *Gesammelte Aufsätze zur Religionssoziologie*, 1920; see also D. Peukert, 'Die "letzten Menschen". Beobachtungen zur Kulturkritik im Geschichtsbild Max Webers', *Geschichte und Gesellschaft*, 12, 1986, pp. 425–44.

18. S. Freud, *Das Unbehagen in der Kultur* (1929–30), in S. Freud, *Studienausgabe*, vol. 9, Frankfurt, 1982, pp. 191–270; the quotation is taken from p. 269.

19. H. P. Schwartz, *Der konservative Anarchist. Politik und Zeitkritik Ernst Jüngers*, Freiburg, 1962; Prümm, *Literatur*; K. H. Bohrer, *Die Ästhetik des Schreckens*, Frankfurt, 1983.

20. M. Weber, 'Wissenschaft als Beruf', in M. Weber, *Gesammelte Aufsätze zur Wissenschaftslehre*, 5th edn, Tübingen, 1982, p. 605.

21. For a general treatment, see Grebing, *Der 'deutsche Sonderweg'*; for a polemical view of issues of cultural history, see Gay, *Weimar Culture*; for a critical summary, see Hepp, *Avantgarde*; for a comparative international account, see W. Lepenies, *Die drei Kulturen*, Munich, 1985.

22. G. Lukács, *Die Zerstörung der Vernunft* (1962), 4th edn, 3 vols., Neuwied, 1983 (trans. as *The Destruction of Reason*, London, 1980).

23. F. Stern, *The Politics of Cultural Despair: A Study in the Rise of the German Ideology*, Berkeley, 1961; K. Sontheimer, *Antidemokratisches Denken in der Weimarer Republik* (1962), Munich, 1983.

24. Vondung, *Das wilhelminische Bildungsbürgertum*; F. Ringer, *The Decline of the German Mandarins: The German Academic Community 1890–1933*, Cambridge, Mass., 1969; R. vom Bruch, *Wissenschaft, Politik und öffentliche Meinung. Gelehrtenpolitik im wilhelminischen Deutschland*, Husum, 1980; B. Faulenbach, *Ideologie des deutschen Weges. Die deutsche Geschichte in der Historiographie zwischen Kaiserreich und Nationalsozialismus*, Munich, 1980; D. Käsler, *Die frühe deutsche Soziologie 1909 bis 1934 und ihre Entstehung-Milieus*, Opladen, 1984; W. Jäger, *Historische Forschung und politische Kultur in Deutschland*, Göttingen, 1984; W. Schivelbusch, *Intellektuellendämmerung. Zur Lage der Frankfurter Intelligenz in den zwanziger Jahren*, Frankfurt, 1985.

25. U. Linse, *Barfüßige Propheten. Erlöser der zwanziger Jahre*, Berlin, 1983; M. Weil (ed.), *Werwolf und Biene Maja. Der deutsche Bücherschrank zwischen den Kriegen*, Berlin, 1986.

26. W. Stapel, 'Der Geistige und sein Volk', *Deutsches Volkstum*, January 1930/1, pp. 1–8, quoted in Kaes, *Weimarer Republik*, p. 510; Haarmann *et al.*, 'Das war ein Vorspiel nur . . .'.

27. Freud, *Unbehagen*, p. 270.

IV. DECEPTIVE STABILITY, 1924–9

10. Revisionist Alternatives in Foreign Policy

1. Key studies include Krüger, *Außenpolitik*; Krüger, *Versailles*, which also contains a survey of recent research; important contributions to the Stresemann debate are included in W. Michalka and M. Lee (eds.), *Gustav Stresemann*, Darmstadt, 1982;

for an account within a wider interpretative framework, see A. Hillgruber, *Die gescheiterte Großmacht*, Düsseldorf, 1980.

2. cf. Heinemann, *Verdrängte Niederlage*.

3. cf. Link, *Amerikanische Stabilisierungspolitik*.

4. cf. the generous account by Krüger.

5. C. Höltje, *Die Weimarer Republik und das Ostlocarno-Problem 1919–1934*, Würzburg, 1958.

6. For a controversial view, see Krüger, *Außenpolitik*, pp. 14ff; Hillgruber, *Gescheiterte Großmacht*, p. 69.

7. Michalka and Lee, *Gustav Stresemann*; E. Kolb, 'Probleme einer modernen Stresemann-Biographie', in O. Franz (ed.), *Am Wendepunkt der europäischen Geschichte*, Göttingen, 1981, pp. 107–34.

8. Link, *Amerikanische Stabilisierungspolitik*; K. Holz, *Die Diskussion um den Dawes-und Young-Plan in der deutschen Presse*, 2 vols., Frankfurt, 1977.

9. Petzina *et al.*, *Materialien*, p. 150; C.-L. Holtfrerich, 'Eine Chance für Europa. Neue Forschungen zur Reparationspolitik vor 1933', *Frankfurter Allgemeine Zeitung*, 14 January 1987.

10. cf. Ziebura, *Weltwirtschaft*; Aldcroft, *Versailles to Wall Street*.

11. Ziebura, *Weltwirtschaft*, p. 46; Petzina, *Deutsche Wirtschaft*, p. 69.

12. Krüger, *Außenpolitik*, esp. pp. 207ff and 269ff; cf. also K. Megerle, *Deutsche Außenpolitik 1925*, Frankfurt, 1974.

13. G. Niedhart (ed.), *Der Westen und die Sowjetunion*, Paderborn, 1983; K. Hildebrand, *Das Deutsche Reich und die Sowjetunion*; H. von Rieckhoff, *German–Polish Relations, 1918–1933*, Baltimore, 1977; G. Campbell, *Confrontation in Central Europe: Weimar Germany and Czechoslovakia*, Chicago, 1975; St Suval, *The Anschluss Question in the Weimar Era*, Baltimore, 1974.

14. H. Pieper, *Die Minderheitenfrage und das Deutsche Reich 1919–1933/34*, Hamburg, 1974; N. Krekeler, *Revisionsanspruch und geheime Ostpolitik der Weimarer Republik. Die Subventionierung der deutschen Minderheit in Polen*, Stuttgart, 1973; R. Jaworski, *Vorposten oder Minderheit? Der sudetendeutsche Volkstumskampf in den Beziehungen zwischen der Weimarer Republik und der CSR*, Stuttgart, 1977; for a central discussion of the problems of national self-determination, see P. Alter, *Nationalismus*, Frankfurt, 1985, pp. 113ff.

15. J. Becker and K. Hildebrand (eds.), *Internationale Beziehungen in der Weltwirtschaftskrise 1929–1933*, Munich, 1980.

11. The Illusion of Domestic Stability

1. cf., for example, the titles used in various accounts of the period 1924–9: 'The stable republic' (Michalka and Niedhart), 'The "golden twenties" ' (Henning), 'The best five years' (Möller); but also 'The semblance of normality' (Winkler) and 'Deceptive stability' (Schulze).

2. A chief source of data is Falter *et al.*, *Wahlen und Abstimmungen*; see also older

accounts by S. Neumann, *Die Parteien in der Weimarer Republik* (1932), 4th edn, Stuttgart, 1977; A. Milatz, *Wähler und Wahlen in der Weimarer Republik*, Bonn, 1968; J. Holzer, *Parteien und Massen. Die politische Krise in Deutschland 1928–1930*, Wiesbaden, 1975.

3. This vulgarized version of the totalitarianism thesis survives mainly as a stick with which contemporary politicians choose to beat one another. It has to be distinguished from the sophisticated and challenging variants of the historical theory of totalitarianism proposed by, for example, Hannah Arendt or Karl Dietrich Bracher. In the author's view, such concepts of totalitarianism are helpful, at least in a heuristic sense, for an understanding of the political crisis of the inter-war period. Cf. K. D. Bracher, *Europa in der Krise. Innengeschichte und Weltpolitik seit 1917*, Frankfurt, 1979; K. D. Bracher, *Zeit der Ideologien. Eine Geschichte politischen Denkens im 20. Jahrhundert*, Stuttgart, 1982; H. Arendt, *The Origins of Totalitarianism*, New York, 1951.

4. H. Weber, *Die Wandlung des deutschen Kommunismus*; H. Weber, *Kommunismus in Deutschland 1918–1945*; H. Weber, *Hauptfeind Sozialdemokratie. Strategie und Taktik der KPD 1929–1933*, Düsseldorf, 1981; Rosenhaft, *Beating the Fascists?*

5. For key studies, see Winkler, *Der Schein der Normalität*; H. Mommsen, *Sozialdemokratie*; Morsey, *Untergang*.

6. Holzer, *Parteien und Massen*; T. Childers, 'Interest and Ideology: Anti-System Politics in the Era of Stabilization 1924–1928', in Feldman, *Nachwirkungen*, pp. 1–19; Jones, 'In the Shadow of Stabilization', pp. 21–41.

7. This tendency cannot, however, be dismissed unhistorically as 'false thinking', for purposes of political education, as Hagen Schulze attempts to do. The question, rather, is what 'correct' actions might have been possible under given sets of circumstances.

8. To this extent we can agree with those authors who date the effective end of the Republic in 1930. See K. D. Erdmann and H. Schulze (eds.), *Weimar – Selbstpreisgabe einer Demokratie*, Düsseldorf, 1984.

9. For a key study, see M. Stürmer, *Koalition und Opposition in der Weimarer Republik 1924–1928*, Düsseldorf, 1967.

10. Schulze, *Otto Braun*; H. Möller, *Parlamentarismus in Preußen 1919–1932*, Düsseldorf, 1985.

11. Boldt, 'Artikel 48'.

12. U. Schüren, *Der Volksentscheid zur Fürstenenteignung 1926*, Düsseldorf, 1978.

13. Bracher, *Zeit der Ideologien*; Bracher, *Europa in der Krise*; K. Newman, *Zerstörung und Selbstzerstörung der Demokratie. Europa 1918–1938* (1965), Stuttgart, 1984; Sontheimer, *Antidemokratisches Denken*.

14. Maier, *Recasting Bourgeois Europe*.

15. At the meeting of the DVP central executive committee, 26 February 1929, quoted in L. Jones, 'Gustav Stresemann und die Krise des deutschen Liberalismus', in Michalka and Lee, *Gustav Stresemann*, pp. 279–303; the quotation is taken from p. 292.

16. M. Martiny, 'Die Entstehung und politische Bedeutung der "Neuen Blätter für den Sozialismus" und ihres Freundeskreises', *Vierteljahreshefte für Zeitgeschichte*, 25, 1977, pp. 373–419; D. Beck, *Julius Leber, Sozialdemokrat zwischen Reform und Widerstand*, Berlin, 1983, esp. pp. 107ff.

17. W. Schneider, *Die Deutsche Demokratische Partei in der Weimarer Republik 1924–1930*, Munich, 1978; L. Döhn, *Politik und Interesse. Die Interessenstruktur der Deutschen Volkspartei*, Meisenheim, 1970; E. Matthias and R. Morsey, 'Die Deutsche Staatspartei', in Matthias and Morsey, *Das Ende*, pp. 31–97; H. Booms, 'Die Deutsche Volkspartei', in Matthias and Morsey, *Das Ende*, pp. 523–39.

18. See also L. Jones, 'Sammlung oder Zersplitterung? Die Bestrebungen zur Bildung einer neuen Mittelpartei in der Endphase der Weimarer Republik 1930–1933', *Vierteljahreshefte für Zeitgeschichte*, 25, 1977, pp. 265–304.

19. Götz von Olenhusen, *Jugendreich*.

20. Morsey, *Untergang*.

21. E. Jonas, *Die Volkskonservativen 1928–1933*, Düsseldorf, 1965.

22. F. Hiller von Gaertringen, 'Die Deutschnationale Volkspartei', in Matthias and Morsey, *Das Ende*, pp. 543–652; H. Holzbach, *Das 'System Hugenberg'. Die Organisation bürgerlicher Sammlungspolitik vor dem Aufstieg der NSDAP*, Stuttgart, 1981; J. Leopold, *Alfred Hugenberg: The Radical Nationalist Campaign against the Weimar Republic*, New Haven, 1977.

23. cf. the subtitle of Erdmann and Schulze, *Weimar – Selbstpreisgabe einer Demokratie*.

12. The Fragmentation of the Political Culture

1. Any monocausal assignment of responsibility to individual anti-republican élite groups is therefore open to question. Nevertheless, while allowing for variations in particular cases, it is impossible to avoid painting a critical overall picture of salient élite group attitudes towards the Republic.

2. For a controversial account, see H. Hattenhauer, 'Zur Lage der Justiz in der Weimarer Republik', in Erdmann and Schulze, *Weimar*, pp. 169–76; also G. Jasper, 'Justiz und Politik in der Weimarer Republik', *Vierteljahreshefte für Zeitgeschichte*, 30, 1982, pp. 167–205.

3. H. Hannover and E. Hannover-Drück, *Politische Justiz 1918–1933* (1966), Hamburg, 1977; D. Blasius, *Geschichte der politischen Kriminalität in Deutschland 1800–1980*, Frankfurt, 1983, pp. 82–115.

4. G. Jasper, *Der Schutz der Republik*, Tübingen, 1963.

5. cf. Jasper, 'Justiz', p. 187.

6. For the 'revaluation dispute', see D. Southern, 'The Impact of Inflation: Inflation, the Courts and Revaluation', in R. Bessel and E. J. Feuchtwanger (eds.), *Social Change and Political Development in Weimar Germany*, London, 1981, pp. 55–76; the ambivalent nature of the reform of juvenile law is discussed in Peukert, *Grenzen der Sozialdisziplinierung*, esp. pp. 68–97 and 240–304.

7. R. Morsey, 'Beamtenschaft und Verwaltung zwischen Republik und "Neuem

Staat" ', in Erdmann and Schulze, *Weimar*, pp. 151–68; B. Wunder, *Geschichte der Bürokratie in Deutschland*, Frankfurt, 1986, pp. 109–37; W. Runge, *Politik und Beamtentum im Parteienstaat. Die Demokratisierung der politischen Beamten in Preußen 1918–1933*, Stuttgart, 1965.

8. Jarausch, *Deutsche Studenten 1800–1970*; M. Kater, *Studentenschaft und Rechtsradikalismus in Deutschland 1918–1933*, Hamburg, 1975.

9. F. Carsten, *The Reichswehr and Politics 1918–1933*, Oxford, 1965; R. Wohlfeil, 'Heer und Republik' (1970), in Militärgeschichtliches Forschungsamt (ed.), *Deutsche Militärgeschichte 1648–1939*, vol. 3/VI, Herrsching, 1983, pp. 11–304; Müller and Opitz, *Militär*; M. Geyer, *Aufrüstung oder Sicherheit. Die Reichswehr in der Krise der Machtpolitik*, Wiesbaden, 1980; K. J. Müller, 'Die Reichswehr und die "Machtergreifung" ', in W. Michalka (ed.), *Die nationalsozialistische Machtergreifung*, Paderborn, 1984, p. 137.

10. Weisbrod, *Schwerindustrie*; M. Schneider, *Unternehmer und Demokratie*; R. Neebe, *Großindustrie, Staat und NSDAP 1930–1933*, Göttingen, 1981; H. A. Turner, *German Big Business*; D. Stegmann, 'Kapitalismus und Faschismus in Deutschland 1929–1934', *Gesellschaft*, vol. 6, Frankfurt, 1976, pp. 19–91.

11. For a stimulating conceptual discussion, see M. Broszat, 'Zur Struktur der NS-Massenbewegung', *Vierteljahreshefte für Zeitgeschichte*, 31, 1983, pp. 52–76, esp. pp. 63ff.

12. Quoted in Jones, 'Gustav Stresemann', p. 286.

13. From the many regional studies, see W. S. Allen, *Nazi Seizure of Power*; R. Heberle, *Landbevölkerung und Nationalsozialismus. Eine soziologische Untersuchung der politischen Willensbildung in Schleswig-Holstein 1918–1932*, Stuttgart, 1963; Z. Zofka, *Die Ausbreitung des Nationalsozialismus auf dem Lande*, Munich, 1979; K. Wagner and G. Wilke, 'Dorfleben im Dritten Reich: Körle in Hessen', in D. Peukert and J. Reulecke (eds.), *Die Reihen fast geschlossen. Beiträge zur Geschichte des Alltags unterm Nationalsozialismus*, Wuppertal, 1981, pp. 85–106.

14. Feldman, *Nachwirkungen*.

15. See surveys of the literature in D. Gessner, 'The Dilemma of German Agriculture during the Weimar Republic', in Bessel and Feuchtwanger, *Social Change*, pp. 134–54; D. Gessner, 'Die Landwirtschaft und die Machtergreifung', in Michalka, *Die nationalsozialistische Machtergreifung*, pp. 124–36.

16. W. Horn, *Der Marsch zur Machtergreifung. Die NSDAP bis 1933* (1972), Königstein, 1980; G. Schulz, *Aufstieg des Nationalsozialismus*, Berlin, 1975; see also the survey of research by G. Schreiber, *Hitler. Interpretationen 1923–1983*, Darmstadt, 1984.

17. Broszat, 'Zur Struktur der NS-Massenbewegung'; E. Jäckel, *Hitlers Weltanschauung*, Stuttgart, 1981; for an example of a more recent regional study of the impact of the National Socialist movement, see R. Bessel, *Political Violence and the Rise of Nazism: The Storm Troopers in Eastern Germany 1925–1934*, New Haven, 1984.

18. R. Mann (ed.), *Die Nationalsozialisten*, Stuttgart, 1980; W. Schieder (ed.), *Fasch-*

ismus als soziale Bewegung, 2nd edn, Göttingen, 1983; M. Jamin, *Zwischen den Klassen. Zur Sozialstruktur der SA-Führerschaft*, Wuppertal, 1984; M. Kater, *The Nazi Party*, Cambridge, Mass., 1983.

19. Jamin, *Zwischen den Klassen*; C. Schmidt, 'Zu den Motiven "alter Kämpfer" in der NSDAP', in Peukert and Reulecke, *Die Reihen fast geschlossen*, pp. 21–44; P. Merkl, *Political Violence under the Swastika*, Princeton, 1975; L. Steinbach, *Ein Volk, ein Reich, ein Glaube. Ehemalige Nationalsozialisten und Zeitzeugen berichten über ihr Leben im Dritten Reich*, Berlin, 1983.

20. For a general study, see J. Falter, 'Die Wähler der NSDAP 1928–1933', in Michalka, *Die nationalsozialistische Machtergreifung*, pp. 47–59; T. Childers, *The Nazi Voter: The Social Foundations of Fascism in Germany 1919–1933*, Chapel Hill, 1983; see also the data in Falter *et al.*, *Wahlen und Abstimmungen*.

21. Roth, *Erfassung zur Vernichtung*; H. Kaupen-Haas, *Der Griff nach der Bevölkerung*, Nördlingen, 1986; Bock, *Zwangssterilisation im Nationalsozialismus*; Peukert, *Grenzen der Sozialdisziplinierung*; Otto and Sühnker, *Soziale Arbeit und Faschismus*.

22. Theweleit, *Männerphantasien*; Prümm, *Literatur*; M. Rohrwasser, *Saubere Mädel, Starke Genossen*, Frankfurt, 1975.

23. T. Koebner (ed.), *Weimars Ende. Prognosen und Diagnosen in der deutschen Literatur und politischen Publizistik 1930–1933*, Frankfurt, 1982; B. Sösemann, *Das Ende der Weimarer Republik in der Kritik demokratischer Publizisten*, Berlin, 1976.

24. G. Orwell, 'England Your England' (December 1940), quoted in J. Stevenson, *British Society 1914–1945*, Harmondsworth, 1984, p. 472.

V. TOTAL CRISIS, 1930–33

13. The World Economic Crisis

1. See the literature cited in note 2 to chapter 5, above.

2. Ziebura, *Weltwirtschaft*.

3. ibid.; Petzina, *Deutsche Wirtschaft*; for a Marxist-Leninist view, see M. Nussbaum, *Wirtschaft und Staat in Deutschland während der Weimarer Republik*, Berlin, 1978; see also H. Mommsen *et al.*, *Industrielles System*; G. Hardach, *Weltmarktorientierung und relative Stagnation*, Berlin, 1976.

4. F. Blaich, *Die Wirtschaftskrise 1925/26 und die Reichsregierung*, Kallmünz, 1977; Hertz-Eichenrode, *Wirtschaftskrise und Arbeitsbeschaffung*.

5. See also chapters 5 and 6.

6. C. Kindleberger, *The World in Depression 1929–1939*, Harmondsworth, 1987; James, *German Slump*; Blaich, *Schwarzer Freitag*; the following statistical data are taken from Petzina *et al.*, *Materialien*.

7. Stachura, *Unemployment*; Evans and Geary, *The German Unemployed*; D. Reber tisch, 'Kommunalpolitik, Konjunktur und Arbeitsmarkt in der Endphase

Weimarer Republik', in R. Morsey (ed.), *Verwaltungsgeschichte*, Berlin, 1977, pp. 107–56.

8. D. Rebentisch, 'Kommunalpolitik'; R. Vierhaus, 'Auswirkungen der Krise um 1930 in Deutschland. Beiträge zu einer historisch-psychologischen Analyse', in Conze and Raupach, *Staats- und Wirtschaftskrise*, pp. 155–75; W. Treue (ed.), *Deutschland in der Weltwirtschaftskrise in Augenzeugenberichten*, Munich, 1976; R. Fischer and F. Heimann, *Deutsche Kindheiten 1932* (1933), Düsseldorf, 1986, is a reprint of a contemporary documentary account.

9. In addition to the works cited in notes 2 and 24 to chapter 5, above, see also G. Plumpe, 'Wirtschaftspolitik in der Weltwirtschaftskrise', *Geschichte und Gesellschaft*, 11, 1985, pp. 326–57; J. von Kruedener, 'Die Überforderung der Weimarer Republik als Sozialstaat', *Geschichte und Gesellschaft*, 11, 1985, pp. 358–76; P. C. Witt, 'Finanzpolitik als Gesellschaftspolitik. Überlegungen zur Finanzpolitik des Deutschen Reiches in den Jahren 1930–1933', *Geschichte und Gesellschaft*, 8, 1982, pp. 386–414; M. Grübler, *Die Spitzenverbände der Wirtschaft und das erste Kabinett Brüning*, Düsseldorf, 1982.

10. M. Schneider, *Das Arbeitsbeschaffungsprogramm des ADGB*, Bonn, 1975; M. Wolffsohn, *Industrie und Handwerk im Konflikt mit staatlicher Wirtschaftspolitik? Studien zur Politik der Arbeitsbeschaffung in Deutschland 1930–1934*, Berlin, 1977; W. Zollitsch, 'Einzelgewerkschaften und Arbeitsbeschaffung', *Geschichte und Gesellschaft*, 8, 1982, pp. 87–115; H. Marcon, *Arbeitsbeschaffungspolitik der Regierungen Papen und Schleicher*, Berne, 1974.

14. The Erosion of Options

1. The political intricacies of the years 1930–33 cannot, and need not, be dealt with in detail here. See the account by G. Jasper, *Die gescheiterte Zähmung*; see also the survey of research by D. Gessner, *Das Ende der Weimarer Republik*.

2. K. D. Bracher, *Die Auflösung der Weimarer Republik*, remains a key study; see also Conze and Raupach, *Staats- und Wirtschaftskrise*; Matthias and Morsey, *Das Ende*; Michalka, *Die nationalsozialistische Machtergreifung*; K. Holl (ed.), *Wirtschaftskrise und liberale Demokratie*, Göttingen, 1978; M. Broszat et al. (eds.), *Deutschlands Weg in die Diktatur*, Berlin, 1983.

3. H. Mommsen, 'Heinrich Brünings Politik als Reichskanzler: Das Scheitern eines politischen Alleingangs', in Holl, *Wirtschaftskrise*, pp. 16–45.

4. ibid; R. Morsey, *Zur Entstehung, Authentizität und Kritik von Brünings 'Memoiren 1918–1934'*, Opladen, 1975.

5. Matthias and Morsey, *Das Ende*.

....uthardt, *Sozialdemokratische Arbeiterbewegung*, 2 vols.; E. Breit (ed.), *Aufstieg ... — Untergang der Republik — Zerschlagung der Gewerkschaften*, ..., *Die KPD im Widerstand*; M. Scharrer (ed.), *Kampflose ...egung 1933*, Reinbek, 1984.

...aat Hitlers*, Munich, 1969 (trans. as *The Hitler State: The*

Foundation and Development of the Internal Structure of the Third Reich, London, 1981); H.-U. Thamer, *Verführung und Gewalt. Deutschland 1933–1945*, Berlin, 1986; D. Peukert, *Volksgenossen und Gemeinschaftsfremde*, Cologne, 1982 (trans. as *Inside Nazi Germany: Conformity, Opposition and Racism in Everyday Life*, London, 1987).

A GUIDE TO THE LITERATURE

The quantity of published materials on the history of the Weimar Republic is almost too vast to assimilate. This guide mentions a few works only: some central texts, and other works which either provide a useful way into the specialist literature or may guide the reader who wishes to pursue a particular interest.

A. BIBLIOGRAPHIES

The best survey of research, with detailed bibliographical references, is E. Kolb, *Die Weimarer Republik*, Munich, 1984 (trans. as *The Weimar Republic*, London, 1988).

For a good guide to archives, research institutes, sources and secondary sources, see W. Benz, *Quellen zur Zeitgeschichte*, Stuttgart, 1973.

The *Bibliographie zur Zeitgeschichte*, which appears as a regular supplement to the *Vierteljahreshefte für Zeitgeschichte*, is one of the most important collections of up-to-date bibliographical data. A systematic compilation of the bibliography up to 1980 is available as T. Vogelsang and H. Auerbach (eds.), *Bibliographie zur Zeitgeschichte 1953–1980*, vol. I: *Allgemeiner Teil*, vol. II: *Geschichte des 20. Jahrhunderts bis 1945*, Munich, 1982.

B. PRIMARY SOURCES

The most important source collections that are easily accessible and suitable for study and teaching purposes are:

J. Flemming *et al.* (eds.), *Die Republik von Weimar*, vol. 1: *Das politische System*, vol. 2: *Das sozialökonomische System*, Königstein, Düsseldorf, 1979 (contains searching introductions and detailed references to the secondary literature).

W. Michalka and G. Niedhardt (eds.), *Die ungeliebte Republik. Dokumente zur Innen-und Außenpolitik Weimars 1918–1933*, Munich, 1980.

W. Abelshauser *et al.* (eds.), *Deutsche Sozialgeschichte 1914–1945*, Munich, 1986 (a careful selection, with a good introduction).

E. R. Huber (ed.), *Dokumente zur deutschen Verfassungsgeschichte*, vol. 3: *Dokumente der Novemberrevolution und der Weimarer Republik 1918–1933*, 2nd edn, Stuttgart, 1966 (out of print; 3rd edn forthcoming).

For a collection with a particularly thorough introduction and commentary, and going well beyond the bounds of its deceptively restrictive title, see A. Kaes, *Weimarer Republik. Manifeste und Dokumente zur deutschen Literatur 1918–1933*, Stuttgart, 1983.

A useful older source collection, still available in many libraries, is H. Michaelis and E. Schraepler (eds.), *Ursachen und Folgen. Vom deutschen Zusammenbruch 1918 und 1945 bis zur staatlichen Neuordnung Deutschlands in der Gegenwart*, Berlin, 1958ff (vols. 1–9 cover the period up to 1933).

For structural questions, the following data collections are well presented and indispensable:

D. Petzina *et al.*, *Materialien zur Statistik des Deutschen Reiches 1914–1945, Sozialgeschichtliches Arbeitsbuch III*, Munich 1978.

J. Falter *et al.*, *Wahlen und Abstimmungen in der Weimarer Republik*, Munich, 1986.

Politics, economics, culture and everyday life are covered in M. Overesch and F. W. Saal, *Chronik deutscher Zeitgeschichte*, vol. 1: *Die Weimarer Republik*, Düsseldorf, 1982.

For more detailed studies, however, it is necessary to go back to contemporary statistical and chronological sources, especially the series of volumes *Statistik des Deutschen Reiches*, the editions of the *Statistisches Jahrbuch für das Deutsche Reich*, ed. Statistisches Reichsamt, nos. 34–53, Berlin, 1919–34, and *Schulthess' Europäischer Geschichtskalender* (Neue Folge), nos. 34–49, Munich, 1922–34; also *Deutscher Geschichtskalender*, nos. 35–49, Leipzig, n.d. (and supplementary volumes).

The following large source editions should be mentioned: *Akten der Reichskanzlei. Weimarer Republik*, Boppard, 1968–, arranged by cabinets and now virtually complete.

Akten zur Deutschen Auswärtigen Politik 1918–1945 cover the Weimar period in two series: Series A, *1918–1925*, Göttingen, 1982–, 4 vols. to date; Series B, *1925–1933*, Göttingen, 1966–83, 21 vols., complete.

The Bonn Kommission für Geschichte des Parlamentarismus und der politischen Parteien publishes the multi-volume edition of *Quellen zur Geschichte des Parlamentarismus und der politischen Parteien*. This edition falls into three component series: *Von der konstitutionellen Monarchie zur parlamentarischen Republik*, *Militär und Politik* and *Die Weimarer Republik*.

Other important editions of primary sources, full details of which cannot be given here, include *Zur Geschichte der Rätebewegung in Deutschland 1918/19*, *Zur Geschichte der deutschen Gewerkschaftsbewegung im 20. Jahrhundert* and collections of records of important committees and of political parties (Centre, SPD and KPD).

For the serious student, the stenographic reports of German parliamentary proceedings (together with appendices) are indispensable: *Verhandlungen der ver-fassungsgebenden Deutschen Nationalversammlung*, vols. 326–43 (continuous numbering of Reichstag proceedings), Berlin, 1919ff., and *Verhandlungen des Deutschen Reichs-tages*, 1920–1933, vols. 344–457, Berlin, 1920ff. For the revolutionary period, the proceedings of the Reichsrätekongresse (Reich Congresses of Councils) of 16–21 December 1918 and 8–14 April 1919 should also be consulted.

It is not possible to give details of autobiographical sources here. For these, and for biographies and collections of papers of individual politicians, see the bibliographical works listed in section A above.

C. SECONDARY LITERATURE.

As far as older general histories are concerned, the following may be consulted: K. D. Erdmann, *Die Weimarer Republik*, Gebhardt: Handbuch der deutschen Geschi-chte, 9th edn, 1973; paperback edn, Munich, 1980.

The best recent general survey and introduction to the state of current research is the book by Kolb mentioned above. Another recent study is H. Schulze, *Weimar. Deutschland 1917–1933*, Berlin, 1982.

For the orthodox Marxist interpretation, see two books published in the Federal Republic and the GDR respectively: R. Kühnl, *Die Weimarer Republik*, Reinbek, 1985, and W. Ruge, *Deutschland 1917–1933*, 2nd edn, Berlin, 1974.

A number of anthologies, representing a broad spectrum of views, cover the range of recent research on the Weimar Republic: M. Stürmer (ed.), *Die Weimarer Republik. Belagerte Civitas*, Königstein, 1980; K. D. Erdmann and H. Schulze (eds.), *Weimar – Selbstpreisgabe einer Demokratie*, Düsseldorf, 1984; H. Mommsen *et al.* (eds.), *Industrielles System und politische Entwicklung in der Weimarer Republik*, Düs-seldorf, 1974; R. Bessel and E. J. Feuchtwanger (eds.), *Social Change and Political Development in Weimar Germany*, London, 1981; G. Schulz (ed.), *PLOETZ – Weimarer Republik. Eine Nation im Umbruch*, Würzburg, 1987.

Vol. 26 (1986) of *Archiv für Sozialgeschichte* also contains important contributions on Weimar.

A number of more extended histories, covering more than the Weimar period, help locate the Weimar Republic within a longer-term context: K. D. Bracher, *Europa in der Krise. Innengeschichte und Weltpolitik seit 1917*, Frankfurt, 1979; H. Aubin and W. Zorn (eds.), *Handbuch der deutschen Wirtschafts- und Sozialgeschichte*, vol. 2: *Das 19. und 20. Jahrhundert*, Stuttgart, 1976; H. Kaelble, *Auf dem Weg zu einer europäischen*

Gesellschaft. Eine Sozialgeschichte Westeuropas 1880–1980, Munich, 1987; W. Conze and R. Lepsius (eds.), *Sozialgeschichte der Bundesrepublik Deutschland. Beiträge zum Kontinuitätsproblem*, Stuttgart, 1983 (which, despite its title, deals particularly with longitudinal trends in social history between 1870 and 1970).

The most important studies of specific topics are cited in the Notes above. Only a few particularly interesting works will therefore be mentioned here.

In the multi-volume series edited by Martin Broszat *et al.*, *Deutsche Geschichte der neuesten Zeit*, the following individual studies dealing with the Weimar period have so far been published: C. Hepp, *Avantgarde. Moderne Kunst, Kulturkritik und Reformbewegungen nach der Jahrhundertwende*, Munich, 1987; P. Krüger, *Versailles. Deutsche Außenpolitik zwischen Revisionismus und Friedenssicherung*, Munich, 1986; H. Möller, *Weimar. Die unvollendete Demokratie*, Munich, 1985; F. Blaich, *Der Schwarze Freitag. Inflation und Wirtschaftskrise*, Munich, 1985; M. Broszat, *Die Machtergreifung. Der Aufstieg der NSDAP und die Zerstörung der Weimarer Republik*, Munich, 1984 (trans. as *Hitler and the Collapse of Weimar Germany*, Leamington Spa, Hamburg and New York, 1987).

An important gap has been filled by the biographical volume W. Benz and H. Graml (eds.), *Biographisches Lexikon zur Weimarer Republik*, Munich, 1988.

For a history of the genesis of the Republic, see U. Kluge, *Die deutsche Revolution 1918/1919*, Frankfurt, 1985.

An older collection of important research studies is E. Kolb (ed.), *Vom Kaiserreich zur Weimarer Republik*, Cologne, 1972. The prehistory of Weimar and the problems of continuity and change in German history, including social and cultural developments, are discussed by D. Langewiesche (ed.), *PLOETZ – Das deutsche Kaiserreich*, Würzburg, 1984.

The classic account of the framing of the constitution and of constitutional practice, from a conservative viewpoint, is E. R. Huber, *Deutsche Verfassungsgeschichte seit 1789*, vol. 5: *Weltkrieg, Revolution und Reichserneuerung 1914–19*, Stuttgart, 1978; vol. 6: *Die Weimarer Reichsverfassung*, Stuttgart, 1981; vol. 7: *Ausbau, Schutz und Untergang der Weimarer Republik*, Stuttgart, 1984.

For a comparative international study of the post-war period, see C. Maier, *Recasting Bourgeois Europe: Stabilization in France, Germany and Italy in the Decade after World War I*, Princeton, 1975.

A recent general history of Germany's foreign policy during the period is P. Krüger, *Die Außenpolitik der Republik von Weimar*, Darmstadt, 1985.

Of the many works on domestic policy, G. Feldman *et al.* (eds.), *Die deutsche Inflation. Eine Zwischenbilanz*, Berlin, 1982 deserves mention. An instance of the big international effort that has gone into research on the inflation problem, and a work which also looks ahead to the years that followed the stabilization of the economy, is G. Feldman (ed.), *Die Nachwirkungen der Inflation auf die deutsche Geschichte 1924–1933*, Munich, 1985.

A key contribution to the political and social history of the labour movement is

H. A. Winkler, *Arbeiter und Arbeiterbewegung in der Weimarer Republik: Von der Revolution zur Stabilisierung* (1918 to 1924), Berlin, 1984; *Der Schein der Normalität* (1924 to 1930), Berlin, 1985; *Der Weg in die Katastrophe* (1930 to 1933), Berlin, 1987.

Domestic instability during the years of 'stabilization' is dealt with by M. Stürmer, *Koalition und Opposition in der Weimarer Republik 1924–1928*, Düsseldorf, 1967. (A considerable number of other studies of domestic policy during the Republic have appeared in the series *Beiträge zur Geschichte des Parlamentarismus und der politischen Parteien*.)

For a magisterial survey of the political and ideological controversies of the period, see K. D. Bracher, *Zeit der Ideologien. Eine Geschichte politischen Denkens im 20. Jahrhundert*, Stuttgart, 1982.

Illuminating accounts of the world economic background to German economic and social history during the period are given by D. Aldcroft, *From Versailles to Wall Street 1919–1929*, Harmondsworth, 1977, and C. Kindleberger, *The World in Depression 1929–1939*, Harmondsworth, 1987.

For a good general economic survey, see D. Petzina, *Die deutsche Wirtschaft in der Zwischenkriegszeit*, Wiesbaden, 1977.

A helpful anthology, W. Abelshauser (ed.), *Die Weimarer Republik als Wohlfahrtsstaat. Zum Verhältnis von Wirtschafts- und Sozialpolitik in der Industriegesellschaft*, Stuttgart, 1987, appeared after the manuscript of the present volume had been completed.

For a Marxist-Leninist interpretation of the period, see M. Nussbaum, *Wirtschaft und Staat in Deutschland während der Weimarer Republik*, Berlin, 1978.

Tendenzen der Zwanziger Jahre, catalogue, 15. Europäische Kunstausstellung Berlin 1977, Berlin, 1977, provides a conspectus of the cultural history of the period from an international perspective.

The German cultural context is dealt with illuminatingly by Neue Gesellschaft für Bildende Kunst (ed.), *Wem gehört die Welt – Kunst und Gesellschaft in der Weimarer Republik*, Berlin, 1977, and by J. Hermand and F. Trommler, *Die Kultur der Weimarer Republik*, Munich, 1978.

A recent analysis of 'Weimar culture' whose scope is much wider than its title suggests is E. Schütz, *Romane der Weimarer Republik*, Munich, 1986.

For a wide-ranging and conceptually stimulating survey of research, see also H. E. Tenorth, *Zur deutschen Bildungsgeschichte 1918–1945*, Cologne, 1985. Tenorth and D. Langewiesche are also the editors of vol. 5 of the *Handbuch der deutschen Bildungsgeschichte*, Munich, 1989, covering the years 1918–45.

J. Boberg *et al.* (eds.), *Die Metropole. Industriekultur in Berlin im 20. Jahrhundert*, Munich, 1986, is an exemplary treatment of aspects of everyday life of the period.

The end of the Weimar Republic and the National Socialists' seizure of power are dealt with by G. Jasper, *Die gescheiterte Zähmung. Wege zur Machtergreifung Hitlers 1930–1934*, an account which summarizes recent research. Three other books on these events may also be mentioned: K. D. Bracher, *Die Auflösung der Weimarer Republik* (1955), 6th edn, Königstein, 1978, a classic, and still unsurpassed; and two more recent anthologies, W. Michalka (ed.), *Die nationalsozialistische Machtergreifung*, Paderborn, 1984, and M. Broszat *et al.* (eds.), *Deutschlands Weg in die Diktatur*, Berlin, 1983.

A recent general history of the Third Reich which goes deeply into the early history of the National Socialist movement before 1933 is H.-U. Thamer, *Verführung und Gewalt. Deutschland 1933–1945*, Berlin, 1986.

The best introduction to recent research and debate concerning National Socialism is I. Kershaw, *The Nazi Dictatorship: Problems and Perspectives of Interpretation*, London, 1985.

INDEX